The Brontës of Haworth Moor

The Brontës of Haworth Moor

How the Three Daughters of a Country Parson Became the Most Revolutionary Novelists of Their Time

DIANE BROWNING

CUT PAPER ILLUSTRATIONS
BY DIANE BROWNING

ROWMAN & LITTLEFIELD
Lanham • Boulder • New York • London

Published by Rowman & Littlefield
An imprint of The Rowman & Littlefield Publishing Group, Inc.
4501 Forbes Boulevard, Suite 200, Lanham, Maryland 20706
www.rowman.com

86-90 Paul Street, London EC2A 4NE, United Kingdom

British Library Cataloguing in Publication Information Available

Library of Congress Cataloging-in-Publication Data

Names: Browning, Diane, author.
Title: The Brontës of Haworth Moor : how the three daughters of a country
  parson became the most revolutionary novelists of their time / Diane
  Browning.
Description: Lanham : Rowman & Littlefield, 2024. | Includes
  bibliographical references and index. | Audience: Grades 10–12 |
  Summary: "This fascinating work shares the intimate details of the
  Brontë sisters' lives and reveals how their imagination, creativity,
  and passion helped them achieve their childhood dreams of being
  published authors"—Provided by publisher.
Identifiers: LCCN 2023024805 (print) | LCCN 2023024806 (ebook) | ISBN
  9781538172315 (cloth) | ISBN 9781538172322 (epub)
Subjects: LCSH: Brontë, Charlotte, 1816–1855—Juvenile literature. |
  Brontë, Emily, 1818–1848—Juvenile literature. | Brontë, Anne,
  1820–1849—Juvenile literature. | Authors, English—19th
  Century—Biography—Juvenile literature. |
  Sisters—England—Yorkshire—Biography—Juvenile literature. |
  Women authors, English—Biography—Juvenile literature. |
  LCGFT: Autobiographies.
Classification: LCC PR4168 .B86 2024 (print) | LCC PR4168 (ebook) | DDC
  823/.809 [B]—dc23/eng/20230612
LC record available at https://lccn.loc.gov/2023024805
LC ebook record available at https://lccn.loc.gov/2023024806

For my sisters, Janna and Barbara,
in memory of our childhood of drawing and painting,
writing stories, newspapers, poems, and plays.
And, as always, this is for my mother.

Contents

Acknowledgments

Endless thanks to my sister, Barbara, for her above-and-beyond tech support, encouragement, and help in editing and research. The book would not exist without her. Thanks to my sister, Janna, for being a shining light and inspiration all my life. I also want to thank my dear friend and agent, Abigail Samoun (my former editor, and cofounder of Red Fox Literary), for her friendship, wisdom, and hospitality—and for suggesting I write the story of the young Brontës. To my editor, Christen Karniski, heartfelt gratitude for her kindness and extreme patience during what was personally a difficult year. Additional thanks to assistant editors Samantha Delwarte and Joanna Wattenberg, designer Chloe Batch, production editor Nicole Carty Myers, and all those who worked on turning my manuscript into a finished book.

No author of a book about the Brontës can fail to acknowledge the scholars and biographers, past and present, who have done the hard work of gathering, deciphering, recording, and preserving the documents and remembrances that reveal the lives of the Brontës. Specifically I must mention Juliet Barker's definitive biography, *The Brontës: Wild Genius on the Moors*. The excellent Brontë Parsonage Museum, which has collected and preserved vital research collections and belongings of the family, is invaluable.

Thank you, SCBWI (Society of Children's Book Writers and Illustrators) founders Lin Oliver and Steve Mooser for your years of leadership. I am grateful for those years of learning.

Many friends in writer/illustrator groups have provided inspiration and encouragement throughout the years. Special thanks go to Joan Charles, Suzy Engelman Block, Kat McDonough, Carol Heyer, Siri Weber Feeney, early mentor Alexis O'Neill, and the members of the SCBWI Illustrators' Westside Lit Mingle and the Illustrators Table. Thank you to Paul Burrows, Anne Boydston, Bob McMahon, Mary-Jo Murphy, Christy Reeves, and Linda Silvestri. Gratitude goes to Sharon Waterbury for sharing gems of wisdom.

And my unbounded appreciation goes to libraries—especially the Los Angeles Public Library, for their large collection of Brontë books, biographies, and reference works. I have grateful memories of Siddie Joe Johnson, legendary Dallas librarian, children's book author, and poet. My sisters and I were members of her children's writing club. She made the dream believable. Thank you, Miss J.

Author's Note

Many fans of the Brontë novels say they discovered *Jane Eyre* and *Wuthering Heights* as teens or young adults. Yet there seems to be little emphasis on introducing young readers to the intriguing young Brontës who created the novels. None of the Brontë siblings lived to be old. Our knowledge of the four who survived early childhood is of young people growing up, playing, studying, making friends, writing, falling in love, finding jobs, and trying to succeed in their chosen careers. Until the end of their lives—through tragedies, disappointments, and depression—they still had hope and anticipation for the future. None of them believed they would die—the optimism of youth, sometimes against all odds. These are attitudes that the young understand.

I have tried to write a biography, not emphasizing gloom and doom, but showing the Brontë siblings as the vibrant, hopeful, and often happy young people they were. This is a story for young people, showing the commonality of youth, no matter the time period or situation.

Who's Who

THE BRONTË FAMILY

Patrick	Father, 1777–1861
Maria	Mother, 1783–1821
Maria	1814–1825
Elizabeth	1815–1825
Charlotte	1816–1855
Patrick Branwell	1817–1848
Emily Jane	1818–1848
Anne	1820–1849

IMPORTANT PEOPLE IN THEIR LIVES

Aykroyd, Tabitha	"Tabby"—beloved maid and cook
Branwell, Elizabeth	Sister of Maria Branwell Brontë
Brown, John	Sexton, mason, and friend of Patrick Branwell Brontë
Brown, Martha	Family's maid and daughter of John Brown
Coleridge, Hartley	Writer who encouraged Branwell
Franks, Elizabeth Firth	Friend of Patrick and Maria; godmother of Elizabeth and Anne
Garrs, Nancy and Sarah	Cook and nursemaid

Gaskell, Elizabeth Cleghorn	Friend and biographer of Charlotte
Grundy, Francis	Engineer, surveyor, and railroad friend of Branwell
Heger, Claire Zoë	Directress of Pensionnat Heger
Heger, Constantin	Teacher at Pensionnat Heger and husband of Claire Heger
Ingham family	Anne's first employer, at Blake Hall
Kay-Shuttleworth, Sir James	"Fan" of Charlotte
Leyland, Francis	Antiquarian bookseller; brother of Joseph Bentley Leyland
Leyland, Joseph Bentley	Sculptor and friend of Branwell; brother of Francis Leyland
Newby, Thomas Cautley	Publisher of Emily and Anne
Nicholls, Revd. Arthur Bell	Haworth curate
Nussey, Ellen	Best friend of Charlotte
Nussey, Revd. Henry	Brother of Ellen and Charlotte's first suitor
Patchett, Elizabeth	Headmistress at Law Hill
Postlethwaite family	Branwell's employers in Broughton
Pryce, Revd. David	Curate and second suiter of Charlotte
Robinson, Revd. Edmund	Lord of the Manor, Branwell's and Anne's employer at Thorp Green
Robinson, Lydia	Wife of Rev. Edmund Robinson
Robinson, Lydia, Elizabeth, and Mary	Daughters of Edmund and Lydia Robinson
Robinson, William	Portraitist and teacher of Branwell
Sidgwick family	Charlotte's first employer as governess, at Stonegappe
Smith, Elizabeth	Mother of George Smith
Smith, George	Publisher/owner of Smith, Elder & Co.
Southey, Robert	Poet Laureate and advisor to Charlotte
Taylor, James	Charlotte's third suitor, manager of Smith, Elder.
Taylor, Mary	Best friend of Charlotte
Thackeray, William Makepeace	Author; literary idol of Charlotte

Weightman, Revd. William	Haworth curate and favorite of Brontë family
Wheelwright, Laetitia	Student at Pensionnat Heger
White family	Charlotte's employer at Upperwood House
Williams, William Smith	Reader at Smith, Elder; "discoverer" and friend of Charlotte
Wooler, Margaret	Headmistress at Roe Head School and friend of Charlotte

Prologue

A Letter from London

[I] used to wonder whatever they did with so much [paper].

In the small village of Haworth everyone knew the Reverend Brontë's daughters—Charlotte, Emily, and Anne. The family lived in the parsonage at the very top of the village, on the edge of Haworth Moor.

As children, the Brontë sisters had not been allowed to play with the rough village children, but they were still part of village life. They sewed and prepared food for the needy in the parish, and Charlotte and Anne taught in the church Sunday school. Shy with strangers and bookish, they could often be seen walking to the lending library. Mr. Brown, who carved the headstones for the graveyard, often saw them set off across the moors on long, windblown walks. Local weavers, peering through the windows of their dark, crowded houses, noticed the lasses passing by on their way to Mr. Greenwood's stationery shop on Main Street where they would purchase stacks of paper. He "used to wonder whatever they did with so much"[1] paper.

In early July 1848, the postman delivered a letter to the parsonage addressed to Mr. Currer Bell, c/o Miss Charlotte Brontë. Did the postman wonder who would send a letter to a gentleman by way of Mr. Brontë's quiet spinster daughter?

This letter would eventually change the way everyone in the village thought of the parson's girls. But when Charlotte and Anne read the letter, they were upset—there had been a misunderstanding. When Emily read the letter, she quickly shook her head—she didn't want to be involved. Charlotte tried all day to convince her sister to accompany them to London, but only Charlotte and Anne left the parsonage that day after a hurried afternoon tea. They walked four miles through a summer thunderstorm to the train station in the next town. Two trains and seventeen hours later, they arrived in London to reveal to their publishers that they were ladies with secret identities.

The Brontë sisters had each been published within a few months of one another, using the names Currer, Ellis, and Acton Bell. Their novels had been received with gossip, speculation, and criticism—but also praise—as the subjects and point of view were unusual for the times. It was assumed the books had been written by three brothers.

The gentlemen at the publishing house must have been extremely curious about their visitors when they realized the quiet daughters of a country curate had written such surprising books. They were not the kind of books women usually wrote. They were bold, even shocking.

What was their story? Who were these three unusual sisters, and how had their dreams of becoming authors run through their lives like a strong, bright, determined thread?

1

The Town, the Parsonage, the Moors

I have a good House, which is mine for life . . .

In April 1820, the Reverend Patrick Brontë moved his young family across the Yorkshire moors to the small, bustling town of Haworth.

When the carters hired for the move first saw the six tiny Brontë children, they may have marveled at how small they were, all under the age of nine. The eldest child, named Maria after her mother, was eight. Elizabeth was seven, Branwell three, and Emily two. Baby Anne was only three months old. It was the day before young Charlotte's fourth birthday, and the children were probably excited by the novelty of the journey and perhaps the hope of a celebration the following day. Also accompanying the family were two teenage sisters, Sarah and Nancy Garrs, who were the family nursemaid and cook/housekeeper.

Once the wagons were loaded with the family's belongings, Mr. Brontë lifted the children to sit amid a jumble of furniture, boxes, and trunks. Mrs. Brontë held baby Anne snuggled in a warm blanket.

As the new perpetual curate of St. Michael and All Angels church, Mr. Brontë felt positive about the move to Haworth. "My salary is not large," he later wrote, adding, "I have a good House, which is mine for life . . . and is rent free. . . . No one has anything to do with the Church but myself, and I have a large congregation."[1] He had high hopes for the future.

The distance was not far in miles, from Thornton to Haworth, but it probably seemed so. Yorkshiremen spoke of Pennine miles, referring to a mile seeming longer when traveling over the steep, rough country of the Pennine mountain range. The horses pulling the heavy carts would have felt the miles, with their load of household belongings—from the Reverend Brontë and his wife's large wooden bed to baby Anne's tiniest silver spoon.

Pausing to rest on a hilltop as they neared their destination would have provided a good vantage point to see the vast, breathtaking sweep of Mr. Brontë's new chapelry—hill after moorland hill, rolling away to the horizon like waves in the ocean. In April, the moors were covered with shades of gray-green and dun-colored bracken, cotton grass, and heather. There were lonely farms dotting the land, sheep scattered over the hills, a few thorn trees twisted by the wind, and stone walls that crisscrossed the moors like stitches on a quilt.

For hundreds of years, gaily decorated packhorses—loaded with farm produce, cotton, wool, and other goods—had passed single file over these hills on their way to market, the lead horse announcing their passage with its merry jingling collar of bells. They followed an ancient, well-traveled network of trails across the moors. In 1820, this route was still used, as raw wool was brought to bustling Haworth and nearby towns to be made into cloth in one of the most important manufacturing areas in the north of England.

Once in the busy little town, Mr. Brontë's hired carts made their way up Main Street, possibly one of the steepest in England. It was paved with setts—rectangular stone blocks, larger than cobblestones. This was to give the horses' hooves a better grip, in an effort to prevent them from slipping backward on the dangerous incline. Riders would need to dismount and lead horses up the street. Pedestrians also benefited from the setts, as the street was usually wet with either mist, ice, snow, rain, or sleet. The gutters ran with sewage from overflowing hand-dug privies (outdoor toilets) and middens (enclosed areas where waste from households and privies was thrown).

What would Mr. Brontë's children have seen in their new town as their cart thumped and jolted almost three-quarters of a mile up Main Street? They passed houses, taverns, shops, and townspeople who stopped their work to watch the new curate and his older children trudging up the street to their new home. It was a stone town—stone houses with stone roofs and stone walls. The stone was to withstand the constant strong winds that swept up from the bottom (as the locals referred to the valley below) and across the moors. The irregular line of soot-darkened structures was crowded together up the narrow, twisting street. Buildings with two or three stories fronting on the lower side of Main Street might have five or six stories in the rear, reached only by stairs down the hillside.

The large homes at the bottom of the hill and on the outskirts of town were where the business owners lived. The working class lived at the top of the hill, in a maze-like tangle of small houses built around stone-flagged yards. Some could only be reached by ginnels or snickets—dark and narrow dirt alleyways—some just wide enough for one or two people to pass through. The cottages seemed to be tumbling down the hillside, with stairs to cellars where several families lived in tiny, damp, and airless rooms where they often ate, slept, and pursued their livelihood of wool-combing—often in one room only. Fires were kept going day and night, to process the wool, and windows were rarely opened to let in light or air from one year to the next.

The damp, unventilated homes were not the only example of unhealthy conditions in the crowded town, for there were no sewers. The outdoor priv-ies were shared by as many as twenty-four families. When a study was made years later, there were fewer than five dozen privies and few pumps and wells, which were often tainted, to be shared by the whole town. Not surprisingly, life expectancy was short. Wool combers might live to be no older than nine-teen. It was safer to be a spinster or a widow no longer bearing children. Their average lifespan was thirty-eight.

In these houses, Mr. Brontë and his assistant curates would visit to offer comfort to the sick and the dying, and to urge parents to swiftly baptize their children.

As the street became level at the top of the hill, the horses pulling the Brontë carts could stop struggling. The open area boasted several shops, an apothecary, two taverns, a barn, and stables. The carts turned into a quiet little lane that delivered Mr. Brontë and his family to the church, the churchyard, and the parsonage—their new home.

An attractive Georgian house, it was built a half century before of dark stone from a local quarry. It faced east, to the church, and was surrounded on two sides by a graveyard almost an acre in size and filled with thousands of gravestones. Just beyond the walled rear yard were miles of open fields and moorland, rising up behind the house in a series of rolling hills. A friend, after her first visit to the parsonage, would later write about "those high, wild, desolate moors, up above the whole world, and the very realms of silence!"[2] The wind off the moors could be fierce. Both outside and inside the house there was a constant awareness of its presence.

While the furniture was being unloaded and the house inspected, Mr. Brontë might have wanted to step into his new church, to look about with satisfaction.

There had been many months of uncertainty and drama after Mr. Brontë was offered the post in Haworth. He had not realized that, although the powerful churchmen in the large neighboring town of Bradford had the right to nominate and appoint the Haworth minister, the church trustees in Haworth could refuse to pay the new curate's salary if they did not agree with the choice. In the Middle Ages, they had been given the unusual privilege of choosing their own minister, for reasons lost in time.

Patrick Brontë wasn't the only cleric who had been rejected, and even treated rudely. He had been told the rejection was not personal, and eventually the power struggle between the Bradford churchmen and Haworth trustees was settled. The two groups joined together to offer Mr. Brontë the plum post of perpetual curate of Haworth—a guaranteed position for life, which included a home in which to raise his six children.

Though they had been happy in Thornton and were reluctant to leave their many good friends there, Mrs. Brontë must have agreed with her husband that the move to Haworth was a good decision. The large front garden, where her children could play, would have been a welcome sight. In their last home at Thornton's parsonage, she surely worried her young ones would run through the front door directly into the town's busy traffic of horsemen, carriages, and carts. Mr. Brontë's previous salary had also been insufficient for their young family, which had grown too large for their Thornton home.

It's easy to imagine the usually lively young children, tired and fussy from the journey, reviving on arrival at their new home. Surely the church sexton would have lit fires in the fireplaces, to take the chill off the April day. Did the older children run through the front door, shouting to one another as they ran from room to room throwing open the inside shutters? If it was a sunny day, the house would then have been filled with light from the curtainless windows. The children would have seen a stone-flagged hall, with walls stained a light, pretty dove color. To the right was the room that would be

MARIA BRONTË

PATRICK BRONTË

their father's study. Across the hall was the dining room/parlor where the children could spend hours studying, reading, writing, and painting. Running down the hall they would find the kitchen, which would be the domain of the sixteen-year-old cook, Nancy Garrs. If they opened a door across the hall, they could peer down dark, spooky, stone steps that led to the double-vaulted cellar—a wonderful place to play! Another door revealed a walled yard with a peat house. (Peat, partly decayed plant material, was cut from the moorland bogs in squares and dried to burn for cooking and heating.) There was probably also a line strung up on which to hang clothes to dry.

Though there was no plumbing in their house or in any other house in the village, there was a two-seat privy in the yard (one conveniently child-sized), and a well and pump for water. The private well and privy were rare luxuries in Haworth. One of the few in town, their well was fed by a stream on the moors. This was fortunate, because no one yet understood that the graveyard was one source of pollution and poisoning of the town's water.

In the hall again, the stairway beckoned them upward to a half-landing with a large arched window that gave a view of the vast moorland—a playground yet to be explored. Upstairs were the bedrooms. The front one, over the dining room, would be their parents'. A guest would later comment on the beauty of the view in moonlight from that window. Because the parsonage sat on higher ground than church and town, the view from the front windows was not of the gravestones but over the town to three separate moors, making the parsonage seem to be surrounded by moorland.

The servants' room was in the back, with a view of Haworth Moor. It could be reached only by an exterior stairway leading down to the yard. From there the sleepy maids could enter the kitchen, to light the stove and begin the work of the day. There were two additional bedrooms upstairs on the other side of the house. It would be crowded for the family of eight and the two servants.

The three oldest children may have tried to imagine which rooms would be theirs. Above the front entry was a small room, which the Garrs sisters would soon name "the children's study." There they would play on rainy days, and paint little watercolor pictures to decorate the walls. But first the six small children must, somehow, be fed and put to bed, exhausted from their trip to this house that would be their home for the rest of their lives.

In their years in the parsonage, so exposed to weather on the edge of the moors, the members of the household would hear every blast of wind and rain when it swept across the hills in blinding sheets, and bundle up against the penetrating chill of ice storms. They would become invisible when the fog enveloped them, or find their home buried by snow in the long, lingering winters.

But the house and the town had other moods. In spring, the streams would run fast and dark (dyed by the chocolate-colored peat high up on the moors), wild flowers would bloom, and larks would be heard—even close to the parsonage. Summer would bring young fern and moss by the streams and bogs. The siblings could spot peregrine falcons, plover, merlins, and curlews. Some sturdy Yorkshiremen have referred to the frequent rain as Yorkshire kisses. Wild weather or soft mists were common throughout the year.

Summers could be cold, but there would also be long, glorious days of sunshine and blue skies. Still, there was the constant wind and the ever-changing clouds forming fantastic shapes, their shadows moving swiftly across the moors. In August and September, the landscape changed color, and the fragrant heather bloomed—a lavender coverlet casually thrown across the moors.

The freedom, solitude, and wild beauty of the moors would inspire the Brontës all their lives. Their love of nature (first instilled in them by their father) and the drama of Haworth's weather contributed to the intensity of their dreams, their poetry, and their novels. It would be a playground for some of the first fanciful games invented by the two oldest girls to entertain their younger siblings.

The very location of their home resulted in ideas for stories. On dark, rainy days or in the black of night, when their lights were hidden behind their shuttered windows, the dark shape of the house looming up on the edge of the moors would have seemed lonely and isolated. It's easy to imagine Branwell daring his sisters to venture among the tombstones after dark. Rumors of grave robbers who once plied their trade just beyond their windows resulted in the writing of shivery tales—even into adulthood, notably in Charlotte's and Emily's famous novels. It was comforting and pleasurable to escape into worlds of their own creation.

It's unlikely they would have written the books they wrote, had they lived elsewhere. Their unusual father and the unconventional education he gave them, their family sorrows, their home on the edge of the moors, and their close, creative childhood are the keys to who they would become and the books they would write—still read, still loved, after almost two centuries.

The strong-willed Brontë girls would overcome many obstacles in their fight to achieve their dreams. But first they would be aided by their young nurse-maids, described as affectionate and warm-hearted, who enthusiastically joined in their fanciful creative play.

When Sarah Garrs was an old woman, married and living in America, she liked to reminisce about working for the Brontë family in the old parsonage on the edge of Haworth Moor. She had lived with the family from the age of twelve. When Mr. Brontë visited the Bradford School of Industry, a charity school for children of the poor, he had chosen her older sister—capable, trust-worthy young Nancy—to be nursemaid for Charlotte. Mr. Brontë returned to the school when Emily was born to employ Sarah, probably at Nancy's request. With Sarah as nursemaid, Nancy—then only fourteen—became cook and assistant housekeeper.

At the charity school, they had been taught skills to enable them to earn their own living. Sewing was considered the most useful accomplishment for the girls. Next was knitting. They were also taught to read, but apparently it was considered the least important of the lessons they would need in their working lives. Clothing was supplied in exchange for the work they produced. They were also given one and a half pence every four months if they attended church, learned prayers and Bible verses, and always carried their sewing implements (and a handkerchief). It was a harsh school, typical of the times. Their hair was cropped, no adornments were allowed, and minor offenses were severely punished.

Mrs. Brontë had never fully regained her health after the birth of Anne the previous January, and she became seriously ill only months after the move to Haworth. Though she could no longer oversee their work, the young Garrs sisters capably fulfilled their duties. Surely unhappy that they were rarely allowed to see their mother, the children were kept busy by the two sisters. Sarah later described their daily life during that time. She washed and dressed the sleepy children upon arising in the morning. Then she and Nancy took them to their father's study for morning prayers, followed by bread and butter and the preferred Yorkshire breakfast of warm oatmeal porridge and milk (so welcome on cold mornings!). Mr. Brontë then gave Branwell and the older girls their morning lessons in his study, after which Sarah again took charge of all six children until midday. When they were older, the children would be taught by their father, according to their gender. Young gentlemen were educated more thoroughly than girls, with the addition of mathematics and the classical languages of Latin and Greek.

The older girls were learning to sew. Sarah cut out and basted together a very small chemise for five-year-old Charlotte to finish sewing, while Maria and Elizabeth worked on more complicated projects. Even Emily would have been included in the lesson, as three was the age at which girls normally received their first sewing instruction. All the sisters, even at a very young age, would create embroidered samplers that were patiently stitched, spelling out Bible verses. The girls would have been able to proudly show their projects to their mother. Charlotte's embroidery was never as neat as her little sister Emily's. Charlotte did not like to sew, although all the sisters would be sewing for themselves and others for the rest of their lives.

At two o'clock, the children joined their father in the dining room for the heartiest meal of the day. Mr. Brontë, thus fortified, visited his parishioners, sometimes walking miles across the moors to far-flung farms. He enjoyed his walks and relished his time out of doors. He believed his children should be raised to appreciate nature as he did, and encouraged their rambles on the wide expanse of moorland just beyond their walled yard. Most days they happily put on their boots, bonnets, and little coats and set out on their walk, accompanied by Sarah, Nancy, or their father, walking hand in hand. The sedate line of little Brontës may have soon broken up, as Sarah reported that their "fun knew no bounds. . . . They enjoyed a game of romps, and played with zest."[3] If the weather turned rainy or too icy to venture outside, there was great disappointment, and probably some tears.

The last meal of the day—"tea"—was waiting when they returned. It consisted of bread and butter and fruit preserves, perhaps made with bilberries or even the hard-to-find amber-colored cloudberries that might be found near the glistening bogs at the top of the moors. Perhaps instead Nancy gave them her freshly made bread, smeared with the strong-tasting heather honey sold in the village by beekeepers who placed their hives on the moors.

After Mr. Brontë had his tea in his study, he gave the children their afternoon lessons. These included a series of questions and answers from a popular textbook, *Mangnall's Historical Questions*, which had been written by the headmistress of a local girls' school and was widely used by schoolteachers and governesses. The girls combined their lessons with sewing tasks, their small heads bent intently over their work. With repetition they learned their lessons by heart, often practicing their assignments in bed after the candles were snuffed out—a technique they would later use to work on story ideas. The next day they would recite the answers in response to their father's question. Did clever young Branwell squirm and wish to go play? Or did he already find the lessons fun—for soon his imagination would lead his siblings into finding stories, not dry facts, in their lessons.

Their *Mangnall's* textbook, first published in 1798, was largely a series of questions and answers on a variety of subjects, such as "Who were the Druids? Priests of Britain, whose principal residence was in the Isle of Anglesea, where they performed their idolatrous worship, and were held in great veneration by the people. How were the Druids clothed when they sacrificed? In long white garments; they wore on their heads the tiara, or sacred crown, their temples were encircled with a wreath of oak-leaves, they waved in their hands a magic wand, and also placed upon their heads a serpent's egg, as an ensign of their order."[4]

It's easy to imagine this lesson inspiring the creative Brontë children to don nightgowns and a wreath of leaves for a play about Druids.

Too soon the day would end, and Sarah would put the children to bed. But first there would be nightly prayers, with special prayers for their ailing mother.

2

Death and Duty

Oh God, my poor children!

By the new year of 1821, Maria Brontë's health had worsened. Mr. Brontë feared his wife would not recover. Meanwhile, all six of his children had become ill with scarlet fever. This was their first serious illness—they had all been healthy since birth. Nineteenth-century children often did not survive babyhood, and half the children in unhealthy Haworth died before the age of six. Patrick Brontë worried he would lose his entire family, but while his wife's health did not improve, the children recovered—though they were slow to regain their strength.

Mr. Brontë was grateful and relieved when his wife's older sister, Elizabeth Branwell, came from Cornwall to help with his wife's care. She had previously spent a year with the family, in Thornton, helping her sister when the older children were born. Still, they would probably have been too young to remember her. When she arrived, weary and stiff from her long, perilous journey by stagecoach from the southwest tip of England, their first impressions of her were likely of her petite size and the immensity of the old-fashioned, lace-trimmed cap she always wore.

Miss Branwell quickly took charge of her sister's sickroom. She was brisk, purposeful, and protective. She instructed the children not to disturb their mama's rest—that her sister needed peace, quiet, and prayers.

In their youth, Elizabeth and Maria Branwell had led secure, privileged lives as the daughters of a prosperous landowner and merchant banker in Penzance, Cornwall. But with their father's death, his businesses were inherited by his brother, as women were not considered capable of managing property and men determined property must stay in the male line. Though they were each left a modest income for life, the four Branwell sisters' lives changed forever. Their home was no longer theirs, and they were expected to either marry, move in with relatives who would take them, or find employment. Sisters Jane and Charlotte Branwell both married.

Twenty-nine-year-old Maria was invited to be assistant housekeeper in her uncle's boarding school for Methodist ministers' sons, four hundred miles away in Yorkshire. Soon the young woman—described as plain but elegant, self-assured, witty, and intelligent—met a tall, handsome, red-haired Irish curate. The young couple fell in love, and soon married.

Maria's elder sister, Elizabeth, was happy and content living with relatives in Cornwall. Her life was pleasant and comfortable, and she enjoyed the gaiety of life in Penzance. She had a wide circle of family and friends who cared for her. She would have happily stayed in Penzance were it not for the call of duty. She agreed to nurse her younger sister in far-away Haworth.

With the stress of Maria's illness, Mr. Brontë did not wish to hear the chatter, laughter, or rowdy games of his children. They were only allowed to see their mother one at a time, and at intervals, as their visits upset her. Bedridden and in great pain, she cried out in despair—"Oh God my poor children!"[1]—at the thought of leaving her six little ones without a mother's love and care.

Elizabeth Branwell was a practical and efficient caregiver, and competent to take over her sister's care. This enabled Mr. Brontë to dismiss the nurse he had hired to care for his wife. The nurse was resentful about losing her job. Years later she made cruel and untrue comments about her former employer and even the parsonage servants. Her lies were vigorously denied by Mr. Brontë, his friends, and the servants. Especially egregious were stories about him being cruel to his wife and children. Unfortunately they are still commonly believed because the falsehoods were included in the first, still widely read biography of Charlotte by Elizabeth Gaskell, who usually wrote fiction and liked great drama. Still in print, it makes many disproven claims.

The Garrs sisters said the nurse was dismissed by Mr. Brontë "for reasons which he thought sufficient"[2] and hinted at inappropriate behavior on the nurse's part. In addition to no longer being needed after Aunt Branwell's arrival, one theory was that the nurse enjoyed dipping into the homemade beer stored in the parsonage's cellar.

Every night, Mr. Brontë led the whole household in evening prayers around Maria Brontë's bed. The children were then allowed to kiss their mother and wish her good night.

Sarah encouraged them to play quietly in the small room at the top of the stairs, or in the warm, fragrant kitchen where her sister Nancy, the cook, would sit them at the table to draw, read, or help with small tasks. And every day, in fine weather, the children would be taken through the gate at the top of Church Lane and on to the moors.

Moorland walks must have been a relief from the subdued, sorrowful mood in the house and their father's and their aunt's anxious admonitions to "hush." These walks were the highlights of their day, and would continue to be so all their lives.

In August 1821, despite the doctor's ministrations and her husband's and sister's prayers and loving care, Maria Brontë died. The entire household was gathered by her bedside to pray and to say goodbye.

As their mother had feared, the absence of her love and influence would affect the children from then on.

While their father struggled with the devastating loss of his wife and his worries about the future, the children were learning to live without their mother. Eight-year-old Maria and seven-year-old Elizabeth did their best to mother their younger siblings. Mature and responsible for her age, Maria read newspapers and magazines aloud to her sisters and brother, and to her father, who was proud of his precocious eldest daughter.

The newspapers of the day included book reviews, fashion reports, exciting articles about explorers and adventurers, gossip, scandals, and politics. (Charlotte later claimed she became interested in politics at age five due to what was read to her, and her father's comments.) The local news also sometimes included articles written by their own father, or even items about him and his church activities.

Being typical, energetic children, the siblings resumed their imaginative and rowdy games and entertainments, which helped distract them from the loss of their mother. Sarah Garrs later said the children's plays were inspired by young Maria's reading to them. The older children began to gather ideas they would later turn into stories. Little Anne, too, would join in their creative play as she grew older. Many of the stories they would write all their lives were about motherless children or orphans.

Their father allowed them to read from his collection of books. The children found John Bunyan's *Pilgrim's Progress*, a tale intended as a spiritual lesson, to also be an imaginative and entertaining adventure. After it was read to her at age six, Charlotte determinedly set out intending to walk to the next town, which she believed must be the Celestial City she had imagined so vividly from the novel.

Mr. Brontë also told his children old legends from his childhood in Ireland. His lessons in history and geography also gave the imaginative siblings ideas for further play.

All six of the children loved tales of fairies and other fanciful creatures. A few months after her mother's death, Charlotte rushed to bring Sarah Garrs to Anne's cradle. Sarah described Charlotte as wild and pale with excitement—she insisted she had seen a fairy above her baby sister's crib. Though no fairy could be found to show to Sarah, nothing could shake Charlotte's belief in its reality.

After a lesson on seventeenth-century British history, the children were excited and full of energy. They grabbed the counterpane off one of the beds and wrapped it like a cape around their young nursemaid, Sarah. In their game, she was the future King Charles II, and the children were his enemies. They chased her through the house, out an upper window, and onto a limb of Mr. Brontë's favorite cherry tree (meant to represent the great oak in which Charles had hidden). The limb tumbled to the ground. Unharmed, but apparently feeling anxious and guilty, teenaged Sarah rubbed soot on the broken stump of the tree and carried the limb away.

When Mr. Brontë next took his chair to sit under his tree, he immediately realized a branch was missing. "Who spoiled my tree?"[3] he asked. The children did not give their friend away, and Sarah remembered them as "always loyal and true."[4] Luckily, when she confessed Mr. Brontë forgave the accident.

Their father was pleased to see his children happily playing together. He later recalled that "as soon as they could read and write, Charlotte and her brother and sisters used to invent and act little plays of their own, in which the

Duke of Wellington, my daughter Charlotte's hero, was sure to come off conqueror; when a dispute would not unfrequently arise amongst them regarding the comparative merits of him, Buonaparte, Hannibal, and Caesar. When the argument got warm, and rose to its height . . . I had sometimes to come in . . . and settle the dispute . . . to the best of my judgement."[5]

Nancy Garrs later recalled that Branwell was "a good lad enough" but willful, and he was "made out to be a good deal worse than he really was." Though he had "fits of fury" as a child, she could handle him at those times, and she believed the naughty little boy loved her.[6]

The children, always close, had each other. They were surrounded with kindness and love from their father and aunt, and the young nursemaid and cook may have seemed like additional sisters. Certainly the two teenagers were their friends and playmates as well as caregivers. But they were missing their mother's love and affection, and their aunt would soon be returning to Cornwall.

Mr. Brontë was overwhelmed by the thought of raising his lively young children alone while fulfilling his many duties as curate of such a large chapelry. He was also in debt from his wife's medical care. There was no longer her annuity to help with expenses.

The Garrs sisters were not well educated, and though kind and responsible, they could not teach Mr. Brontë's daughters to be ladies or Branwell to be a gentleman. He could raise his son, but the girls needed a role model to teach them the strict rules of young ladies' behavior demanded by society. He struggled with the question of how he was to manage. He decided the only solution was to remarry.

Patrick Brontë was now forty-five years old, and still a handsome man— tall and upright in his top hat, long black coat, and thornwood walking stick. Most widowers eventually remarried, but it was his concern for his six children that determined his ill-advised decision, so soon after the loss of his wife, to approach the twenty-four-year-old godmother of young Elizabeth and Anne with a proposal of marriage. Elizabeth Firth had been a good friend of his late wife. She was a prosperous young gentlewoman, and soon to be engaged to an admirer with better prospects. She was offended. She felt it was shockingly inappropriate for Mr. Brontë to think of remarrying only three months after her friend's death, and did not speak to him for two years.

A few months later he approached Isabelle Dury, the sister of a clergy-man friend. Though sounding very mercenary, she actually expressed a very pragmatic reason for refusing Mr. Brontë's proposal. In a letter to a friend, she wrote, "I think I never should be so very silly as to have the most distant idea of marrying anybody who had not some fortune, and six children into the bargain."[7]

Finally, Mr. Brontë bravely contacted Mary Burder, a still-unmarried for-mer sweetheart who had been his first love. His proposal of marriage received a bitter and sarcastic "no." There had been obstacles and a misunderstanding concerning their engagement many years before. Patrick had taken a curacy in another town. Her family objected to him, there was confusion concerning letters, and Patrick had gone on with his life, considering their relationship over. Mary, however, had continued to believe Patrick would come back for her. His desire to return to her fifteen years later was met with anger. She felt she had been treated badly, had not forgiven him, and would not.

By 1824, Mr. Brontë had given up any idea of remarriage, but still had to find a way to ensure his children were raised properly. With no other solu-tion forthcoming, he asked Elizabeth Branwell, who was eager to return to her home in Cornwall, to stay until the four oldest girls could be sent away to school. Her help with the care of his children, the education of his girls, and the overseeing of the parsonage housekeeping was invaluable. Mr. Brontë and Elizabeth Branwell were close in age. Though it might have been practical for them to marry, it was against the law at that time to marry one's sister-in-law or brother-in-law. With no knowledge of genetics, first cousins were allowed to marry, but in-laws were considered too closely related—even though they were not blood relatives.

Patrick Brontë's extreme anxiety for his family must have been obvious to his sister-in-law. Perhaps in a spirit of pious self-sacrifice, she decided to abandon her plan to return soon to Penzance, with its fresh sea air, warmth, bright flowers, and her family and friends. She did not like the local people, so different from Cornish folk. She did not like Haworth. The cold and the constant wind rattled the doors and moaned at the windows, "piping and wailing . . . round the square unsheltered house in a very strange unearthly way."[8] Though she settled in, and seemed content, she continued to miss her life in Cornwall and to reminisce about her former life.

AUNT BRANWELL

It's likely Miss Branwell did appreciate being needed. She had become the children's stern, but not unkind, Aunt Branwell. Her word was usually law with the children, and she seems to have not been a very affectionate aunt. Charlotte later gave her credit for instilling good habits—such as neatness, order, and punctuality—in herself and her siblings. The townspeople said they could set their clocks by her regimented routine. Nancy Garrs later described her as "a bit of a tyke,"[9] meaning she was stingy because she doled out only a gill—five fluid ounces—of beer a day for the Garrs sisters to share. (Ale was a common beverage, as was tea—plain water was often polluted.) Aunt Branwell's attachment to sweet-natured, golden-haired baby Anne and precocious young Branwell, her sister's only son (who even as a child was likely a charmer), probably influenced her decision to willingly stay longer and care for her sister's motherless children. The two would remain her favorites, though she was probably always fair in her treatment of all the children.

Tiny Elizabeth Branwell wore old-fashioned high-waisted silk dresses, either black or in her favorite shades of mauve or purple, with a shoulder shawl to ward off the chill of the old house. Peeking from under her unfashionably large cap's ruffle was a youthful fake fringe of light auburn curls. A pious lady with perfect manners, she apparently also had a bit of an independent streak. She relished describing scenes of her youth in Cornwall where, though a staunch Methodist, she had a busy social schedule and apparently had been quite a belle. She enjoyed surprising visitors with her use of snuff, which she carried in a pretty little gold box she produced in company with a laugh, a small flourish, and probably a charming little smile. The sniffing of snuff (pulverized tobacco) was an old-fashioned habit popular in the eighteenth century, when Aunt Branwell was a young woman. Even then it was considered by many to be inappropriate for a lady, and it was rarely seen by the 1820s.

Despite her tales of her carefree youth, Elizabeth Branwell had been raised in an Evangelical church and had strong religious beliefs. She shared with the children her Methodist church magazines, which Charlotte once described as "mad . . . full of miracles and apparitions, and preternatural warnings, ominous dreams and frenzied fanatacisms."[10] Mr. Brontë was a curate of the Anglican Church of England (which referred to Methodists as Dissenters). He and Elizabeth Branwell did not see eye to eye with all of each other's beliefs, but they enjoyed discussing their differences.

She got along well with her brother-in-law and liked to read aloud to him on summer afternoons. Their many animated discussions during dark winter days touched on politics as well as religion. An intelligent conversationalist, she did not hesitate to disagree or express her own opinions, and Mr. Brontë was, for the most part, an unusually liberal cleric in his opinions of others' religious beliefs. The loss of his wife, coupled with his financial worries, had caused the once "saucy Pat"[11] (as his wife had teasingly called him) to sometimes appear austere and forbidding, but his sister-in-law was not daunted. Their discussions were a welcome diversion, and Mr. Brontë was very grateful for the aid of his wife's sister.

Anne was raised from babyhood by her aunt, at times even sharing a room in the crowded house. Though enjoying snuff and not opposed to dancing, Aunt Branwell still may have exposed Anne to stricter beliefs than those of her father.

The children respected their aunt but cheekily liked to sass her, too. They were amused when she wore outdoor overshoes inside the parsonage. Wood and metal pattens were ordinarily worn in the rain, snow, and mud—a helpful addition to boots. Though they could be awkward to wear, they were necessary on the dirty streets of Haworth. Their aunt was often heard, however, loudly clattering about in them indoors. The pattens raised her feet above the stone floors, protecting them from the cold. Some people found the sound they made annoying, even outdoors. Years later Charlotte may have thought of her aunt when she visited Kensington Gardens on one of her trips to London. A sign on the entrance gate announced that dogs and women wearing the dreaded pattens were prohibited from the gardens!

Aunt Branwell's favorite room was her own bedroom, overheated all year round. She fought a constant battle against the cold. She did not feel guilty about the cost of the fuel bills she incurred, for throughout her time in Haworth she insisted on paying her own way, contributing to the household expenses from her inheritance. She believed the children's care and the overseeing of the housekeeping were her sisterly duties.

Their aunt took over the girls' lessons in sewing and embroidery in her room. Charlotte found sewing tedious and was still not as adept with a needle as Emily. But throughout their lives, sewing would be a necessary skill, and they were expected to learn to make and mend their own clothing, and sew shirts and collars for their brother Branwell. Aunt Branwell also determined they would make clothing for charity, which she considered good for their souls.

3

The School at Cowan Bridge

. . . to teach them to clothe themselves with shame-facedness and sobriety . . .

Mr. Brontë was thinking of his daughters' minds, as well as their souls, when an advertisement in the newspaper caught his eye. He was worried about finding an appropriate school for his girls—and one he would be able to afford. Money for their schooling was among his most difficult problems to solve. Maria and Elizabeth had briefly attended a very fine boarding school founded by Mrs. Mangnall, who wrote their study book, but the expenses there were too high for all five girls to attend.

Reading an advertisement in the December 4, 1823, *Leeds Intelligencer* gave him hope. A school for the daughters of poor clergymen appeared to be exactly what he had been looking for: "[T]he great Object in View will be their intellectual and religious Improvement; and to give that plain and useful Education, which may best fit them to return with Respectability and Advantage to their own Homes, or to maintain themselves in the different Stations of Life to which Providence may call them."

The fees for the school were half the amount for schools his friends had recommended. Scandalous stories about inexpensive schools had appeared in local papers. They either did not catch Mr. Brontë's eye or were ignored because the Clergy Daughters School at Cowan Bridge had a long list of wealthy, well-known, and influential patrons—two of whom were men who had assisted him financially in the past. The founder of the Clergy Daughters School, the Reverend William Carus Wilson, was a well-respected cleric. Mr. Brontë may have believed he and Mr. Wilson shared opinions on education and religious instruction. He was totally confident he had chosen the perfect school for his five young daughters. He was determined *his* daughters would be well educated.

Mr. Brontë was born Patrick Brunty, the eldest son of a poor Irish farmer. Though he was born in a two-room cabin, his family soon moved to a larger house. Over the next twenty years, Patrick grew more and more determined to keep improving his situation. He was intelligent and ambitious, loved books, and believed education was the way out of poverty. As a boy, he had worked for a blacksmith, and had overheard his employer telling a customer that young Patrick was a "gentleman by nature."[1] The remark made a strong impression, and probably encouraged him to dream of becoming what society, at the time, determined was a *true* gentleman—educated, and in a gentleman's profession.

Patrick's father allowed his bookish son to stay in school, perhaps as a student/part-time teacher, at a time when farmers' children left school early to work. He may have studied more advanced subjects with a local clergyman. Amazingly, by age sixteen Patrick opened a school of his own, apparently teaching young sons of the gentry. After five or six years, he moved on, becoming a tutor to the children of an influential clergyman who taught him Latin and Greek. A classical education was necessary to attend university, which was Patrick's goal.

By his own efforts, and with the aid of two mentors, he was able at the age of twenty-five to travel to England to attend university. He received a scholarship but still struggled with expenses. He worked hard and was an excellent student. While at Cambridge University, Patrick Brunty changed his Irish surname (possibly at the suggestion of one of his mentors) to the more gentlemanly sounding Brontë. Meaning thunder in Greek, it was a name an ambitious, strong-minded young classical scholar would have found appealing. Making it even more attractive, Horatio Nelson—admired by Patrick as a hero of the ongoing wars with France—held the title of Duke of Brontë. The military and the church were the only ways at that time that a young man with no fortune could advance in life. Mr. Brontë may have been attracted to the military, but he was committed to the church. A friend wrote later that, with his discipline and asceticism, he would have made an excellent soldier.

In 1806, Patrick Brontë received his degree at St. John's College, Cambridge. This was an amazing accomplishment. At the time, there were few Irishmen accepted to the university, especially ones so poor. He was ordained into the Church of England and would serve as curate in several parishes before he attained the perpetual curacy in Haworth, where he would spend the rest of his life.

Patrick Brontë would always be known for his strong beliefs and commitment to improve the lives of his parishioners. He was said to have had a quick temper, but was also kind, gentlemanly, and courageous—even, as a young curate, saving a boy from drowning. He was well liked and had many friends. He was noted for his tall, upright carriage; his long, swift stride; and his ability to cover great distances carrying a stout thornwood stick. His friends jokingly called him "Old Staff."[2] Before Patrick met twenty-nine-year-old Maria Branwell in 1812, he had a broken engagement behind him. Considered very handsome and full of energy and determination, he was also believed to be somewhat eccentric.

The eccentricity of Patrick Brontë is often mentioned in biographies—few explanations for the opinions are ever given. Possible reasons early in his career were that he had a thick Irish accent, and his nose was often in a book. He wrote poetry. He ate frugally and had ascetic tastes. He enjoyed long walks and loved nature. His parishioners were English, and he was Irish. He would continue to be labeled as eccentric, and new reasons would later be added to the list.

The young curate's children would grow up with more opportunities than he ever thought possible as a boy growing up in Ireland. His only son would have a gentleman's education in the classics, which would qualify him to attend university. To Patrick Brontë, education was one of the most important gifts he could ensure his children received. But before he had daughters, he had expressed the opinion—popular at the time—that as a general rule girls needed little education. In his novelette, *The Maid of Killarney*, he wrote, "The education of a female ought, most assuredly, to be competent, in order that she might enjoy herself, and be a fit companion for man. But, believe me, lovely, delicate, and sprightly woman, is not formed by nature, to pore over the musty pages of Grecian and Roman literature, or to plod through the windings of Mathematical Problems. . . . Her forte is softness, tenderness, and grace."[3] He wrote this even though his wife was something of a "bluestocking" (not considered a compliment)—an intelligent, educated woman—with an interest in writing, herself.

Perhaps Mr. Brontë changed his mind due to his wife's influence, or when he realized how clever his own daughters were. The education of his three youngest would rival that of his son. Working-class girls might only need enough education to be able to find employment as maids, seamstresses, or shopkeepers, but the Brontë girls could not pursue working-class jobs. Thanks to their father's status, they were young *ladies*. They were, however, *poor* young ladies who would have to work, and they were bright and eager to learn. With his finances limited—and debts to pay—he may have borrowed from his friends or applied for aid from the church for their school fees as well as new clothing for each girl.

Along with a Bible and a prayer book, the Clergy Daughters School determined that an extensive wardrobe was to be brought with each girl. A partial list includes day shifts (slips), night shifts (nightgowns), night caps, corsets, cotton stockings, linen pinafores, a short jacket called a spencer, petticoats of both flannel and wool, shoes, and pattens. Also on the list were sewing supplies and assorted accessories. For a required fee, some items were provided by the school. Their uniforms were plain purple wool dresses and cloaks for winter. (Purple was a color associated with continued mourning—appropriate considering the sad and dreary conditions at the school.) In summer, there were simple off-white dresses, straw bonnets, and nankeen cotton frocks for every day.

Upon their arrival, the little girls' pretty hair was cut short in order "to teach them to clothe themselves with shame-facedness and sobriety, not with braided hair and costly apparel."[4] Usefulness and humility were goals at the school—but they would soon learn that so was fear and humiliation. The plain, identical uniforms and the shorn haircuts were meant to remind the girls of their status as charity children—something Charlotte, especially, would always remember with resentment.

Precocious Maria and sensible Elizabeth were the first of the little girls to be taken by their father by coach to the school at Cowan Bridge, forty-five miles from Haworth. The Clergy Daughters School was located in a row of sixteenth-century stone cottages, which had been built near an ancient stone

bridge across the little River Leck. The school felt very isolated in open countryside. Coaches from Leeds passed by without stopping until they reached
Kirkby Lonsdale—three miles up the road. William Carus Wilson had added
wings at right angles to each end of the cottages to provide schoolrooms, with
dormitories upstairs. There was also a covered walkway for exercise, as well as
a walled garden in the center of the buildings large enough for each girl to cul-
tivate a small plot of her own. There were nine staff members and six servants.
The school site was beautiful, with views of moors, woods, and mountains,
which Mr. Brontë would have appreciated. At first sight, the school made a
good impression.

Charlotte soon joined her older sisters at school. At eight, she was described by a teacher as a "bright, clever little child."[5] A grown-up Charlotte
believed she had been grave and quiet, though her father said that at home
she'd been a chatterbox who was apt to make funny, surprising comments.
When Mr. Brontë had important guests, Charlotte liked to spy on them. After
they left, she would mimic them so accurately that, though he tried to resist
the temptation, he would burst out laughing.

None of the girls at Cowan Bridge were to be educated in preparation for
university, for women were not allowed to attend. But girls like the Brontë
sisters (who had no dowry, prospect of inheritance, or beauty, and might be
unlikely to marry) were to be trained to be governesses or schoolteachers. For
this, Mr. Brontë paid an extra fee. He also paid extra for Maria to have music
lessons. Tidy, order-loving Elizabeth would be trained for the useful job of
family housekeeper, predetermining that she would probably remain single.
But governesses usually did not marry either, spending their lives with other
people's children.

At Cowan Bridge, the harsh conditions may well have alarmed the Brontë
girls, accustomed to a kind, close family and healthy food. The schoolgirls
were always hungry, as the cook was dirty and the food badly cooked. Sometimes the students preferred not to eat at all, so spoiled or inedible was the
food. Breakfast porridge was usually burned and had "offensive fragments
of other substances discoverable in it."[6] For dinner a "mess . . . of indifferent
potatoes and strange shreds of rusty meat"[7] were served. Twice a week, the
students were given beef that "had often become tainted from neglect."[8]

The site of the school was apparently not healthy. It was frequently damp
from fog and rain as well as cold, in both summer and winter. The wind blew

icy air from over the snowy mountain range to the north. It was a struggle for the younger or weaker girls to fight for a place by the fire in the cold evenings. The pupils were only allowed to write home once every four months, and though the Brontë sisters must have yearned to return to their home, they did not complain to their father.

That September, while Maria, Elizabeth, and Charlotte were frightened and miserable at Cowan Bridge, Branwell, Emily, and Anne experienced an alarming and troubling incident on Haworth Moor. On a fine afternoon at the beginning of the month, Sarah and Nancy took the three children, ages seven, six, and four, for a walk on the moors. They had recently been ill, and their father wanted them to have exercise and fresh air. When they were not home by six, Mr. Brontë grew anxious and went upstairs to look out a window facing the probable route the children had taken over the moors. He saw a dramatic, darkening sky with thunder, lightning, blowing dirt, and the threat of an impending rain storm. There was an eerie sense of stillness in the house, then the sound of a far-off explosion, a shaking of the floor, and a rattling of the windows. The dramatic event was a bog burst—a combination of an eruption, landslide, and flood, probably due to drought, followed by heavy rainfall. The real problem was overcutting of the peat and other mismanagement at the Crow Hill bog, only four miles over the moors behind the parsonage.

A frantic Patrick Brontë set out to find his children, Sarah, and Nancy. He located them—terrified and shivering—where they had taken shelter, the children huddling under Sarah's cloak, in the doorway of an isolated house. The little group barely escaped being swept away by the fast-moving flood of water, mud, and peat rushing down the valley from Crow Hill. Luckily an alarm had been raised, and the teenagers had rushed the terrified children to safety, away from the seven-foot-high torrent.

Afterward it was reported that thousands of sightseers came to view the wreckage. Houses were flooded and mills damaged. Cows and sheep were drowned, and even fish didn't survive, trapped and drowned in the mud. Bogs, fields, trees, walls, and bridges had been swept away. The polluted water brought the wool industries in the area to a halt for days. When investigators came, they downplayed the drama of the event, saying the bog burst was not caused by an earthquake but by a waterspout.

Mr. Brontë disagreed with the report. He had strong opinions of its cause, and delivered a powerful sermon and sent dramatic letters to local newspapers about the disaster and its impact. He had his sermon printed and wrote a poem for children so they could understand what he believed had happened. As an Evangelical, he believed the end of the world would one day occur and had felt during that frightening afternoon that the end was imminent. He still believed the bog burst was a sign and a warning. His warning, however, wasn't only about biblical predictions. He wanted to warn as many of his parishioners as he could of the danger of destroying their natural resources by mismanagement. The fears and concerns of most of the locals, however, were not for the possible end of the world or for men's mismanagement of Crow Hill bog, but for the disaster causing still further problems for the wool trade.

The fear, religious fervor, and upset following the bog burst would seem to have been yet another trauma for the young children. They would have been cautioned to be watchful on their walks, and to have great respect for the power of nature. The frightening event did not, however, diminish the children's love for the moors. Charlotte, who did not experience the bog burst, was the only one who ever expressed anxiety on their moorland walks. Emily, famous for her love of the moors, apparently never felt any fear of further disasters there. Outwardly, at least, the young children didn't appear to have suffered lasting harm from their brush with death.

The excitement of the bog burst died down, and changes at the parsonage were being made. Soon Emily would be taken to join her older sisters at the school at Cowan Bridge. A place was being held there for Anne in two or three years, when Mr. Brontë felt she would be old enough to leave home. Aunt Branwell could then return to Cornwall. Mr. Brontë's anxieties about his household were easing. There was a sense of anticipation building at the parsonage, and there was more than one reason for the flurry of activity.

Sarah and Nancy Garrs were busy assisting Aunt Branwell in sewing the large wardrobe required for little Emily to take with her to school. After she left, Nancy was to marry a young man from Bradford. Mr. Brontë teased her about marrying another Pat, and she answered, "Yes, sir . . . and if he prove but a tenth part as kind a husband to me as you have been to Mrs. Brontë, I shall think myself very happy in having made a Pat my choice."[9] Sarah would also be leaving. Mr. Brontë had found the eighteen-year-old a job traveling with a wealthy lady and her daughter as her maid/companion, but Sarah's mother was very much against the plan. Instead, Sarah would return to her parents' home and soon be apprenticed to a dressmaker, using the skills she had learned at the School of Industry. Before they left, Mr. Brontë gave each young woman a gift of £10, a considerable amount of money at the time. The Garrs sisters leaving meant Mr. Brontë would be able to save the money needed to pay for Emily's schooling by replacing the two girls with one elderly housekeeper/cook from the town, Tabitha Aykroyd—known as Tabby.

Nancy and Sarah had been with the four youngest children all their lives. Their steady presence as nurses, playmates, and confidants was vitally important after Mrs. Brontë's death. They had wiped away tears and made the children laugh. Their absence would be one more loss in the children's short lives.

Five years later Sarah married, too, and eventually immigrated to America with her husband and children. She remained devoted to the family that had taken her and her sister out of the School of Industry, giving them jobs and a home. A lock of hair from each family member, from Maria's dark brown hair to a curl of pale gold belonging to little Anne, was taken by Sarah to America. The household servants were always treated like members of the family, and remained loyal to the Brontës all their lives. When Mrs. Gaskell's biography of Charlotte was published, criticizing Mr. Brontë, Nancy was furious. She proclaimed he had been "outrageously misrepresented . . . a kinder master . . . never drew breath."[10] Sarah, Nancy, and the Brontës kept in touch with each other and always remembered one another fondly.

Years later eleven-year-old Martha Brown, one of the sexton's daughters, would join the household to assist Tabby. She would become equally devoted and remain with the family for the rest of their lives.

Except for staying with her sister for brief periods, the children's dearly loved Tabby lived in the parsonage until her death at the age of eighty-five.

Though he had personally delivered four of his daughters to the school at Cowan Bridge, Mr. Brontë can't have noticed any ill effects of the school's policies. It would have been unusual at the time for children to disagree with a parent's decision. Perhaps the girls wished to avoid upsetting their father, who was so pleased and optimistic about their school. They had made no complaints to him about their treatment or the conditions at the school, so in November Mr. Brontë delivered Emily to Cowan Bridge. She was apparently a charmer and one of the youngest at the school. Sweet and adorable at six years old, Emily showed little or none of the extreme shyness and avoidance of people for which she would later be known. She was well treated and fussed

over by the school staff. They described her as a "darling child . . . the pet nursling[11] of the school."

The treatment of her oldest sister, Maria, was very different. So loved and admired by her family, Maria was bullied and often punished by the school staff. Though intelligent and respectful, she was often ill, forgetful, and late to class. When washbasins were frozen in the mornings, Maria was singled out for punishment for not washing herself sufficiently. Punishment included a beating with a switch and wearing a sign (The Badge of Shame) for various misdemeanors. Maria would have been made to wear the sign naming her as a slattern—a rude word applied to an untidy person. Punishments were meant to humiliate, and it was difficult for Maria's three little sisters to watch her being bullied. Maria never complained. Little Elizabeth was also a patient and stoic child. When suffering from a bad cut to her head in a school injury, her courage and lack of complaint impressed the teacher who attended her.

In bad weather, the girls' uniforms and thin shoes, even worn with pattens, were inadequate for long walks. Still, the students were required to make a two-mile trek each way across the fields to Sunday worship at Tunstall church. The weather was often harsh, so arriving wet and tired was a common condition. In the ancient, gloomy, and unheated stone building, the little girls were alarmed by stories of the terrors of hell. Day-long sermons were only interrupted by a cold lunch in an equally cold room upstairs. After the walk home, however, their meal was a *whole* slice of bread with a tiny scrap of butter, as opposed to the usual half slice. Next they repeated their catechisms and Bible verses. The day concluded with another sermon.

The school's founder, William Carus Wilson, was an Evangelical but also a Calvinist whose interpretation of church teachings was extremely strict and harsh. He believed only a chosen few—the elect—would be saved and endless suffering was the fate of most of mankind. His sermons, and the books required to be read by the children in his school, told the fate of little girls who lied or were jealous, bad-tempered, vain, or selfish. The children were taught that those girls always met with terrible fates and would not go to heaven. The two clerics—William Carus Wilson and Patrick Brontë—differed greatly in their beliefs about the teachings of the church as well as how children should be taught, or treated.

The girls slept two to a bed in a long dormitory crammed with beds on both sides of the room. Respiratory illnesses were easily passed back and forth among the girls. Constant threats and predictions of a fearful future were a daily diet. Education may have been a priority, and cleanliness was stressed, but there seemed to be little concern on the part of the school for providing healthy food for the students, keeping them warm and dry, or notifying their parents when they became ill.

A common treatment for respiratory disorders was a blistering plaster (made of a preparation of dried beetle mixed with fat or wax) applied to the skin as an irritant, causing painful blisters. This was meant to draw out deep inflammation and poisons. The plasters were used from the Middle Ages into the twentieth century. When the painful irritant was applied to Maria's side by a doctor at Cowan Bridge, she felt so ill and in pain that she wished to stay in bed but—fearing the anger of her teacher—she tried to dress for class. The impatient teacher who had come to see why Maria was late grabbed her and jerked her across the room, not caring that the little girl was ill and in distress. Maria was then loudly berated for being dirty and slovenly, for which she was punished.

Charlotte would never forget or forgive her traumatic experiences at Cowan Bridge. Years later she would describe the harsh rules, cruelty of the teachers, frightening lessons, and inedible food in sharp, detailed language in her novel, *Jane Eyre*. The school in the novel—which she called Lowood— would be unforgettable to anyone who read the book, and would also be recognizable.

The Clergy Daughters School was not the only harsh and unhealthy school at the time, but it was unfortunate for any weak or sickly child to have been placed there—especially in the first year of the school's existence. The conditions there and the recurring bouts of fever and illness that swept through the school led to more serious diseases for many of the girls at Cowan Bridge, including Maria and Elizabeth Brontë.

Eleven-year-old Maria Brontë was at Cowan Bridge, seriously ill with the symptoms of tuberculosis (then called consumption), and her father was not told. When he was finally notified in mid-February of her illness, he quickly brought her home. Elizabeth, Charlotte, and Emily were frightened. Many of their fellow students were ill with a low fever (possibly typhus), which could have been caused by unsanitary conditions at the school. In fact, during the time the sisters were at Cowan Bridge, seven girls died of various illnesses—including tuberculosis—either at school or shortly after returning to their homes.

Maria was in the final stages of the disease, and by the beginning of May she was gone. Elizabeth, Charlotte, and Emily—still at Cowan Bridge—were not able to tell their sister goodbye. At the parsonage, the remaining family was devastated. Eight-year-old Branwell was overwhelmed with grief. His eldest sister Maria, though so young, had apparently been a motherly figure to him, providing the affection and sense of security his mother's loss had taken from him.

A month later, the pupils who had no symptoms of illness—which included Charlotte and Emily—were sent to Mr. Wilson's vacation home on the coast in Lancashire. They had to leave Elizabeth, who (very ill and probably infectious) was quietly taken home that same day by a school servant in a public coach. Mr. Brontë had not been notified of her serious condition, either. Had he known, he would have insisted Charlotte and Emily be brought home as well. As Elizabeth was suffering from the same symptoms as Maria, the anxious father immediately rushed to bring the younger girls home. They were confused and grief-stricken at the loss of Maria, and fearful of losing Elizabeth. Did they think about all the sermons they heard and the books they read at Cowan Bridge, about children punished by painful death? At least their father could comfort them with his kinder and more loving faith. In mid-June, Elizabeth died.

The deaths of the two girls at ages ten and eleven were a shock to the entire household. Charlotte later believed the harsh treatment at the school had killed her sisters, and the inadequate nutrition there had resulted in her own tiny stature. She was only four feet ten when fully grown. Her father was more than six feet in height, and Emily, the tallest of the girls, would grow to five feet six, considered very tall for a woman at that time.

Now the eldest child, Charlotte worried about the responsibility of looking after her brother and sisters. She thought often of Maria's example as an image of perfection that she wished to emulate. She believed she must guide and protect her siblings, especially her sisters—a determination she never relinquished as long as she lived, though Emily and Anne may have wished otherwise.

Nine-year-old Charlotte and seven-year-old Emily's grief, their rushed trip home, and even the absence of the Garrs sisters would have been very unsettling for the young girls even if they knew beforehand of the teenagers' departure. The new member of the household, Tabitha Aykroyd, may have quickly fit in with the family, however. She was outspoken, sharp-tongued, and opinionated, but she was also a rough, motherly, sensible, and loving Yorkshire woman whose steady presence would continue to provide a sense of security and safety. From then on, she would probably always be the supplier of comforting hugs for the children in the parsonage. Perhaps almost as important to them at the time, however, was that Tabby was a storyteller with many a diverting tale to tell.

The children were again recovering from trauma and loss, but they were home, and together again. Years later, in Emily's novel *Wuthering Heights*, she would write of a maid's desire to console bereaved children. As the maid (usually believed to be partly based on Tabby) neared the door of the fictional children's room, she realized: "The little souls were comforting each other with better thoughts than I could have hit on: no parson in the world ever pictured heaven so beautifully as they did, in their innocent talk."[12] Hopefully Emily was writing from her own memories of herself and her brother and sisters confronting their own loss of Maria and Elizabeth.

The children's father, aunt, and the new maid—concerned for their health, both emotional and physical—made sure to return them to their comforting routine of lessons, walks, and playtime. With Tabby's healthy food, they slowly recovered and resumed their imaginative games. There may also have been the comfort of a dog or cat for the children to play with and to accompany them on moorland walks. Mr. Brontë loved dogs, and there was probably always one in the parsonage, even in the early days in Haworth.

Apparently the children soon felt free to tease Tabby and even terrorize her, shrieking and playing exuberantly. She once took brief refuge at her nephew's nearby house, fearful of their wild games, vowing not to return to the parsonage. But she soon became accustomed to the children's play, and considered the "childer" to be hers. Tabby remained loyal, devoted, and protective of the entire family all her long life.

The warm, cozy kitchen was now Tabby's domain. The children spent a great deal of time there, and as they grew older, the girls helped with the cooking, baking, and cleaning alongside Tabby.

After moorland walks on dark winter afternoons, it was perhaps Tabby's light in the kitchen that would guide the children home. Rushing in—

sharing their recent adventure, their dog barking, the scent of the wind in their clothes, and their pink cheeks cold to the touch—they might have demanded their tea and perhaps one of Tabby's stories. Tabby's old Yorkshire tales entertained the children and probably helped win their affection. The elderly woman, in her colorful local dialect, swore she had known people who had seen the moorland fairies frequent "the margin of the 'beck' [stream] on moonlight nights"[13] long ago, probably delighting the wide-eyed young Brontës. (That was before the mills and factories, with their noise and dirt, had driven the fairies away!) Her stories contributed to the children's growing desire to invent their own tales, and to write them down.

4

The Twelves

Papa bought Branwell some wooden soldiers at Leeds.

Young Maria Brontë may have been the first of the children to construct small paper books, just as she had led the way inventing their first games and plays. The books were easily put together—just a cover and a few bits of paper sewn together, meant to look like the books on their shelves. Charlotte's first surviving book was written at age ten and was a gift for five-year-old Anne. It told the story of a little girl named "Ane." She was the only child of wealthy parents—who traveled with her mother by ship to a fine castle near the great city of London. When her mother became ill, Ane nursed her lovingly and saved her life. The tiny book is written in a round childish script and is approximately one inch by two inches, with a cover of white, blue, and gray printed wallpaper. Charlotte even illustrated her story with tiny watercolor pictures.

As in many large families, the children were taught early to look out for one another. The older ones entertained the younger, telling stories and giving them little gifts, such as Charlotte's book for Anne. Charlotte and Emily also made many sketches labeled "for Anne" throughout their childhood. Anne was especially cherished by the family. She was treated with affection and with extra efforts to protect her all her life. Around the same time Charlotte made her gift, Branwell created his own small book, "The Battell Book," with watercolor images of cannons and soldiers in red and blue uniforms. His story is about the British and Americans fighting in the War of 1812—a war only fourteen years before, and still fresh in the memory of the adults.

Mr. Brontë would have been aware from his children's chatter that they were imaginative and creative. Their efforts at storytelling would not have been a surprise because he himself was a writer. Unlike most fathers at the time, he allowed his children to read what they chose from his library. He liked to discuss current events with them, so they were encouraged to read newspapers and magazines, too, as their reading abilities grew. Though books were expensive, Mr. Brontë had a small, well-loved selection of mostly second-hand books. In his college years at Cambridge, he had received prize books from his professors and gifts from pupils he tutored. Many of his books were worn and well thumbed. Hopefully he didn't mind his children's scribbles, annotations, and sketches in the margins and on the end-papers of his books. He himself wrote many notes and comments in his copy of Graham's *Modern Domestic Medicine*. Among his books were poetry collections, biographies, classics, and geographies. The children saw them all as a possible source of ideas for their plays and games.

The siblings were proud that their own father's published books were displayed on the shelves in the parsonage. Perhaps one day they might be published, too? The idea grew, as did their abilities to make their own handmade, miniature books, looking as similar as they could to the ones they read every day. Mr. Brontë's few published books had shared his religious and political beliefs and his joy in the beauty of nature, which he felt expressed God's love. He greatly enjoyed writing. In the parishes he had served, he was seen as a minor celebrity for his literary accomplishments. He put effort into his plots and characterizations and tried to entertain his readers, though he always felt the need to instruct them. His most successful novella, *The Maid of Killarney*, was a love story as well as a religious and moral tale. It also included poetry and descriptive passages on nature and the beauty of Ireland. The book was a great influence on his children, and they imitated his style in their earliest writings. By the time the family moved to Haworth, his writing only consisted of articles for local papers. He had probably sadly realized he had neither the time nor the talent for great literary accomplishment.

Money was always strictly budgeted, and Mr. Brontë was in debt at times with no savings or other income to rely on in hard times. Still, he managed to find the funds for his children's toys, entertainment, and lessons. All the children shared a set of ninepins (a bowling game), brightly painted alphabet blocks, and a small toy village. Mr. Brontë gave Branwell his first box of twelve carved wooden soldiers the summer he turned seven. They were bought in Bradford and cost one shilling and sixpence. They would remain his favorites, though he would have several sets of the toys, including Indians and Turkish musicians.

The girls may not have found Branwell's toys of interest that summer. They had wax-headed dolls with little muslin dresses and tiny hats. Their father, or perhaps Aunt Branwell, had given them a wicker-work doll's cradle, and there was a child-size tea party set with a charming verse painted on the saucers. Many years after the Brontës were all gone, a loose floorboard in the children's study was discovered. When lifted, a hiding place was found containing a forgotten child's toy top and building bricks, believed to have belonged to the Brontë children.

Branwell was a careless boy and hard on his toys, especially his favorite carved soldiers, which according to Branwell himself were usually broken, burned, or lost on their moorland battlegrounds. During the long, mournful year after the loss of Maria and Elizabeth, Branwell, sadly, had no toy soldiers left at all. His grieving father may have been too distracted and anxious to think of children's toys.

At eight, precocious, red-haired Branwell, called Bany by his sisters, apparently looked like a miniature version of his father. He was full of energy and ideas and confident of his father's spoiling of him. He told his father what he wanted for his ninth birthday in June—a new set of twelve wooden soldiers. Both Charlotte and Branwell later thought what happened next was a momentous event, and important enough to record in their *History of the Year 1829*. Charlotte wrote:

"Papa bought Branwell some wooden soldiers at Leeds; when Papa came home it was night, and we were in bed, so next morning Branwell came to our door with a box of soldiers. Emily and I jumped out of bed, and I snatched up one and exclaimed, 'This is the Duke of Wellington! This shall be the Duke!' When I had said this, Emily likewise took up one and said it should be hers; when Anne came down, she said one should be hers. Mine was the prettiest of the whole . . . and the most perfect in every part. Emily's was a grave-looking fellow, and we called him 'Gravey.' Anne's was a queer little thing, much like herself, and we called him 'Waiting Boy.' Branwell chose his, and called him 'Buonaparte.'"[1] Branwell wrote his version of the occasion, too, adding that he had given the soldiers to his sisters to take care of, although they were his. Soon he gave the soldiers to them to keep.

The children, especially Branwell and Charlotte, inherited their father's interest in the military. There were many wars between the English and the French throughout history. Charlotte was born just a year after the end of a long war with their traditional enemy. Mr. Brontë probably shared stories with his children about the war with France, and his time in the militia. He had followed the esteemed careers of Lord Nelson and the Duke of Wellington, the heroes of the war's most famous battles. As a young student at St. John's College, Cambridge in 1803, Patrick Brontë had been one of thousands of men who joined militias when invasion by the French was feared. More than one hundred students were taught to use firearms, and they proudly paraded in the market square. There was an agreement that the student militia would be used only in event of invasion—they would not be sent abroad to fight. Eighteen-year-old Lord Palmerston was the elected officer of the thirty-five members of the St. John's contingent. (Only members of the aristocracy could be officers.)

Mr. Brontë was proud all his life that he had trained for nine months under the command of Lord Palmerston, who only five years later was appointed minister of war. The young officer would later become foreign secretary and, twice, prime minister. For years, there were invasion scares. Lord Nelson's victory at Trafalgar ended the worst fear of invasion, but the war didn't end until 1815. When the British and European armies defeated Napoleon at the famous battle at Waterloo in the Netherlands, the Duke of Wellington led the British forces.

For years, Branwell and Charlotte wrote about their imaginary versions of the Duke of Wellington and his famed adversary, the French general and emperor, Napoleon Bonaparte.

Many of the siblings' happiest childhood memories were centered on the toy soldiers (known as The Twelves, or The Young Men). The Twelves excited their imaginations and provided characters for their plays. They played with them upstairs, downstairs, in the cellar, and on the moors. The girls' dolls and a set of ninepins—and later new sets of Turkish musicians and Indians—stood in for other characters, and their adventures with their toys became more and more inventive and exciting. Soon the children began to write down the histories and activities of The Twelves, in the little books young Maria had shown them how to make. They were an appropriate size for the soldiers themselves to read. The children transcribed their tiny text to look like book print. An advantage of the books being so small was that it could be difficult for adults to read the tiny print, which gave a fun, secretive feeling to the whole venture. But to keep production going, they had to find a paper source.

Paper was expensive, so they salvaged their supplies from various sources. For their book covers, they were especially imaginative. They used wrappings from packages that came for their father; advertisements from books, with intriguing descriptions; floral-patterned wallpaper; and the blue cone-shaped paper package wrappers, still smelling sweetly of the sugar they had contained. The children must have been like little magpies, happily gathering newly found treasures—gray, brown, yellow, or blue; with text, or patterned, or plain—to save for the next tiny edition. The girls had, in their workboxes, scissors, needles, thread, and yarn, which they needed to cut the paper and stitch the sheets together. They all had art boxes containing watercolor cakes, brushes, and small dishes for water, to illustrate their books with tiny paintings.

When the children read a story, they usually wanted to make it into a play, adding imaginative additions with enthusiasm. Bossy and self-confident Branwell was the ringleader of their little troupe of actors, writers, and publishers. He created most of the early stories.

One of his plays for The Twelves was called "Our Fellows." It was inspired by one of their favorite books: *Aesop's Fables*. "Our Fellows" was probably played on the moors, since it involved Branwell's preferred game—battles—which his sisters were beginning to find tiresome. The girls also disliked Branwell killing their favorite characters—it was painful to lose even imaginary people. They often used a magical process to bring them back to life. They didn't want anyone to die. They had found a way to control their little make-believe worlds as they had not been able to do in their own lives.

In "Our Fellows," the children pretended to be giants ten miles high, except for Emily, who for some unknown reason was only four miles high. The basic story line of "Our Fellows"—upheaval in governments, unrest, rebellions, and wars in which The Twelves would take part—underwent variation upon variation.

The children participated in their plays as themselves, or as genii—the term borrowed from *The Arabian Nights*. Each child was a Chief Genii: Brannii (Branwell), Tallii (Charlotte), Emmii (Emily), and Annii (Anne). They spoke in dramatic, trumpet-like voices when playing their roles as Chief Genii. The genii were all-powerful. They could read minds. They could protect and rescue their own favorite character. They could also discipline them.

In the "History of the Rebellion of Our Fellows," Branwell wrote, "Good man was A Rascal and did want to Raise a Rebellion."[2] Good Man (Charlotte) had written to Little Bany (Branwell) declaring war on him. One can imagine what may have partly inspired the plot. The siblings were normal children— sometimes argumentative, rowdy, and competitive. Charlotte lost the war and had to pay homage—probably reluctantly—to Branwell (aptly named Boaster in the play).

Also intriguing was the name given to Anne—Clown. Described earlier by Charlotte as "a queer little thing," was she a delightfully comic little girl, making faces and perhaps unintentionally hilarious comments? Apparently the children also humorously called characters in "Our Fellows" the "O Dears" as they were so often in trouble, as perhaps the children were as well. Aunt Branwell may have despaired of ever keeping the girls from joining in unladylike and exuberant games with their brother.

While the children were happily involved with their play, their father was planning a visit to the neighboring town of Keighley, where a famous visitor was expected. A cleric friend of Mr. Brontë was hosting William Wilberforce, who had been one of the most important and vocal leaders in the movement to abolish the slave trade, trying to undo wrongs, and introducing new, progressive programs.

Aside from wishing to hear William Wilberforce speak at the Keighley vicarage, Mr. Brontë would perhaps have wanted to thank the great man in person for the aid he had twice given him. Finances had been the young Irishman's greatest problem when he was a student at St. John's College. He had sought the aid of an influential cleric who was sympathetic to Patrick Brontë's aspirations to enter the church. The cleric had in turn appealed to the wealthy Wilberforce—a graduate of St. John's himself—on behalf of the Irish student. Wilberforce had agreed to personally sponsor him. Patrick Brontë had attracted the attention of more than one important man due to his outstanding qualities, dedication to his work, and efforts to fight injustice—such as his attempts to secure the release of a man falsely accused of deserting the army. Wilberforce had helped Mr. Brontë by contacting Lord Palmerston to intervene in the case, which resulted in the man being set free.

The children would have also appreciated that William Wilberforce had urged the creation of a society to prevent cruelty to animals. The children (especially Emily and Anne) were beginning—and would continue the rest of their lives—to collect a menagerie of pets. There would be a steady parade of dogs, cats, and birds as time passed, though Aunt Branwell was strict at first about what room in the parsonage they were allowed to enter. Fortunately for the children, their aunt lost the battle of limiting their number, as Emily and Anne collected more and more pets, some of whom moved freely about the old house.

Only a month after the excitement of the Wilberforce visit, there was a thrilling and unusual event of even more interest to children. Charles Green, the most famous aeronaut of the nineteenth century, embarked on a balloon flight, leaving from Keighley—just four miles away. Huge crowds gathered there to watch the famous balloonist ascend, crossing Haworth Moor to Colne, in Lancashire. The delighted Brontë children could have watched from the moors, or even from their own upstairs windows, where there would have been a clear view. The balloon flight and the brave Mr. Green fired up their imaginations, and balloon flights were to be featured in many of their childhood writings, including what they considered their next "great play"[3]—*The Tale of the Islanders*.

On a typical night with her siblings and Tabby, eleven-year-old Charlotte recorded a charming example of the children's method of story development. Her creative spelling and punctuation has been made legible here.

"The play of the 'Islanders' was formed in December, 1827, in the following manner. One night, about the time when the cold sleet and stormy fogs of November are succeeded by the snow-storms, and high piercing night winds of confirmed winter, we were all sitting round the warm blazing kitchen fire, having just concluded a quarrel with Tabby concerning the propriety of lighting a candle, from which she came off victorious, no candle having been produced. A long pause succeeded, which was at last broken by Branwell saying, in a lazy manner, 'I don't know what to do.' This was echoed by Emily and Anne.

"*Tabby*. 'Wha ya may go t'bed.'

"*Branwell.* 'I'd rather do anything than that.'

"*Charlotte.* 'Why are you so glum to-night, Tabby? Oh! suppose we had each an island of our own.'

"*Branwell.* 'If we had I would choose the Island of Man.'"[4]

The sisters chose the isles of Wight, Arran, and Guernsey. Charlotte chose the Duke of Wellington as her chief man. The others each chose their chief men.

Charlotte ended the report, "Here our conversation was interrupted by the, to us, dismal sound of the clock striking seven, and we were summoned off to bed. The next day we added many others to our list of men, till we got almost all the chief men of the kingdom."[5]

The children were to be protectors of their islands in their roles as Little King (Branwell) and Little Queens (the sisters), who were the equivalent of Chief Genii. The "Tale of the Islanders" was Charlotte's first long series of connected stories. There were adventures, including a dark and vaulted subterranean dungeon for wayward children. Presumably the play took place in their own cellar.

Their story included a school rebellion, an intrigue with a quarrelsome version of Princess Victoria, and the Duke of Wellington arriving in a balloon! The duke ended the rebellion by threatening to bring a thousand bloodhounds. After the surrender "the school prospered as before but we, becoming tired of it, sent the children of[f] to their own home's & now only fairy's dwell in the Island of a dream."[6]

Charlotte alone carried on the story for a while, but she finally lost interest, too. The last chapter included quarrels (possibly real) incited by the Little King (Branwell), who was always causing trouble, according to Charlotte. Her attitude to her brother was often humorously patronizing. She enjoyed emphasizing his spoiled misbehavior in her stories.

Charlotte and Emily, who slept in the children's study at that time, invented a secret play one icy night at the end of 1827. After the candles were extinguished, they came up with a probably spooky and mysterious tale, as befitted the cold winter night. (Both girls especially loved scary stories and would continue to do so, even as adults. Charlotte's novels, *Jane Eyre* and *Villette*, and Emily's *Wuthering Heights* were to have elements of mystery and Gothic touches, which were first introduced to them by their father's and Tabby's tales and the books they read as girls.) Did their father knock on their adjoining wall to stop the whispering and giggling as the two little girls made up the tales they called bed plays? It probably was fun to hint to their siblings about a secret kept not only from the adults but also from Branwell and Anne—stories they were not going to share. Charlotte claimed she would never forget the tales, so (to the regret of later readers) they were not recorded.

5

Scribblemania

. . . we must now conclude for we are dreadfully tired.

Mr. Brontë often took his young children on walks in Haworth and neighboring Keighley. One of their stops was at the studio of artist John Bradley. He was well known locally, and had shown his work at exhibitions in Leeds. A friend of Mr. Brontë remembered seeing the cleric's children in the studio studying the artist's work with avid attention.

The thorough education Mr. Brontë wanted to give his children included the arts. When they showed interest in drawing and painting, he arranged for classes with Mr. Bradley. The primary method of teaching at the time was to copy the work of well-known artists from art books. It probably was Mr. Bradley who first saw talent in eleven-year-old Branwell, encouraging him to try difficult copy-work as well as working from life. The girls were equally determined to improve their skills, and many sketches were made by all of them throughout 1828. Perhaps Mr. Bradley suggested the career of professional painter to Branwell, or at least inspired him to dream of being an artist. Charlotte shared the same dream, though the career was frowned upon for women, making success more difficult. Each of the Brontë children showed talent, and in the following years, the sisters created very accomplished and detailed drawings and watercolor paintings.

When the children showed an interest in music, their father arranged for them to have lessons with the parish organist, Abraham Sunderland. (He was to appear as a character in one of their stories, as Mr. Sudbury Figgs.) Sunderland was enlisted to teach Branwell the flute, organ, and piano. The girls had piano lessons, too. Charlotte had to abandon her efforts to learn, as her eyesight was too poor to read the sheet music. Music was worked into their stories, as was most of what they learned or encountered in their everyday lives.

With their studies, their writing, and their art and music, they were happy and busily occupied. Evenings often found them all writing stories on their ink-stained lap desks or opening their painting boxes to create little paintings, including several charming portraits of their pets. They also meticulously copied detailed studies of birds from Thomas Bewick's *History of British Birds* or little scenes from their well-thumbed copy of his *Fables*. Charlotte would later describe her fictional Jane Eyre admiring the delightful illustrations in one of Bewick's books as she hid behind a curtain in her cruel aunt's home.

The siblings went to the workshops of cabinet maker and carpenter William Wood, Tabby's great-nephew, to obtain frames for their drawings and paintings. He would probably have given them for free, as they were made from scrap wood. But they wouldn't take them without paying, so they traded some of their small paintings for frames. At one time, Mr. Wood had a drawer full of their art work, but his children played with them and they were soon tattered and lost. He later wished he had kept them.

Twelve-year-old Charlotte reported on the family's activities on an ordinary day in March. "I am in the kitchen of the Parsonage, Haworth; Tabby, the servant, is washing up the breakfast-things, and Anne, my youngest sister . . . is kneeling on a chair, looking at some cakes which Tabby has been baking for us. Emily is in the parlour, brushing the carpet. Papa and Branwell are gone to Keighley. Aunt is up-stairs in her room, and I am sitting by the table writing this in the kitchen. Keighley is a small town four miles from here. Papa and Branwell are gone for the newspaper, the 'Leeds Intelligencer,' a most excellent . . . newspaper . . . Mr. Driver lends us . . . 'Blackwood's Magazine,' the most able periodical there is."[1]

One of the most important literary influences on the children's imaginations and their development as writers was a monthly Scottish publication, *Blackwood's Edinburgh Magazine*. It was lively and entertaining, and often satirized the famous and the infamous. The editors had been threatened and sued for libel more than once for their sometimes outrageous claims. The children delighted in it and avidly read it, cover to cover. There were knowledgeable articles, poetry, and stories. The variety of subject matter ranged from explorations and reports of military campaigns to reviews of art exhibitions. The articles supplied the children with enough ideas to fill many of the hundred or more tiny books they created over the next thirteen years. Once, reading an old issue from 1818, they were excited to find an advertisement for their father's novel, *The Maid of Killarney*. And when they found that James Hogg (their favorite writer on the magazine) had named his character's dog O'Brontë, they were delighted, finding it hilariously funny.

When Branwell was seventeen, he wrote to the editor, hoping to write for his favorite publication. "I cannot express . . . the heavenliness of . . . articles . . . read and re-read while a little child. . . . I speak so, sir, because as a child 'Blackwood' formed my chief delight."[2] He wrote a total of six times to the periodical over the years. They never responded to his letters.

The children read a review in *Blackwood's* of Thomas Edward Bowdich's book *The Mission from Cape Coast Castle to Ashantee: With a Statistical Account of That Kingdom, and Geographical Notices of Other Parts of the Interior of Africa*. They were inspired, as usual, to mix fact with fiction to tell the next adventures of their wooden soldiers—the Young Men. Sailing from England, the brave band landed on the coast of Africa to found their own imaginary lands—the Glasstown Federation—divided between the siblings' favorite soldiers.

As they grew older, some of the early, humorous, names of the Young Men were changed, becoming more dignified. Emily renamed Gravey after real-life explorer Sir William Edward Parry, whose expedition to find the North-West Passage the children had read about in *Blackwood's Magazine*. Anne's soldier's name was changed from Waiting Boy to Sir James Clarke Ross. Ross had traveled to the Arctic with Parry. Branwell's Napoleon went through many name changes—Sneaky, Rogue, and finally Northangerland—as well as changes to his personality.

Branwell drew a detailed map of their lands on the coast of Africa. They were named Stumpsland, Monkeysland, and Frenchyland. He invented the "old young men tongue."[3] It was apparently an ancient language, which he demonstrated by speaking in the local Yorkshire dialect while holding his nose, perhaps causing giggles from the younger children and older-sister distain from Charlotte. Branwell wrote elaborate details of the history of Glasstown—city facts, figures, and geography.

At twelve, Branwell created his own tiny version of *Blackwood's Magazine*, a miniature book like the others the children had created. It looked as much as possible like the original printed magazine, with decorated covers, illustrations, and many of the other details common to a periodical. He included humorous, often witty letters to the editor as well as reviews, fiction, commentaries, articles on travel, and poetry. He even included humorous advertisements. It was a publication for The Twelves, in Glasstown. Branwell named it "Branwell's Blackwoods Magazine."

A favorite article in *Blackwood's* had consisted of conversations of a group of actual and imaginary writers in an Edinburgh tavern. The children's version was recorded as a play, conversing in the personas of their favorite characters—supposedly in Bravey's Inn in Glasstown, but probably acted out in the parsonage parlor.

Branwell experimented with writing verse plays, heroic verse, and medieval tragedies, and Charlotte followed his lead. By writing in different genres, and as different characters, they were growing as writers. There would be a monthly issue of "Branwell's Blackwoods Magazine" for the next two years. The years 1829 and 1830 were a very creative time for all the siblings. Eighteen tiny books have survived from 1829 alone. Branwell, studying Latin with his father, liked to include the ancient language in his stories. But the most clever use of his new knowledge was his name for their extremely enthusiastic scribbling—*furor scribendi*—scribblemania.

Mr. Brontë admired the work of the famous, popular artist John Martin. Several mezzotint prints of his fantastic, theatrical, dark, and ominous visions of biblical scenes adorned the walls of the parsonage. The children were fascinated by the elaborately detailed paintings of tiny figures amid apocalyptic surroundings of massive architecture, dark stormy skies, and turbulent seas.

The dramatic narrative features of Martin's paintings gave the siblings details to add to their vision of Glasstown. Charlotte loved to write lengthy, overwrought, descriptive passages in her stories, inspired by Martin's work. In "Tales of the Islanders," she wrote "from a beautiful grove of winter roses & twining woodbine towers a magnificent palace of pure white marble whose elegant & finely wrought pillars & majestic turrets seem the work of mighty Geni [sic] & not of feeble men."[4]

One of Martin's paintings is of enormous buildings reflected in the still, glassy waters of a river. Viewing that painting probably inspired the name of the children's imaginary African capital cities—all called Glasstown.

Artists, writers, and even engineers have been influenced by Martin's images. The power of his work to inspire has continued for almost two hundred years. Films—from Cecil B. DeMille's biblical movies to George Lucas's science fiction—owe much to Martin. The Brontë children, standing transfixed before his print of *Belshazzar's Feast* displayed in their dining room, may have been among the first to find inspiration from his work.

There was a pattern to the creation of their projects. Branwell had creative ideas, led the way in developing them, took part for a while, became bored, and moved on to pursue his next idea. After six months as editor of his magazine, he tired of it and turned the position over to Chief Genius Charlotte, who renamed it the "Young Men's Magazine." He promptly started a newspaper he called "The Monthly Intelligencer." He continued to make contributions to the magazine, but Charlotte filled it primarily with her own poetry and prose—especially tales of her imaginary version of the Duke of Wellington (an imposing, attractive man in real life) and his two imaginary sons, whose personalities changed a great deal as her stories progressed. She still favored the inclusion of mystery, magic, fairies, elves, and old legends, which Branwell scoffed at. She had fun with the advertisements (as Branwell had), such as "THE ART OF BLOWing ones Nose"[5] and "*How to Curl One's Hair*, by Monsieur Whats-the-reason."[6]

After a few months, Branwell announced he would no longer be involved with his former creation—blaming Charlotte for the silly romances and frivolity, which had changed what he liked to claim, unbelievably, had been a more serious, sober publication! She answered by heralding the end of dullness.

Branwell and Charlotte both wrote comical satire aimed at each other. They never missed a chance to poke fun at and insult one another, which they enjoyed immensely. They were writing partners whose competitiveness inspired them both, and they enjoyed reading each other's new creations.

The children's stories were an expression of inventive minds, and a way to escape reality. They often were also very humorous, which must have resulted in a great deal of laughter as they shared their work with one another. Charlotte wrote a spoof aimed at reviving a fainting Glasstown poet (Branwell). It involved the use of "hartshorn, cold water, vinegar salvolatic . . . and sal everything else."[7] Inspired by the names of characters in John Bunyan's *Pilgrim's Progress*, which included Great-Heart, Much-Afraid, and Mr. Ready-to-Halt, the children imaginatively came up with their own characters' names, such as Mr. Blatant, Alexander Rogue, Henry Fearnothing, Skulker, and Young Man Naughty.

In Branwell's version of a literary commentary, he ended with "this is one of the most long winded Books that have ever been printed we must now conclude for we are dreadfully tired."[8]

The children wrote quickly—they didn't worry about spelling, grammar, or punctuation. Length seems to have been valued. Charlotte bragged about the fourteen pages she had written in two days.

She often made fun of Branwell's pomposity and the poetic pretension that he was a budding Romantic poet like Lord Byron. The well-aimed barbs may have been good for him. But perhaps not so beneficial for her little sisters was Charlotte's amusing but unkind spoof of Emily and Anne's make-believe world. From the beginning, both Charlotte and Branwell had teased the younger girls and were patronizing about their more childish efforts at writing. Emily and Anne cared more about dolls than soldiers.

The two oldest children always took precedence over the younger ones in all their games and plays. Emily and Anne's roles were too often unimportant—and may have resulted in arguments and tears. Their chief men would never be taken as seriously as the magnificent Duke of Wellington or any of the varied versions of Napoleon Bonaparte.

Branwell and Charlotte were also the main contributors to the Glasstown stories. Although the early writings of Emily and Anne were all either lost or destroyed, the younger girls were also involved. They controlled their own soldiers in the adventures, and made their own little books. By 1829, or even earlier, they were writing partners, just as Charlotte and Branwell had become a team.

Thirteen-year-old Charlotte was working on a piece for the "Young Men's Magazine" for the October 1829 issue. Using her pseudonym of Lord Charles Wellesley, she turned her attention to her younger sisters' Parrysland, which was as unlike her own Wellingtonsland—with its magnificent architecture, heroes, and villains—as possible. Emily and Anne preferred the familiarity of a setting similar to Haworth and its moors and mills rather than hot, exotic Africa. Charlotte had not been impressed with Branwell's old young men's tongue, but she used a version of it—a combination of Yorkshire dialect and baby talk—in her tale, to emphasize her sisters' childish world. Her dismissive and sarcastic Lord Charles wrote a description of his arrival on a trip to Parrysland:

"I . . . was immediately struck with the changed aspect of every thing. Instead of tall . . . muscular men going about . . . with guns on their shoulder . . . I saw none but little shiftless milk-and-water-beings, in clean blue linen jackets & white aprons[.] all the houses were ranged in formal rows. they contained four rooms each with a little garden in front. No proud Castle or splendid palace toweres [sic] insultingly over the cottages around."[9]

Parry's Palace was an unpretentious building with a moderate sized garden with "rows of peas, gooseberry bushes . . . & a grass place to dry clothes on." A paddock had one milk cow and "one horse, to draw the gig, carry their majesties, & bring home provisions from market."[10] There were also "three cats, two dogs, five rabbits & six pigs."[11]

At tea, "Parry took from the cupboard a napkin, which he directed me to pin before my clothes lest I should dirty them, saying in a scarcely intelligible jargon 'that he supposed they were my best as I had come on a visit & that perhaps my mama would be angry if they got stained.'"[12]

According to Charlotte, she and Branwell discussed art, literature, and politics in their stories, while Emily's and Anne's characters conversed in babyish language about the latest dolls' clothes. "Aun . . . moide Trahl a nou clouk of flouered muslin waud punk rubun ot de bottom & faul saulk belt."[13] Charlotte continued with more baby talk, but roughly translated it reads that Anne made a new cloak of flowered muslin with pink ribbon at the bottom and full silk belt, and that the latest dress Emily had made was a beautiful pale crimson trimmed with yellow green and purple, and a feather in his cap of a rich lilac color. If Charlotte's spoof of her sisters' creations represented actual elaborately designed doll clothes they had created, it's in stark contrast to Emily's later reported lack of interest in her clothing.

The dinner at Parry's Palace was simple Yorkshire fare. After dinner, Lord Charles (Charlotte) wrote, "I felt a strong inclination to set the house on fire, & consume the senseless gluttons."[14] Ross apparently overate, and became so ill "Death was . . . expected . . . had not the Genius Emily arrived" and "cured with an incantation & vanished."[15] Lord Charles reported he "found my visit intolerably dull."[16]

Charlotte's story was, of course, an exaggeration. But she was ridiculing her eleven- and nine-year-old sisters who were envisioning an imaginary world, and apprenticing as writers too, in their own small books. But they had different tales they wished to tell than those of their older sister and brother. It is no surprise they were beginning to break away from their siblings, and the world of Glasstown.

While the children were busily constructing their made-up worlds, their father was trying, by writing letters to local newspapers, to influence his countrymen to bring about change in the real world. He was joining other reformers throughout England to petition the government for the abolition of slavery in the entire British Empire. Still other petitions were aimed at changing the criminal code, which gave the same punishment—hanging—for the theft of a sheep as for a murder. Neither effort produced results, but the fight continued.

In the summer of 1830, exhausted by his parish duties, his seemingly failed efforts for reform, and probably depressed and run down, Mr. Brontë became seriously ill with an inflammation of the lungs.

6

Roe Head School— and Home Again

. . . to bend our inclination to our duty.

Mr. Brontë was confined to his bed for weeks, unable to perform his clerical duties. The family and Tabby were fearful he would not recover. For months, he was weak and depressed. He slowly regained his health, but, newly reminded of his own mortality, he worried about his children's futures. His girls especially were in danger of being left without a home or support should he die. He decided it was time for fourteen-year-old Charlotte to go back to school to learn the skills she needed to begin her life as a governess. Charlotte's school fees would have been a problem, which he may have solved by borrowing what was needed from friends. He'd had to seek loans in the past, but he always paid his debts.

Unlike many clerics, Mr. Brontë had no property or inheritance of his own to leave his children. Most of the money he could save would be put away for university or art training for his son—bright and spoiled young Branwell. The whole family was confident Branwell was destined for an impressive future, even a great future. But what was to become of the girls? If his daughters did not marry, they must have employment. Their choices were limited, however, by the societal rules of the day. There was a rigid class structure. As daughters of a man of the church they were considered ladies, and the only professions acceptable for them by society were governess or teacher. But even these respectable careers lowered their position in society. They would be not *quite* equal to their employers, although theirs was a higher status than that of the servants.

Roe Head school was a genteel boarding establishment on the outskirts of Mirfield. Charlotte traveled twenty miles from Haworth in a horse-drawn covered carrier cart, arriving feeling miserable, conspicuous, and already homesick. The other girls arriving at the school were in fancy gigs or carriages.

The school was in an impressive three-story house that had previously been a private home. It had distinctive double bow windows and was large and comfortable, with pleasant lawns and gardens. There were woods wrapping around one side and the rear of the house. This gave a feeling of privacy from the traffic on the road into town. The property was well placed in an area away from the polluted air of the mills and factories on the valley floor.

The boarding school had been recommended to Mr. Brontë by friends, and most of the pupils were the young daughters of powerful local manufacturers. Margaret Wooler was the headmistress. She was part of a close knit family, and owned and ran the school with her four sisters. Mr. Brontë considered her intelligent, respectable, and motherly. A well-spoken woman, she was popular with the girls and had a talent for making her pupils interested in their studies. At thirty-five, she was described as short and stout—not pretty, but graceful. Always strikingly dressed in white, she looked like an imposing and dignified lady abbess, the girls thought. She wore her long hair in braids coiled on top of her head, resembling a crown. A few long ringlets completed her striking appearance.

As only seven to ten students were accepted at a time, the teachers could give each girl personal attention. Best of all, Mr. Brontë had made sure the school bore no resemblance to Charlotte's first school, at Cowan Bridge. Though the regimen at Roe Head was disciplined, the teachers were kind and understanding, and there would be outdoor games as well as dances and plays during the school year. And "on Saturday half-holidays they went on long scrambling walks down mysterious shady lanes"[1] and up the hillsides, where there were views over the countryside.

Charlotte knew she was fortunate to be attending the school, but she found it difficult to fight her misery. There was little time for daydreaming and writing stories. She missed her family and Tabby. She felt awkward with strangers, and often believed she was misunderstood and too different from her classmates to be liked, too far behind in the curriculum to succeed, and too plain to be admired. Very soon, however, she made several friends, who would remain her closest friends for life—especially pretty, gentle, and conventional Ellen Nussey, with her ringlets and heart-shaped face, and outspoken, clever, and independent-minded Mary Taylor.

The Brontë siblings had never played with other young children and learned the usual childhood games—they had made up their own. Even wishing to fit in at school, Charlotte could not be convinced to join in the lively games her classmates played on the lawns. Headmistress Margaret Wooler, however, encouraged all the girls to exercise. When the weather was too inclement to go outside during the day, Miss Wooler walked with them around the parlor in the evening. It was a companionable exercise that also included discussions (and probably gossip). Charlotte enjoyed it, and when they returned home, she and her sisters would continue the practice for the rest of their lives.

Charlotte wanted to share personal details about herself with her new friends. She wanted to tell them how she and her brother and sisters spent their time at home—their plays, their handmade books and magazines, and their enjoyment of long walks on the moors. She soon realized, however, that what was important to her and to her siblings was considered eccentric by her school friends. Mary Taylor remarked to Charlotte that the creative play that absorbed her and her siblings seemed to be "like growing potatoes in a cellar. She said, sadly, 'Yes! I know we are!'"[2] (Thirteen-year-old Mary also thoughtlessly told Charlotte she was rather ugly. She later apologized for her unkind comment, but Charlotte answered, "You did me a great deal of good, Polly, so don't repent of it."[3]) Charlotte did share with her new friends her sorrow over the loss of her two older sisters. She cried as she spoke of them—especially when she spoke of her eldest sister, Maria, whom she continued to idolize and wished to emulate. Though Charlotte enjoyed her new friendships, nothing could rival the close, dependent relationship she shared with Branwell, Emily, and Anne.

At fourteen, Charlotte was neat and quiet, but she was mocked and laughed at by her fellow students for her appearance as well as her strong Irish accent, picked up from her father. (Even as an adult, she was described as having a Yorkshire-Irish accent.)

Since Cowan Bridge, Charlotte had refused to eat meat, unable to forget the spoiled and inedible fare, but by the end of her time at Roe Head, she had been persuaded to return to her former diet.

Aunt Branwell apparently had no understanding of the discomfort of being young and different in a new school. She always dressed Charlotte, Emily, and Anne in old-fashioned dresses like those worn when she, herself, was young. Charlotte arrived at school in a dark, rusty-green dress, long out of style. Ellen Nussey, on her first day at school, had encountered Charlotte sitting alone and crying. Ellen had been comforting and confided her own homesickness. She later insisted Charlotte was not as unattractive as she was sometimes described. But Ellen admitted Charlotte had a "crooked mouth,"[4] a square face, and "want of complexion (reddish skin)."[5]

Charlotte's eyesight was very poor (made worse by years of creating minuscule details in her artwork and tiny script in her handmade books). To read, she had to hold her book only inches from her face and squint her eyes to see the text. According to Ellen, Charlotte had an "invincible objection to wearing glasses,"[6] possibly fearing she would be considered even more plain. Later, as her eyesight worsened, she relented and wore spectacles—round and wire-rimmed like Branwell's.

Because of her shyness and tiny, thin figure, Charlotte gave the impression she was younger than she was. She found visits to her godmother (Frances Atkinson, who lived less than a mile from Roe Head) particularly upsetting. She felt humiliated and angry at being thought of and treated as a very young child.

Aunt Branwell had taught the girls to curl their hair with metal curling tongs, which were heated by holding them over flames. This could singe their hair, as well as perhaps burn an ear or neck during the process. The goal was curled ringlets, and is possible with the tongs, but somehow Aunt Branwell's method resulted in a combination of a frizzy fringe and tight little curls. Fourteen-year-old Charlotte's hair style was as unflattering as her dress, and was also out of style. More popular with her schoolmates was the technique of rolling strands of damp hair onto homemade curl papers or rag strips. The papers or rags were then twisted or tied. Once the hair dried and was unrolled, the results were soft ringlets that could be arranged in a variety of attractive ways. One popular source of curl papers among the schoolgirls was their used exercise books, which they may have been happy to destroy by cutting them into strips.

Charlotte wrote home weekly—usually to Branwell, whom she may have missed most, especially since they were closest in age and had spent so many years on joint projects and in friendly competition. One of her happiest days at the school was a surprise visit from thirteen-year-old Branwell. He had missed Charlotte so much his father allowed him to walk the twenty plus miles to Roe Head and back in one day, just for a brief visit with her.

Before long, the girls who had laughed at Charlotte's differences from themselves, and originally considered her hopelessly ignorant and odd, grew to recognize and admire her talent, diligence, and lack of ego. It probably helped that Ellen Nussey and Mary Taylor—who were popular girls—had befriended her. The three girls were all intelligent and at the top of their class. Mary was also stubborn and rebellious, and had forfeited a month's dinners for refusing to do an assignment. Charlotte had shown she was knowledgeable about subjects the other students knew little about. She impressed them when she quoted poetry and spoke about literature, authors, art, and famous painters she had studied at home. They also enjoyed her storytelling at bedtime, especially her ghost stories inspired by books she had read and Tabby's tales of the fairies and spirits that roamed Haworth Moor. One of her dramatic tales—of raging seas, a castle, and a sleepwalker—upset a classmate so much that Charlotte refused to tell more of her frightening tales, though that decision most likely disappointed her schoolmates. Her stories also resulted in the only trouble she got into while at school—for "late [night] talking."[7]

After the worst of her homesickness wore off, Charlotte appreciated her time at school. She knew it was difficult for her father to pay her tuition, and she was determined to learn all she could, as quickly as she could. She was studying subjects her father may not have stressed, such as geography, the rules of grammar, and spelling—all four children were poor spellers, perhaps because their father had concentrated on oral lessons. At Roe Head, she was also learning the genteel social rules of society, and manners, a calm and ladylike demeanor, music, dancing, drawing, and needlework. These accomplishments were important parts of the curriculum for her, considering they were necessary skills she must teach when she became a governess.

Above all, Charlotte was being taught to be dutiful, not to do as she pleased (writing stories and wandering the moors) but to be a pleasant, obedient girl who behaved well and did what was expected of her. All of this would have pleased Aunt Branwell, who may have worried she could never instill a more ladylike and less exuberant behavior in the girls, used as they were to their lively play with their brother, feet propped on fireplace fenders, and romps on the moors.

Charlotte's classmates were being prepared to make good marriages, and to hire their own governesses. Two years before she entered Roe Head, twelve-year-old Charlotte had dramatically written in her journal that she didn't believe she would ever marry. She admired her new friend, pretty and outrageous Mary Taylor, who did not plan to marry or work at a profession she disliked. Her family appeared to be comfortably well off, and it did not seem likely she would have to support herself, though Mary may have confided there were financial worries at home. Mary's younger sister, Martha—a boisterous, high-spirited girl—was also at the school and was friendly to Charlotte.

At school holidays, Charlotte enjoyed visiting Ellen and Mary, though her friends' homes made her more aware of the difference in their social status and wealth. Ellen Nussey's beautiful home was in Birstall, five miles from school. Her father, who had been a wealthy manufacturer, had died five years before and there had been some financial losses, but they still lived well. Her large family of much-older brothers and sisters meant the house was always full of family and friends.

Mary Taylor's home was in Gomersal, even closer to Roe Head. Charlotte may have enjoyed visiting Mary's interesting, comfortable, and rowdy family the most. Her five energetic young brothers and sister were all close in age. Their home, built by a Taylor ancestor in 1600, was called the Red House. It was brick—uncommon in a town built of the usual Yorkshire stone. In fact, brick had become unfashionable by the 1830s, but the house was very attractive, with tall French windows, vine-covered trellises, and graceful lawns. A beautiful stained-glass window was an unusual feature of the house. The Taylor family were bankers and cloth merchants—their woolen mill was only two miles from their home. The family fortune was made by producing red cloth for the British army—the fabric of the "Redcoats," famous around the world. Mr. Taylor had gone bankrupt years before, partially caused perhaps by the cessation of the wars with America and France—which had required so many soldiers (and red cloth!). He was an honest man and was repaying his debts

MISS WOOLER

MARY TAYLOR

ELLEN NUSSEY

while trying to rebuild the family's fortune. The oldest son would finally clear what was owed after his father's death.

The Taylors were respected, cultured, well traveled, and unconventional. They were also Dissenters (Methodists), and had radical political beliefs— the opposite of the Brontës, who were Tories and loyal to the Crown. Mary came by her independent spirit naturally. The Taylors believed the country should change from a monarchy to a republic. The political discussions (and arguments) may have annoyed Charlotte at first—especially when she had to defend the Duke of Wellington from criticism—but the opinions must have been expressed cheerfully and without rancor, perhaps even with laughter, for Charlotte found their discussions fun, exciting, and stimulating. Years later, Mary wrote about those spirited discussions with Charlotte: "Neither she nor we had any idea but that our opinions were the opinions of all the *sensible* people in the world, and we used to astonish each other at every sentence."[8] Charlotte believed "the society of the Taylors is one of the most rousing pleasures I have ever known."[9]

Sadly, when Charlotte reluctantly visited her parents' old friend, Elizabeth Firth Franks (Anne's godmother), Charlotte felt inferior. She distrusted kindness and was awkward and uncomfortable when she was given a dress and a shawl—she felt she was the recipient of charity. She would have preferred to spend her holidays at home or with her friends.

Elizabeth Firth Franks lived in Huddersfield, a few miles from Roe Head. It was an area where riots had occurred years before, when Charlotte's father was a curate nearby. Visiting her there, Charlotte met people who had witnessed the events. Newly invented machinery of the Industrial Revolution had destroyed the livelihood of weavers and other hand-workers. Luddites, named after their probably mythical leader, Ned Ludd, had angrily rioted against the mill and factory owners who were depriving them of their ancient home industries. Interested in everything, Charlotte listened to the stories and would one day write a novel, *Shirley*, about those troubled times. Today the word *Luddite* is still used to describe anyone who is resistant to new technology.

Charlotte had quickly caught up in her studies. In fact, she had risen from the bottom of the class to the top. At the end of each term, she won awards—for fulfillment of duties, industry, manners, and speech—and, most important to her, the French prize. The medals were usually passed to the next class's winning student, but the Wooler sisters decided that Charlotte was so outstanding that she could keep her trophies when she returned home.

While she was at school, Branwell was writing his longest story so far, about the history of Glasstown. Charlotte and Branwell often sabotaged or mocked each other's youthful efforts, but it was his next volume—"Letters from an Englishman"—that inspired thirteen-year-old Emily to deface the front of Branwell's latest miniature book (in her best schoolgirl French—with errors). She wrote that he had written it well, and that she didn't think he would. But then she added, goodness, what a bad boy he was, and that he would be a shocking man. The story she referred to included cattle rustlers, poachers, and "rare lads"[10] (thieves and brawlers).

Charlotte was busy with school work and her new friends, and had written little until the end of the year. During the Christmas vacation, she wrote a poem that began "The trumpet hath sounded."[11] Charlotte and Branwell were considering the destruction of their whole imaginary world. Two weeks later she had moved on to another Glasstown poem, and there was no question of the saga not continuing.

She was at Roe Head for a year and a half. She had enjoyed her time at school. Miss Wooler's tact in handling oversensitive Charlotte had eased her time spent there. She would be a mentor and lifelong friend. Charlotte was proud she had mastered the entire school curriculum, but she was delighted to return to her home, her family, and her writing.

Though Charlotte was still uncomfortable with strangers, her social skills had improved, and her world was widening. Nevertheless, she was well aware that, as Miss Wooler had instructed her students, they would in their lives often be compelled "to bend our inclination to our duty."[12] She probably thought it was especially true of herself and her sisters who, though they had no desire to become governesses, apparently must do so.

Emily was fourteen and Anne twelve when Charlotte returned from school. It was a happy homecoming, but the summer stretched ahead for Charlotte, with the knowledge that she must teach her sisters what she had learned at school.

Mr. Brontë would have been happy to turn over his youngest daughters' education to Charlotte. He was very busy with church business. He had worked hard to bring about the building of a Sunday school, with the National School Society. It was across the lane from the church, and would give the village children a basic education for a small fee. There was an emphasis on reading, so they could read the Bible on their own. The school opened that summer, and Charlotte, though only sixteen, was made superintendent. All the Reverend's children were expected to teach in the school, though somehow Emily managed to avoid it. Anne probably helped with the littlest ones. "I used to think Miss Anne looked the nicest and most serious like," one of the sexton's daughters later remembered, adding she had "a good face."[13]

Fifteen-year-old Branwell was an unwilling teacher, and apparently annoyed by the task. When the village children dawdled, read slowly, or stumbled over their lessons, he lost all patience. The children could also be cheeky and outspoken to their young teacher. At least one walked out of Branwell's class. Indicating the villagers may have still seen the family as outsiders, the boy referred in a rude way to Branwell's Irish lineage as he stomped out. The students had little respect for his authority because they had noticed that the parson's son was no better behaved than they were, often fidgeting and reading novels during his father's sermon.

Charlotte and Anne probably disliked their new Sunday jobs as much as their brother. As well as teaching in the Sunday school, it was Charlotte's annual duty to act as hostess when the female teachers were invited to a special tea in the schoolroom. With her shyness, the Teachers Tea was undoubtedly an uncomfortable chore.

There had been a chapel in Haworth since the Middle Ages. The church of St. Michael and All Angels, however, was built in the previous century, incorporating only the much-older square tower. It had a double-gabled roof, and fifteen arched windows of green glass, which may have given the interior a murky, underwater dimness. Much of the light from the windows was blocked out as well by wooden galleries that provided space for parishioners who could not afford to pay to have their names neatly painted on the doors of reserved, waist-high box pews. The Brontës' larger pew was next to the altar and underneath the organ loft. It had green baize cushions, and diminutive Charlotte had a footstool because the bench was so high. The girls usually entered the church together, very quietly, through a back door. There were three services on Sunday.

Mr. Brontë's sermons were given from high above the congregation, in a tall, three-decker pulpit. Many of the congregation were illiterate, and Mr. Brontë usually preached simple texts he delivered without notes. He timed his sermon exactly to one hour with the aid of his pocket watch, carefully placed where he could see it.

Before the service began, William Brown, the sexton, walked along the aisles "knobbing"[14] (poking) dozing members of the congregation with a long staff. He would shake his head disapprovingly at the sleeping parishioner or threaten restless or unruly children. According to a visitor, the church became quiet once Mr. Brontë began, and all eyes were on the speaker as they listened to his simple sermon.

Even with all her church duties and teaching responsibilities, Charlotte was glad to be home. She did, however, miss the happy times she spent with her new friends at school. She described her life at home in a letter to Ellen: "one day is an account of all. In the mornings, from nine o'clock to half-past twelve, I instruct my sisters and draw, then we walk till dinner; after dinner I sew till tea-time, and after tea I either read, write, do a little fancy [needle] work, or draw, as I please. Thus in one delightful, though somewhat monotonous course, my life is passed."[15] It's very likely Emily and Anne did not entirely enjoy having their bossy older sister as their instructor, just as Charlotte didn't enjoy teaching them.

Charlotte exaggerated the monotony of her life, but when she was first home she had trouble concentrating on her writing again, even though she had missed that activity above all. Branwell, however, was still deeply involved in his Glasstown stories and long poems. The story he had written when Charlotte was at Roe Head was "The History of the Young Men." She would soon join him in writing new tales.

Happily, at the end of September Charlotte was invited to visit Ellen Nussey. Mr. Brontë agreed to the trip and rented a two-wheel gig for Branwell to drive her the twenty miles to Ellen's home, Rydings. Charlotte was delighted to return. The house was elegant, complete with turrets, a rookery, and fine old-growth chestnut trees. Charlotte made drawings of a dramatic tree on the grounds that had been split by lightning. The house made a great impression on her, and is believed by some to have been the inspiration for Thornfield Hall in her novel *Jane Eyre*. Even a lightning-damaged tree and the heroine's love of drawing found their way into the novel.

Years later Ellen would write about Branwell's reaction to her home— concluding that the fifteen-year-old must never have traveled far from home, as "he was in wild ectasy with everything . . . he was *then* a very dear brother, as dear to Charlotte as her own soul; they were in perfect accord of taste and feeling, and it was mutual delight to be together." The house and grounds thrilled excitable Branwell so much that he was reluctant to leave. Ellen recalled him stating with his usual intensity that he "was leaving her [Charlotte] in Paradise, and if she were not intensely happy she never would be!"[16]

The two-week visit went well despite Charlotte's crippling shyness with strangers. When the two girls were allowed to forgo the company of the daily visitors, Charlotte enjoyed herself very much. Branwell returned in mid-October to drive his sister home. They brought with them Ellen's gift of apples from the orchard at Rydings, for Emily and Anne. Charlotte's sisters were delighted at her return. They had missed her.

A Visitor

. . . the pleasantest manner of spending a hot July day . . .

Charlotte started the new year of 1833 feeling guilty about her lack of inter-est in self-improvement, which she had credited with her rapid progress at school. She was again enthusiastically writing Glasstown stories.

Branwell was engrossed in scribbling another very ambitious and lengthy tale. His stories had become more realistic, and for the first time, he was changing the format of his writing—leaving behind the miniature books the siblings had all eagerly created since childhood. His new story was in a book-let four times larger than the original miniature books. However, he contin-ued to print in the same tiny scale as before.

Charlotte was still concentrating on romantic tales. She enjoyed the story of her parents' courtship and the dramatic loss of her mother's trousseau and bridal veil. When the date was set for her wedding, Maria Branwell had re-quested that her sisters send her belongings by ship from Penzance rather than by the long, dangerous, and more expensive overland route by stagecoach. The ship, however, foundered in a fierce storm off the coast of Devonshire, and most of her belongings (dresses, bonnets, paint set, and books) were destroyed. What did survive the wreck however—tucked in her waterlogged trunk—were bound copies of the *Lady's Magazine; or, Entertaining Companion for the Fair Sex.* They were salt-stained by the sea, but still readable. Aunt Branwell allowed Charlotte to read the romantic stories, believing them superior to the fiction currently being written for women and girls.

Charlotte loved the magazines. Her own stories were influenced by what she read in them. She wrote later that she had "read them as a treat on holiday afternoons or by stealth when I should have been minding my lessons—I shall never see anything which will interest me so much again." Her father, however, had come upon her immersed in reading one of the "foolish love-stories"[1] and was disapproving, not understanding the appeal to his young daughter. Perhaps wishing his children to read only well-written literature (or fearing a flighty, romantic nature in Charlotte), he scolded her and destroyed the magazines. Years later Charlotte still lamented the loss of the stories she had loved as a girl. "With all my heart I wish I had been born in time to contribute to the Lady's magazine."[2]

Charlotte's stories had become the vivid imaginings of a teenage girl who thought a great deal about romance, and whose life was quiet and sheltered. All the siblings craved drama and excitement. Sir Walter Scott's romances and adventures and Lord Byron's appalling personal life and dramatic poetry made a huge impression on them. They also read what was referred to as "silver fork" romantic novels, which were popular and featured the manners and habits of the aristocracy. Charlotte's main focus for her stories was now the triumph of love against all odds. The theme would continue into her adult books.

The young woman, who felt she was ugly and made squat little unattractive sketches of herself, peopled her writings with aristocratic, haughty, but submissive beauties. The men were predictably masterful and courageous. Charlotte enjoyed writing long, detailed descriptions of the facial beauty and fashionable clothing of her characters. Her plots were dramatic and full of romance. As in her childhood, she still liked to introduce supernatural elements, mysteries, and portentous omens.

Branwell and Charlotte were again working on the same stories, and the plots were often elaborate. Charlotte would introduce characters, and Branwell would change them or do away with them. She would bring them back to life. Or she would alter the plot line of Branwell's evil or disreputable characters. Each quickly responded to new plot lines and kept writing.

Mr. Brontë was not oblivious to the fact that his children were still straining their eyes by writing in the tiniest print they could manage. In an effort to change that habit, at Christmas he gave Charlotte—and perhaps each of his children—a notebook with the following inscription: *"All that is written in this book must be in a good, plain, and legible hand.—P.B."*[3]

Charlotte, at least, tried to follow his direction, writing several long poems suitable for a father of a teenage poet to read. She continued to record her exciting new stories in the same minute eye-straining printing, meant just for herself or her siblings. Concerning what he may have recognized as the obsessive and secretive nature of his children's writing, Mr. Brontë perhaps did not know what to do.

Charlotte was seventeen and Branwell sixteen, and they were creating more grown-up stories. With their new maturity, they agreed that the Great Glasstown capital should be given a more literary, elegant, and sophisticated name. They settled on the name Verdopolis. They were soon to create a new kingdom on which to focus their attention. Angria fired their imagination with new, fresh ideas. Many more stories and poems resulted. They included scandalous affairs of the wealthy, as well as crimes of highwaymen, poachers, and murderers. The children were intrigued by the poet Lord Byron, who was famously described as "mad, bad, and dangerous to know."[4]

Branwell liked to include references to drunkards and scenes in taverns, in even his early tales, leading biographers to speculate he was experimenting with alcohol. This was unlikely at that time—Branwell's aim was to appear older, bolder, and more worldly than he was.

Glasstown had been fantastic, foreign, and exotic—Angria was more realistic. Charlotte was slow to give up the elegant aristocratic world of her Glasstown stories. She believed the new English setting of Angria was bleak, and too familiar. There was even a village—Howard—very much like Haworth. She soon came to appreciate that the Angrian setting gave her an even better chance to satirize her town and family in her work—especially her brother, Branwell.

Charlotte's character, Benjamin Patrick Wiggins, was an egotistical braggart—pretentious, talkative, and ambitious. He had carroty hair, and spectacles perched on a prominent Roman nose. Wiggins considered himself extraordinarily talented and that he had a great future. His attitude to his three sisters was condescending.

Emily and Anne had been so often teased or left out of their older siblings' collaborations that they decided to abandon their Glasstown contributions, or only participate occasionally. Perhaps Branwell and Charlotte's shift of interest to Angria gave them the idea to leave the Glasstown story line behind. They began writing about an imaginary world of their own creation, separate from their sister and brother, called Gondal. Branwell wrote a scathing editorial in his "Monthly Intelligencer," accusing his young sisters of running off and deserting Glasstown.

Emily and Anne's stories took place on islands they named Gondal and Gaaldine. The manuscripts were all lost or destroyed, but there are some very beautiful surviving poems from the saga, which give hints to the story lines. Names and brief descriptions of characters and locations survived on loose bits of paper, backs of poems, and in Emily's copy of a gazetteer. In it she wrote of the imaginary geography and climate of Gondal, in the North Pacific, and Gaaldine, in the South Pacific.

There are similarities throughout their new creation to Charlotte and Branwell's Angria. The siblings had always incorporated versions of each other's ideas and even adopted characters and names to use in their own stories. They each were inspired by, or borrowed landscapes from, their favorite writers. Sir Walter Scott was a particular favorite of Emily, and his work influenced how both she and Anne pictured Gondal and Gaaldine. Combining the beautiful Scottish border settings of Scott's novels with their beloved Yorkshire landscape provided the setting of Gondal.

Emily and Anne's imaginary worlds were inhabited by new versions of aristocratic and royal young people who engaged in rebellions, passionate romances, and political intrigues. The characters were often imprisoned and dreaming of freedom, expressed beautifully in their evocative, elegiac poetry. Charlotte and Branwell's Angria was dominated by men, and the women were often weak and powerless. Emily and Anne's heroines may have been inspired by the new young Queen Victoria. A woman could be in charge of a nation—she could be powerful. The women of Gondal were strong, ambitious, and equal to their men. They played a more important part in the progression of their stories than the Angrian women.

The four siblings all had lap desks, which each had locks. The portable writing desks would have been their only private place for their papers and keepsakes. Emily liked to take hers and a small three-legged stool into the garden, and perhaps even onto the moors. In fair weather, she would sit in the shade of a wind-twisted hawthorn tree, her lap desk perched on her knees, and write for hours. The mauve velvet interior was splattered with ink; probably eager to write her ideas down swiftly, she seems to have been particularly messy with her quill pens. Pens with metal nibs would not be invented until ten years later.

All four young people wrote with concentration and intensity. Charlotte once described Anne bent over her desk, so absorbed by her writing she could not be lured away, even for a walk on the moors.

Carriages traveling up Church Lane, the narrow by-lane that turned off Main Street and led to the parsonage, would have passed the sexton's house where Mr. Brontë's curates rented rooms. Next was the new Sunday school's long, low building where the townspeople's children were being taught to read and write. A stone barn where the sexton and his sons plied their trade as stone masons was at the end of the lane, as was the gate that opened onto the fields and the moors. Passengers arriving to visit the Brontës alit from their carriages beside the gate to the parsonage garden.

What sounds might they have heard in this small world of parsonage, church, and outbuildings? They probably would hear the monotonous chip-chipping of sexton/stonemason William Brown and his sons' endless task of carving memorial tombstones for the dead. There might be the too-often-heard mournful passing bell announcing a funeral at St. Michael's. Or, more cheerfully, a visitor may have heard the village children's shouts and laughter from the town, or the sound of Emily and Anne playing a duet or practicing scales on their cabinet piano in their father's study. The family dog might bark at their arrival. If it was Sunday, there may have been bells ringing at St. Michael's and at churches in the valley. Or perhaps they would only hear the sound of the wind sweeping across the moors, rattling the windows, trying to get in.

In the summer following her stay with Ellen Nussey at Rydings, plans were finally in place for Charlotte to welcome Ellen to the parsonage.

Years later Ellen wrote about her first visit to her friend's home. A gracious Mr. Brontë greeted her at the door, making sure—as was his practice—that her driver was given refreshment before his return journey. Charlotte was there waiting, having heard the approach of the horse and gig. A gracious Miss Branwell then took charge, making sure Ellen was settled comfortably. Charlotte's longed-for visit of her friend had begun.

Ellen's memories supply the best recorded descriptions of the family. She found the Reverend daunting, impressive, austere, and "very venerable" with his snow-white hair and "tone of high-bred courtesy."[5] When she noticed the thick silk-wrapped cravat he wore, she may not have known how very ill he had been three years earlier, with severe respiratory and bronchial infections. She believed the long length of silk fabric, wrapped around his throat many times, indicated he was a hypochondriac, and very odd. His fear of illness was largely due to anxiety for his children should he die. The label of eccentric, however, was confirmed for Ellen when she awoke, alarmed by his discharging his pistol each morning from a bedroom window.

Mr. Brontë had told his children of his own experiences during the Luddite riots years before, when jobs were being replaced by machinery in mills and factories. He'd had to arm himself for protection from the desperate and unhappy workers. A mill owner had been shot at and another attacked and murdered. There continued to be sporadic trouble from those who still fought against the inevitable as their world changed. So he still carried a pistol on his long journeys to visit parishioners on the lonely moors, and slept with the gun at hand. In the morning he fired it, for safety, as there was no other way to unload the shot. He had taught Branwell and Emily to shoot. His son hunted pheasants on the moors in the autumn hunting season. And Emily may have been taught to use a gun at a time when both her father and Branwell were going to be away from the parsonage and there was trouble in the area. This was still more evidence (along with their wide-ranging education) of his unusual—for the times—rearing of his daughters.

Because of her more privileged family background, breakfast fare at the parsonage was a surprise for Ellen. Oatmeal porridge was the favorite Yorkshire working-class breakfast, just as it had been Mr. Brontë's when he was growing up in Ireland, and it was the breakfast of choice of the Brontë family.

During the meal, Ellen probably remembered Charlotte's storytelling skills. Her ghost stories had entertained all the girls at Roe Head, and she now realized Charlotte's father was a storyteller as well. At breakfast time, his tales of wild Yorkshiremen who once lived in the far reaches of the moors disturbed Ellen. The Brontë teenagers loved their father's stories. They appreciated the dark side of his humor, but Ellen, who was a timid girl and lacking in imagination, found the stories "grim"[6] and disturbing. Still, she loved the time she spent with the young people of the house.

At night the entire household assembled for prayers, after which the adults retired to their beds. Mr. Brontë paused to tell his children and Ellen good night, and not to stay up too late. He wound the grandfather clock on the stair landing every night at nine o'clock, on his way to bed.

Teenage Ellen thought tiny Aunt Branwell was old-fashioned, quaint, and even amusing as she witnessed the lady clicking about the parsonage in her outdoor pattens. But she was shocked when Charlotte's prim aunt offered her a pinch of snuff from a little gold box.

Tabby, too, she judged to be quaint in appearance. She would have been about seventy then, but she seemed to be very active, and felt a great responsibility for her "childer." If Branwell couldn't escort his sisters on their moorland walks, Tabby would insist on accompanying them to keep them safe. With her ear for a good tale, she may have entertained the siblings with gossip from town—but she wouldn't talk about the Brontë family with townspeople. When villagers were curious and asked Tabby questions about the family, she was fiercely protective and loyal, and refused to gossip—as when she was asked whether they were "fearfully larn'd." She "left them in a 'huff'"[7] and, returning home, reported the nonsense she had heard to her "bairns," knowing they would laugh.

Tabby would be given credit years later by Charlotte's biographer, Elizabeth Gaskell, as to her importance in inspiring the budding young storytellers in the household. Mrs. Gaskell wrote that Tabby "had many a tale . . . of bygone days of the country-side; old ways of living, former inhabitants, decayed gentry, who had melted away, and whose places knew them no more; family tragedies, and dark superstitious dooms."[8] Charlotte and Emily had both taken note of Tabby's large trove of local lore.

It's easy to imagine Emily as a quiet, unobtrusive presence, listening in on her father and parishioners who had stopped by to talk and gossip "with t'parson" about the old folks and the old ways. Years later there would be shocked questions about how the author of *Wuthering Heights*—the quiet spinster daughter of a country cleric—knew about the lives of such people. She had heard their stories all her life, and perhaps had even spoken with the moorland storytellers themselves on her lonely walks.

At fifteen, Emily was the tallest of the siblings but had a "lithesome, graceful figure,"[9] according to Ellen. She was usually described as the best looking of the sisters. Ellen wrote that at that time her hair "was naturally as beautiful

EMILY BRONTË

as Charlotte's,"[10] but that it, too, was frizzed and curled in the same unflattering style. "She had very beautiful eyes . . . but she did not often look at you:
she was too reserved. Their color might be said to be dark gray, at other times
dark blue, they varied so."[11] Ellen said, "One of her rare expressive looks was
something to remember through life, there was such a depth of soul and feeling, and yet a shyness of revealing herself—a strength of self-containment
seen in no other."[12] And "[s]he talked very little. She and Anne were like
twins—inseparable companions."[13]

"Anne—dear, gentle Anne—was quite different in appearance from the
others. . . . She had lovely violet-blue eyes, fine penciled eyebrows, and clear,
almost transparent complexion."[14] Her hair was brown but with an auburn
tint, from the red-haired Irish Brontës, and "fell on her neck in graceful
curls."[15] It was fairer than her sisters', and she was the only one with naturally
curly hair. A plait of her hair, cut off in the previous spring, was kept by her
father. Was the comic little girl now quiet and sedate at thirteen?

Though the plainest of the girls, Charlotte's luminous eyes were often
commented on, as well as her neat little figure, and sweet voice.

Years later one of the villagers recalled that the girls usually dressed alike.
In summer, they wore pastel print dresses accessorized with pale-colored
bonnets. Her memory of them was that "[t]hey looked grand."[16]

Ellen had little to say about Charlotte's bright, excitable sixteen-year-old
brother, Branwell, who resembled his father. His shock of red hair—the same
color his father had in his youth—was, however, worn long and brushed forward in the style of Romantic poet Lord Byron. Mr. Brontë, despite his modest background, possessed aristocratic features—an aquiline Roman nose and
high forehead—which his son had inherited. But Branwell did not inherit his
father's height (more than six feet); he was small in stature, and is believed to
have been five feet two. On his nose were always perched round wire-framed
glasses. Like his father and Charlotte, his eyesight was poor.

During Ellen's visit, he was much occupied. It's likely he was deeply involved with his current Angrian story. Due to being surrounded by a house-
ful of females, Branwell also sought out masculine companionship and had
joined a boxing club, which met upstairs above the Black Bull Inn. His idol,
Lord Byron, had boxed, and references to boxing in *Blackwood's Magazine*
had probably inspired his choice of sport. Of course, his Angrian noblemen
were boxing in his imaginary world. Branwell was also studying with his

father, and painting in preparation for a planned career as a professional painter. No matter what Ellen thought of him at the time, she would later judge him harshly.

Ellen believed the furnishings of the parsonage were austere, blaming Mr. Brontë's personal taste and a lack of consideration for his children, rather than recognizing his limited finances. Fashionable well-off Victorian households were generally over-filled with furniture, curios, and other decorative items—very different from the parsonage. But she, as had others, noticed and appreciated the cleanliness and refinement of her friend's home.

The garden of the parsonage contained little more than stunted trees and shrubs, perhaps because the soil was too poor and the wind too strong to sustain any but hardy plants. Later Ellen would please Emily with the gift of Sicilian peas and crimson cornflower seeds for the garden. Anne and Emily planted a few currant bushes, but they were more likely to find a superior variety of plump, tasty berries on the moors, and probably carried their finds home in baskets, bonnets, or shawls. Their favorite berries would find their way into Charlotte's first published book, comforting a lost and hungry Jane Eyre, struggling across the moors and finding "ripe bilberries gleaming here and there, like jet beads in the heath."[17] Jane ate them with her scrap of bread and they gave her strength to go on.

The young Brontës had enjoyed studying plants, flowers, and birds on the moors since childhood. They read about the country walks and botanizing habits of the Romantic poets who, in their own wild places, collected varieties of ferns and wild herbs to press between the pages of their books.

Either Mr. Brontë or his children carefully placed healing herbs in their botany guidebook. Plants were also found in their copy of *Songs in the Night*. Perhaps the girls also put moorland flowers in a pitcher on the kitchen table to surprise and please Tabby. In *Agnes Grey*, Anne's first book, her heroine is given primroses by the man with whom she is secretly in love. She presses the petals in the pages of her Bible, and says she will keep them forever.

Charlotte wrote later that when Emily was walking on the moors "every moss, every flower, every tint and form, were noted and enjoyed."[18] A never-finished poem of Emily's declared "Every leaf speaks bliss to me."[19] The entire family—but especially Patrick Brontë, Emily, and Anne—associated nature with the sacred.

Ellen and Charlotte may have spent a great deal of time talking and gossiping about shared school friends, but every afternoon, when weather permitted, the girls walked on the moors with Branwell as escort. The Brontës were all great walkers. Branwell perhaps thought he made a fine figure—a young gentleman striding across the hills with his walking stick. It was a time, though, when females rambling about the countryside would provoke frowns and disapproval. Seeing Mr. Brontë's daughters on the moors, with (or later, without) a chaperone, would have been no surprise to the villagers. Later, when questioned about the sisters, they always mentioned seeing the girls setting off on their moorland walks. They were used to the eccentricities of their curate and his family.

We can imagine the siblings happily closing the gate that led to the moors behind them, and following their own well-worn footprints across the brown landscape in winter, or on paths amid the fragrant purple heather in early autumn. Did they time themselves to ensure they did not wander too far, so they could return before tea and early candlelight?

Years later Emily would beautifully express her own love of the moors in *Wuthering Heights*, through the comments of two of her fictional characters. The first declared "the pleasantest manner of spending a hot July day was lying from morning till evening on a bank of heath in the middle of the moors, with the bees humming dreamily about among the bloom." Another character prefers "rocking in a rustling green tree, with a west wind blowing, and bright white clouds flitting rapidly above; and not only larks, but throstles, and blackbirds, and linnets . . . pouring out music on every side . . . and the whole world awake and wild with joy."[20]

Ellen Nussey won Emily's friendship during that first visit by allowing the family dog, a terrier named Grasper, to sprawl across her lap without complaining about his exuberant attentions. Emily and Anne judged people by their treatment of animals, so Emily set aside her reserve and joined the happy party. Ellen noticed how the younger girl came to life on the moors, enjoying everything she saw.

Emily, Branwell, and Anne led the way across the moors. They placed stepping-stones across the streams for timid, lady-like Charlotte and Ellen. Emily's sense of humor has been described as "wicked," and she liked to tease Charlotte with reminders of the possible dangers of the moors—falling boulders, slippery rocks, lightning storms, and even wild animals. (Charlotte was afraid of cows.)

The two youngest girls had a favorite walk they wanted to share with Ellen. They followed Sladen Beck, which led to the spot where it joined other streams. Together the streams flowed over a rocky crag, where the fall of water formed a pool. Emily and Anne had given this site the romantic and important-sounding name, the Meeting of the Waters. They named it after a poem by Thomas Moore, an Irish friend of Lord Byron and one of Emily's favorite lyricists. Ellen wrote that "Emily, half reclining on a slab of stone, played like a young child with the tadpoles in the water, making them swim about, and then fell to moralizing on the strong and the weak, the brave and the cowardly, as she chased them with her hand."[21] The isolation of the spot was part of its appeal to the two youngest sisters. Their sharing of their special place with Ellen was undoubtedly a sign of their acceptance of her as a friend.

Ellen's visit coincided with the annual Sunday School Teachers Tea. Insight into the townspeople's relationship with the parson's family was clear to Ellen when the teachers—mill and factory girls—spoke casually to the Brontë sisters, using their given names and inviting them to join their games. (The townspeople called Charlotte "Charlotty.") Ellen had only experienced the class system that required everyone adhere to their place in society. She was shocked by the familiarity with which the teachers addressed their employers. When Ellen suggested the family require they be addressed more respectfully, Emily's response was, "Vain attempt!"[22] The familiarity did not shock the Brontë girls. The idea of *games* did.

Years after the entire family was gone, townspeople were asked about the sisters. They replied fondly that they were gentle and kindly. Some, though, added that they were also odd, but admitted they did not see much of them except on Sundays.

Before Ellen returned to her home, a last entertainment was planned. Branwell and the sisters each counted out their pocket money, and Branwell rented a "shabby looking"[23] phaeton (a light horse-drawn vehicle) for a special outing. Very early in the morning, the excited party of young people crammed into the phaeton, probably amid much laughter, and left Haworth for a day trip to imposing Bolton Abbey—the ruins of a twelfth-century Augustinian monastery.

Branwell had studied the route and, as self-appointed tour guide (though he had never been there before), shared a constant patter of place-names, sea level, and view spots. The young Brontës may have especially looked forward to stopping for breakfast at the Devonshire Arms as it was popular with poets and artists, including their idol William Wordsworth. This was where Ellen's family would meet them for their visit to the Abbey, and then take her home. They were all happy and excited until they felt the hotel employees were judging them disdainfully because of their disreputable conveyance. (Fine carriages were definitely a status symbol.) The experience was initially made worse—embarrassing the siblings again—when Ellen's family arrived in a fancy carriage pulled by *two* horses. But when it became clear the two groups were friends, the hotel staff became more polite.

The party strolled through the ancient Abbey grounds, another place where Wordsworth had found inspiration for his poetry. Branwell was charming and amusing but seemed over-excited, too, speaking too fast and quoting poetry, but apparently successfully entertaining Ellen's family. Branwell may have told the Nusseys and his sisters about the famous cow, which had been bred on the Bolton Abbey estate years before. Britain's largest cow, it weighed 312 stone (4,368 pounds) and was more than seven feet tall! Charming people was "one of the things he did well,"[24] Ellen later reluctantly admitted about Branwell. Emily and Anne wandered off together—in their own world—only speaking to one another.

Charlotte wrote to Ellen after her friend returned home, telling her what a good impression she had made on her father and aunt, who held Ellen up as an example for Charlotte—and probably Emily and Anne, as well—to emulate. She reported that her sisters said they "never saw anyone they liked so well as you" and that "Tabby, whom you have absolutely fascinated, talks a great deal more nonsense about your ladyship than I care to repeat."[25] It was fortunate that Ellen met with Tabby's approval. She possessed a keen Yorkshire sense of perception and could be outspoken about those she disliked.

Despite what she considered the eccentricities of Charlotte's family, Ellen had enjoyed her visit. She had become a valued friend of the whole family, to be welcomed often as a guest in future. Ellen liked to call herself and the Brontë girls "the Quartet." She wished to be one of them, not realizing that, though accepted as a friend, she could never be one of their circle of sisters. The siblings' close relationship could not be replicated with someone who had not been an intimate part of their lives—their sorrows and their shared creativity. Still, Ellen's friendship was very important to Charlotte—and Emily and Anne were always happy to see her. She was missed when she returned home.

Soon after Ellen left, Emily showed herself to be fearless in a dangerous situation. It's believed that during one of her kind attempts to help a stray dog she had offered it a bowl of water, and had been bitten as her reward. As one sign of rabies is a fear of water, Emily thought the dog might be rabid. The sixteen-year-old then took a red-hot iron and cauterized her own wound. (Cauterization was the medical advice for rabies bites at the time.) Though she was ill, with weakness and painful inflammation, the danger of rabies passed, and the burn and the bite healed. Only then did she confess the cause of the wound. She had kept her terrible fears to herself to spare her family, and perhaps to avoid becoming even more frightened herself, from seeing the terror in their eyes.

There was an incident involving a later parsonage dog (Keeper, a fierce bull terrier and Emily's devoted companion) who engaged in a fight with what seems to have been an equally ferocious dog. Men from the town stood watching, making no attempt to stop the fight, and when Emily was told of the combat she ran to stop it. She separated the animals with the aid of black pepper applied to their noses, and her own strength. She angrily took Keeper home, leaving the men astonished at what she had done.

8

Young Writers, Musicians, and Artists

. . . we want to go out to play.

Ellen Nussey traveled to London to stay for six months with her older brother—the court physician. From there, she would visit another brother who lived in the resort town of Bath. Charlotte missed Ellen but also was jealous of her travels. She had dreamed of visiting London since childhood. Knowing Ellen was there made her discontented with her life in Haworth. To make it worse, Ellen didn't even seem to appreciate being in London, with all its possibilities and diversions. Charlotte complained to Ellen that she had no news to report—there was nothing of interest in *her* life. She never discussed her passion for writing with Ellen.

Haworth was growing, however, and there was a surprising variety of entertainment available. There were lectures that would have been of interest to the whole family. There were often concerts in Haworth or the larger neighboring towns. The Haworth Philharmonic Society—founded more than fifty years before—put on yearly events at the Black Bull, situated at the top of Main Street, next to the church steps. A local Yorkshire tenor, Thomas Parker, had entertained the townspeople at local concerts, even at the church itself. He would later sing for Queen Victoria. Mr. Brontë helped secure a new organ, thrilling Branwell (who loved organ music) and inspiring Charlotte to write another stinging satire about Benjamin Wiggins (alias Branwell) and his ecstatic enthusiasm for the first organ recital held in the church.

The siblings inherited their love of music from their father. It's very likely he had fond memories of the haunting Irish folk music performed by his fiddle-playing brothers when he was a young man in Ireland. Emily and Anne were still having lessons with piano teacher Abraham Sunderland. The girls were collecting sheet music, copying their favorites into notebooks, and learning to play solos, duets, and waltzes on the small upright cottage piano Mr. Brontë had bought in Leeds. They were learning classical pieces as well as hymns, ballads, and traditional songs. Emily was already a very talented pianist. Anne had a sweet voice and sometimes sang to her own or Emily's accompaniment, probably entertaining the household with their musical recitals. Each of the sisters was said to have a pleasing voice. Along with musical evenings at home, Emily enjoyed reading aloud to the family or reciting poetry—a popular form of entertainment at the time.

It's unknown if the Brontës ever attended any of the concerts in Halifax. It's possible they could have been entertained by some of the greatest and most popular classical composers and musicians of all time. Paganini, Liszt, Mendelssohn, and Strauss had included the growing town of Halifax on their concert tours of England, and Halifax was only twelve miles from Haworth.

Mr. Brontë and Branwell loved oratorio—sacred music—such as works by Haydn and Mozart. Charlotte loved martial music. There were many bands made up of mill and factory workers in town. And Emily and Anne loved the piano. There were opportunities to enjoy all their preferences in Haworth. The young Brontës themselves may have performed in local concerts or entertainments—certainly Branwell was not shy. He played the organ for church services and could have been involved in musical organizations. He played several instruments and a range of melodies from church music to popular songs of the day (including one with the intriguing title "Oh No, We Never Mention Her").

Charlotte had not given up on the dream of being a professional artist. She was spending more time bent over her drawing paper—with pencil, pen, or brush in hand—than scribbling romances or writing teasing stories about her pretentious younger brother.

All the siblings meticulously copied engravings from art annuals. For their copies of copper-plate engravings (which can capture very fine details) they utilized a slow, patient, stippling technique that duplicated the look of the engravings to an amazing degree.

Charlotte proudly but nervously submitted two of her drawings—one of Bolton Abbey—to the Royal Northern Society for the Encouragement of the Arts, in Leeds. It was a prestigious event, where even master painters such as Sir Thomas Lawrence and J. M. W. Turner showed their new paintings. Charlotte, only eighteen, must have been thrilled to have her drawings in the same exhibition as the work of such artists, and having her family see her work displayed there was assuredly a source of great pride. But Charlotte's work was only two of more than four hundred pieces of art, and her drawings were not noticed. They remained unsold. Charlotte may have hoped that if her drawings were purchased she could convince her father to let her pursue a career in art, as Branwell was. Perhaps she expected too much from her first show, but she would have known her dream was an unrealistic one for a woman at that time. Women were not even allowed to be members of the Royal Academy of Art. Discouraged and depressed, she gave up her dream. Her artist's eye, however, would aid her in her writing, helping her visualize scenes and paint them with words. This was true for all the siblings.

It was at the Leeds exhibition, however, that Mr. Brontë noticed the work of a local portrait painter, William Robinson. Perhaps he even inquired at that time whether Mr. Robinson would accept his son as a student of portraiture in oils. So Branwell was the one who would benefit from being present at the exhibition, not Charlotte.

Emily and Anne were only a year and a half apart in age. They played together, wrote stories together, studied the piano together, and decided to keep a diary together. They'd read that Lord Byron had kept a youthful journal in which he recorded what was happening around him as it happened, and they decided to follow his lead. They planned to record their current surroundings and activities, as well as those of their family, pets, and the characters in their stories and poetry. Their diary was always written on a scrap of paper (approximately two and a half inches by four inches), in the same minute print as their handmade books. The paper was then folded to the size of a sixpence and stored in a small tin box. They decided that they would reread them every four years and update them. All the diary papers are little gems, giving us a glimpse of the family's world. It's almost as though we had a short but treasured film clip. This one briefly catches the usually elusive Emily as her authentic sixteen-year-old self.

Emily was very bright, but none of the siblings worried about grammar. This diary paper of Emily's, intended just for her eyes and Anne's, is the way she wrote it. Her casual lack of punctuation and poor spelling, along with the informality (teasing, sassiness, hopefulness) of her writing, create a charming written sketch of what a typical busy Monday washday was like with four teenagers in the Brontë parsonage. Emily was likely sitting at the kitchen table when she began the diary entry with the news that on that morning she had fed Rainbow, Diamond, and Snowflake (believed to be their three cats) and their pet pheasant, Jasper.

The diary papers almost always mentioned the family pets. Aunt Branwell had long ago lost the battle of limiting their number. There was probably always a dog in the parsonage. If the siblings were ever told by their father—as children so often are—you may keep pets if you take care of them yourself, they must have taken his words to heart. The two youngest accumulated a variety of possible strays over the years. Did neighbors know they could bring unwanted kittens to them? Perhaps they found more than one injured avian on the moors, and did they come home from the yearly Haworth Fair with Dick, the canary, in his cage?

Of all the family, Emily and Anne were the ones who most devotedly cared for the pets, even as far as sharing their breakfasts of oatmeal porridge with their dogs and cats in the kitchen. Charlotte and Branwell did not seem to ever have their own animals, though Branwell apparently took one of the dogs with him when he went hunting on the moors. Charlotte did usually report news about the pets to Ellen, as when she wrote of Emily's grief over the death of a favorite little cat named Tom.

Emily and Anne had peeled apples so Charlotte could make dessert for their dinner. Emily reported her older sister's witticism: "Charlotte said she made puddings perfectly and she was of a quick but lim[i]ted intellect Tab[b]y said just now come Anne pillopatate [peel a potato] Aunt has come into the Kitchen just now and said where are your feet Anne Anne answered on the floor Aunt" (Aunt Branwell was still trying to cure fourteen-year-old Anne of the unladylike habit of propping her feet on the stove or fireplace fender.) "papa opened the parlour Door and gave Branwell a Letter saying here Branwell read this and show it to your Aunt and Charlotte." Seamlessly, but confusingly, Emily then wrote. "The Gondals are discovering the interior of Gaaldine Sally [M]osley is washing in the back-Kitchin [sic]."[1] Sally was a woman from the village, hired to help with the laundry.

Mr. Brontë had had a second kitchen added for washing and heavy household jobs. This was perhaps due to repeated complaints about the limited space in Tabby's small kitchen with so many tasks to do, and too many children underfoot. Lost was the view from the original kitchen's windows—of the yard and the moors beyond—which were blocked off by the new addition.

Sounding very young, Emily added, "It is past Twelve o'clock Anne and I have not tid[i]ed ourselv[e]s, done our bed work or done our lessons and we want to go out to play We are going to have for Dinner Boiled Beef Turnips, potato's and applepudding the Kitchin is in a very untidy state Anne and I have not Done our music exercise which consists of b majer [sic] Tab[b]y said on my putting a pen in her face Ya pitter pottering there instead of pilling a potate I answered O Dear, O Dear, O dear I will derictly [sic] with that I get up, take a Knife and begin . . . pilling the potatos."[2]

Emily closed with "Anne and I say I wonder what we shall be like and what we shall be and where we shall be if all goes on well in the year 1874 . . . hoping we shall all be well at that time we close our paper Emily and Anne"[3] To later readers of the diary, this is a very poignant wish made by the girls.

Arrangements were made for Branwell to travel to Leeds to study with painter William Robinson who, when only a little older than his new student, had gone to London to study art. While there, perhaps because he showed great promise. Mr. Robinson had received free lessons from the great artist Sir Thomas Lawrence (president of the Royal Academy of Art at that time). He had also studied at the academy before returning to Leeds. The Brontës would also have been impressed that Branwell's teacher had painted a portrait of the Duke of Wellington. Mr. Robinson could certainly have given Branwell information about applying to the Royal Academy and told him what it was like to study there, as well as giving helpful advice about living in London.

Unknown to Mr. Brontë and Branwell, William Robinson was apparently not a good teacher. Considered a fine portrait painter himself, his instructions to Branwell—for the mixing of oil pigments, application of paint, basics of composition, and anatomy—were sadly inadequate. The quality of Branwell's paintings was uneven, usually exhibiting an absence of lifelike skin tones, and the subjects of his portraits were usually stiffly posed.

As part of his instruction to practice working from life, Branwell managed to persuade his sisters to model for him, at least twice. This would have involved their sitting or standing for what could be a lengthy amount of time. He left space on each canvas to add himself to the group portrait. Anne may have been the most patient and agreeable model, as she was painted or sketched more than once by both Branwell and Charlotte. There are similarities between their portraits of Anne, indicating that they may have captured a true likeness of her. She appears to have been a delicate, fine-boned, and interesting-looking young girl.

In her biography of Charlotte, Mrs. Gaskell described Branwell's *Three Sisters* portrait as a "rough, common-looking oil-painting,"[4] but she thought Branwell had captured Charlotte's likeness. She never met Emily or Anne, and it's been suggested she misidentified the two younger girls, confusing their positions on the canvas and therefore incorrectly naming them—an intriguing supposition.[5] It is tempting to consider it, although no one who had known them ever seems to have disagreed with her identification. The painting was a practice piece and may have been one of seventeen-year-old Branwell's first efforts to paint in oils. The technique is especially poor. It's impossible to know if he did achieve a good likeness of his sisters. The painting shows three teenagers, who are neither truly plain nor conventionally pretty, in identical, simple dresses. Branwell, not content with his own painted image, wiped himself from the canvas. Over the years, as the paint degraded, a vague outline of him has reemerged. Charlotte apparently disliked the painting. Years later she wrote, "I grieve to say that I possess no portrait of either of my sisters."[6] Did she forget the painting, not think it was a good enough likeness of either Emily or Anne to acknowledge, or did she mean that they had not been photographed?

The only confirmed images of Charlotte are Branwell's portrait of her and a later, reportedly flattering, drawing by talented portrait painter George Richmond. Perhaps a true likeness lies somewhere between the two.

Most of Branwell's second practice portrait of his sisters was later destroyed, although a badly done tracing had been made. The painting was called *The Gun Group* because in it Branwell, flanked by his sisters, was holding a gun—a brace of pheasants lying on the table in front of him. As in the *Three Sisters* painting, Branwell painted himself taller than his sisters. This apparently unattractive student piece had pride of place in the parsonage for years. Mr. Brontë may have preferred it, as it included all his children, but a visitor described it as being very badly executed. To be fair to Branwell, he may not have wanted to have an unfinished practice painting framed and mounted on the wall, for all to see. All that survives of the *Gun Group* painting is a piece that was cut off and preserved. The only part of the painting considered to be a good likeness, and which was identified by reliable source Arthur Bell Nicholls. It is one of Branwell's most sensitive portraits: a profile of a pretty young woman—Emily, at sixteen.

Societal ideas of beauty change over time. Even personal opinions as to who is attractive vary between people. Among those who knew the Brontës, some—including Martha Brown—claimed Emily was the prettiest of the sisters. Others said Anne was. There were those who said all the sisters were plain. Branwell, who was usually considered handsome, might not be so judged today. His often-mentioned charm and wit, however, would probably still convince us of his attractiveness. The girls, in today's world, might not be considered as plain as they were described during their lifetimes. They were often described as interesting looking. Anne was said to have a pleasing appearance. In today's world, interesting and pleasing might be considered the same as attractive. Victorians liked plump, helpless, fainting beauties with large eyes, long necks, and bouncing ringlets. The Brontë sisters did not fit that image. The mystery of what they looked like remains.

9

Rebellious Writers

I am just going to write because I cannot help it.

Charlotte was happy at home for two years, but in late July 1835, she finally worked up her courage to return to Roe Head School as a teacher. Ironically she would be instructing the girls on the rules of grammar. (She would later express relief when her publishers checked her grammar in her manuscripts before they were published.)

Emily would be enrolled as a new student. Her only formal schooling was a brief tragic memory of Cowan Bridge, and returning to a formal school would not be a welcome experience. Emily was old to be just starting at Roe Head. She and all her siblings had benefited from their father's instruction, and Charlotte had spent the summer after she returned from her schooling at Roe Head teaching her and Anne what she had learned. All the siblings were self-educated in subjects they found interesting. It's unknown why the decision had been made to send her to school at this time. At least the sisters would be together, and Charlotte liked and respected Miss Wooler. She and Emily did not realize, however, just how much they would find their time at the school intolerable.

Apparently their father worried that the two young women—Charlotte was of marriageable age at nineteen, and Emily, who turned seventeen the day of her arrival at school, might not be "beyond the reach of temptation" away from his and their aunt's watchful eye. Though he expressed that "as far as I can judge their principles are good . . . but they are very young, and unacquainted with the ways of this delusive and insnaring [*sic*] world."[1] Fearing an unsuitable attachment for either of the girls, he wrote to his old friend, Elizabeth Firth Franks (to whom he had once disastrously proposed), with a request. As she and her husband lived near Roe Head, he asked that they keep in touch with the girls, and write to him if they thought there was something going on he should know about. He didn't mention the letter to Charlotte or Emily. He knew his daughters. They would have been indignant.

Emily may have been rebellious and depressed from the beginning of her stay. This seems to be the period where she changed from a happy, well-adjusted young girl to the almost reclusive, unapproachable young woman others later described. Unlike Charlotte, there are gaps in our knowledge of the lives and activities of both Emily and Anne. Few letters or papers survived their lifetimes. There have been, and will continue to be, many speculations about Emily, especially. They include an early romantic attachment, which would explain the unusual letter Mr. Brontë sent Mrs. Franks. There is no evidence to prove the supposition. Though new bits of information pertinent to their lives do keep coming to light, it's unlikely there will ever be confirmation of any of the theories surrounding what is unknown about the Brontës.

Emily was able to attend school because Miss Wooler was allowing her tuition to be covered by Charlotte's salary. But even the relief of being at Roe Head together did not alleviate the sisters' unhappiness. As Charlotte had feared, she didn't like teaching and was having a hard time adjusting. She thought her pupils were empty-headed dolts that lacked the seriousness she had when she was a student at the school. She believed they were unimaginative and had no interest in learning. She resented not having time for her favorite pastime—imagining new scenes set in her dramatic world of Angria.

Charlotte seems to have barely tried to hide her misery at the school. She was irritable with everyone, from the youngest student to Miss Wooler herself. One night she took a piece of paper and wrote: "Well, here I am at Roe Head. It is seven o'clock at night. The young ladies are all at their lessons, the school-room is quiet, the fire is low. A stormy day is at this moment passing off in a murmuring and bleak night."[2] She had begun keeping a journal— really just loose pieces of paper stored together in her lap desk. She may have found writing her complaints was an outlet for her anger and frustration at having to teach, and being away from home. She also used it to write a flood of dramatic, evocative new stories.

Charlotte was yearning to be at home with Branwell, who had not stopped writing Angrian stories even as he studied with painter William Robinson. She scribbled in her journal, "About a week since I got a letter from Branwell containing a most exquisitely characteristic epistle from Northangerland to his daughter." The Duke of Northangerland was governor of a province in Angria, and an ongoing character in their stories. "It is astonishing what a soothing and delightful tone that letter seemed to speak. I lived on its content for days. In every pause of employment it came chiming in like some sweet bar of music, bringing with it agreeable thoughts such as I had for many weeks been a stranger to."[3]

Charlotte had made friends when she was a student at Roe Head and ultimately had enjoyed her time there. Emily did not. She never adjusted to life in the boarding school, with its strict routine and the constant companionship of loud, boisterous girls. Sharing a bed with a classmate she didn't know, and having no privacy, may have seemed unbearable. Her age, her height, her unfashionable clothes, and her frizzy hair—possibly even her cleverness—would have set her apart.

Emily was certainly depressed. She pined for her home, family, pets, and the liberating sense of freedom and solitude she found on Haworth Moor. She couldn't write. The siblings had been deeply involved in their fantasy world for most of their lives. All the sisters felt a loss of freedom to write when they studied or worked away from their home. "Nobody knew what ailed her . . ." Charlotte wrote later. "I knew only too well."[4] Emily lasted only six months at school. She became ill, and Charlotte, having lost two sisters to illness, feared for Emily's health.

She arranged for Anne to replace Emily at school with the same arrangement, using her salary as Anne's tuition. Mr. Brontë was reluctant to part with the baby of the family. He had wanted to keep Anne home one more year. At fifteen, she had never attended a formal school at all, and she had rarely been away from home. But gentle, shy, and quiet Anne would prove again and again to have a stronger sense of discipline, responsibility, and determination than any of her siblings. Anne was a conscientious student and dutiful, though she, too, did not want to become a teacher or a governess. There's no reason to believe she suffered less in the school setting than Charlotte or

Emily, but she quietly pursued her studies and did not complain. She soon made a friend at Roe Head, as Charlotte had before her. (Sadly, her young friend died the next year.)

Branwell had finished his series of classes with William Robinson only to be advised by his teacher that he needed further lessons in anatomy and classical painting. After the next series, however, Branwell does not appear to have applied to the Royal Academy. The reason for the decision may be lack of money, or even his teacher's opinion that Branwell was still not ready.

After a Christmas holiday at home, Charlotte and Anne returned to Roe Head—their lives there just as depressing as before. Unlike his sisters, though, Branwell had more than one attractive possibility before him. Apparently father and son may not have given up the idea of the Royal Academy yet. The most exciting idea that was considered was an art study tour of the Continent, painting, visiting museums and galleries to see—and probably copy—great works of art, which was a common method of study. The tour would give added prestige to Branwell's art education and help him enter the academy and establish his painting career. Needing contacts abroad, he joined the Freemasons (an international men's organization for aiding one another in times of hardship, as well as helping others). Branwell was given a special dispensation to join, as he was under the age of eligibility. His good friend John Brown—now church sextant after the death of his father—was Master of the Lodge and may have been instrumental in his acceptance. Branwell faithfully attended the meetings of the Masonic Lodge of Three Graces in Haworth. Perhaps because it was believed his travels were to begin soon, he was promoted very quickly. In only a month, he was a Master Mason.

It may have been because funds for the trip could not be raised that Branwell never made his art tour of the Continent—perhaps it was postponed until he could earn money for the adventure. He seemed not to have been devastated by the decision, however. He had written yet another letter to *Blackwood's Magazine*, applying for a job. Again there was no answer, but Branwell was busy writing poetry, attending Masonic meetings, practicing boxing upstairs at the Black Bull—and painting. Did he still even wish to pursue a career as a painter? He didn't seem to have decided, though he may not have shared that with his father.

It was agreed between father and son that Branwell would try to establish himself as a portrait painter in Haworth, presumably as a way to make money for his grand European tour. One of his sisters' rooms could be used as a studio while they were away at Roe Head. Half of his known paintings are of local residents. The quality varies, but he did paint a very attractive portrait of his friend John Brown. He also painted prosperous mill owners, as well as famed local opera singer Thomas Parker. It's likely fellow Masons from the Three Graces Lodge also sat for portraits.

At Roe Head, Charlotte was still angry at her work schedule. She grabbed any spare moment to lose herself in the "unseen land of thought."[5] "The ladies went into the school-room to do their exercises & I crept up to the bed-room to be *alone* for the first time that day. Delicious was the sensation I experienced as I laid down on the spare-bed & resigned myself to the luxury of twilight & solitude. The stream of thought, checked all day, came flowing free & calm along its channel."[6]

It was becoming even more difficult to hide the rage she felt at the lack of privacy, and at having to teach the young ladies she found so annoying. Her only escape was listening to the "still small voice alone that comes to me at eventide. . . . Last night I did indeed lean upon the thunder-wakening wings of such a stormy blast as I have seldom heard blow, & it whirled me away like heath in the wilderness for five seconds of ecstasy. And as I sat by myself in the dining-room while all the rest were at tea, the trance seemed to descend."[7]

In Charlotte's journal she was recording her feelings, and even her location at the moment, as Emily and Anne did in their diaries. But Charlotte was also letting her imagination carry her to Angria, writing long, detailed stories about their intrigues and passionate romances. She wrote thousands of words and was always irritated when she had to break her deep concentration, which she sometimes referred to as a trance. "I knew I was wide awake and that it was dark and that moreover the ladies were now come into the room to get their curl-papers they perceived me lying on the bed and I heard them talking about me. I wanted to speak, to rise it was impossible—I felt that this was a frightful predicament. . . . I must get up I thought and I did so with a start . . . tea's ready Miss Wooler is impatient."[8]

Charlotte was a restless, rebellious twenty-year-old who felt her youth was slipping away. "The thought came over me am I to spend all the best part of my life in this wretched bondage."[9] Summer was a particularly painful time to be kept in the school where she did not want to be, working at a profession she did not want to pursue. "Must I from day to day sit chained to this chair prisoned within these four bare walls, while these glorious summer suns are burning in heaven and the year is revolving in its richest glow, and declaring at the close of every summer's day, the time I am losing, will never come again?"[10]

On a windy autumn night, Charlotte wrote: "That wind, pouring in impetuous current through the air, sounding wildly, unremittingly from hour to hour, deepening its tone as the night advances . . . that wind I know is heard at this moment far away on the moors at Haworth. Branwell and Emily hear it and as it sweeps over our house down the church-yard and round the old church, they think perhaps of me and Anne."[11]

Emily was grateful to have escaped Roe Head. All the siblings were now expressing themselves in poetry as well as prose. Possibly it was after a wild, windy day on Haworth moors that Emily wrote this exciting, rousing poem. She may even have been remembering the dramatic bog burst she had experienced as a small child on Crow Hill.

> High waving heather 'neath stormy blasts bending,
> Midnight and moonlight and bright shining stars;
> Darkness and glory rejoicingly blending,
> Earth rising to heaven and heaven descending;
> Man's spirit away from the drear dungeon sending,
> Bursting the fetters and breaking the bars.
>
> All down the mountain-sides wild forests lending
> The mighty voice to the life-giving wind;
> Rivers their banks in the jubilee bending,
> Fast through the valleys a reckless course wending,
> Wilder and deeper their waters extending,
> Leaving a desolate desert behind.
>
> Shining and lowering, and swelling and dying,
> Changing for ever from midnight to noon;
> Roaring like thunder, like soft music sighing,
> Shadows on shadows advancing and flying,
> Lightning-bright flashes the deep gloom defying,
> Coming as swiftly and fading as soon.[12]

The mood was festive when the Christmas holidays arrived and everyone was at home. Change came quickly, however, when Tabby fell on steep and icy Main Street. She shattered and dislocated her leg—which could not be set until the next day. She was seriously ill. The three anxious girls insisted they would nurse her as well as take over all the household tasks. Aunt Branwell wanted Tabby removed to her sister's house to recover. She believed it was time for her to retire and leave the parsonage for good. The sisters were upset at the suggestion and stubbornly persisted that they should take care of Tabby now she was old, as she had cared for them for most of their lives. An argument ensued, which the girls finally won—after going on a hunger strike. Even caring for Tabby and taking on her household duties did not keep them from finding time to write. Anne, happy to be home, concentrated on the Gondal saga.

Since childhood, all the siblings had dreamed of being published. With the beginning of their lives as wage-earners, Charlotte and Branwell, together again, discussed their very serious longing to earn their living by writing. What if they could find satisfaction in the work they did?

In January, Branwell wrote to *Blackwood's*, again expressing his desire to be hired as a writer. Unwisely, his tone was arrogant and belligerent, seeming to demand work. Not surprisingly, there was again no answer to his letter. He and Charlotte then decided to send examples of their work to two of their favorite poets, requesting their writing be critiqued—and hoping, perhaps, for aid in being published. William Wordsworth, who had so greatly influenced all the siblings' writing, was Branwell's choice, but that letter was not answered either.

Charlotte had chosen to write to the poet laureate of Great Britain, Robert Southey, confiding to him her wish to be forever known. Not for Charlotte was an *ordinary* writing career—she wished to be a great writer, a memorable writer. She may have given up hope of hearing from the famed poet by the time his answer arrived, three months later. He indicated the belief that she had some talent, and expressed the thought that she should write for her own pleasure but not for fame. He advised her to engage in the "proper duties" of a woman, stating, "Literature cannot be the business of a woman's life, and it ought not to be." These words have angered countless women ever since they first appeared in print. He warned her, "The day dreams in which you habitually indulge are likely to [make] the world seem to you flat and unprofitable."[13] He tempered this with an understanding tone, telling her that being published would not guarantee her happiness. Interestingly, his second wife was a poet. Charlotte sent Mr. Southey an answering letter, and he responded with a surprising invitation—if she was ever in the Lake District—to stop by his home and talk. (By the time she could afford such a trip, he had died.)

Charlotte had indicated she would follow Robert Southey's advice—but she still continued to write and dream of being published one day. She had earlier recorded in her journal, "I am just going to write because I cannot help it."[14] Still, she was troubled. The famed poet had warned against what was her own secret fear—she knew she spent too much time in the imaginary worlds of her writing, and that she had already found it more compelling than her own life.

As a young writer, Mr. Brontë had come to the unhappy conclusion that "creating an imaginary world which" the novelist "can never inhabit" would only "make the real world . . . gloomy and unsupportable."[15] He had warned all his children of the danger, but interestingly, he never curtailed the time they spent scribbling stories and poems. Perhaps he understood they would not heed his advice.

As winter turned into spring over Haworth Moor, Emily was not worried by thoughts of guilt due to her writing. She was composing a personal poem that expressed her feelings of contentment at being home, and her hope for the future.

> All day I've toiled, but not with pain,
>   In learning's golden mine;
> And now at eventide again
>   The moonbeams softly shine.
>
> There is no snow upon the ground,
>   No frost on wind or wave;
> The south wind blew with gentlest sound
>   And broke their icy grave.
>
> 'Tis sweet to wander here at night,
>   To watch the winter die,
> With heart as summer sunshine light,
>   And warm as summer sky.

O may I never lose the peace
   That lulls me gently now,
Though time should change my youthful face,
   And years should shade my brow!

True to myself, and true to all,
   May I be healthful still,
And turn away from passion's call,
   And curb my own wild will.[16]

   With summer's arrival, Charlotte and Anne eagerly returned home for their school break from Roe Head. On the cool but summery afternoon of Branwell's twentieth birthday, the two younger girls decided to write their new diary papers. They were in the drawing room, and had been writing poetry. Emily recorded that Branwell was reading to Charlotte in their aunt's room, and "papa—gone out. Tabby in the Kitchin [sic]—the Emperors and Empresses . . . preparing to depart from Gaaldine to Gondal to prepare for the coranation [sic] which will be on the 12th of July Queen Victoria ascended the throne this month."[17] The young woman who was crowned queen at only eighteen years of age was of great interest to the sisters. She was the same age as Emily, and the lavish details of the ceremony were an inspiration to Emily and Anne for the coronation they were planning in their imaginary world of Gondal. They had acquired two pet geese, which the teenagers gave the magnificent royal names of Victoria and Adelaide, after the queen and her aunt.

   Emily continued, "Northangerland in Monceys Isle—Zamorna at Eversham. all tight and right in which condition it is to be hoped we shall all be on this day 4 years. . . . I wonder where we shall be and how we shall be and what kind of a day it will be then let us hope for the best Emily Jane Brontë—Anne Brontë."[18]

   But both Charlotte and Anne were suffering from private worries, which they didn't share with each other or the rest of the family. When they returned to school after their summer holiday, Charlotte again paid little attention to Anne, as had been her behavior to Emily when she was at the school. Anne became ill with a high fever plus an asthma attack, made worse by severe anxiety of which Charlotte had not been aware. It had plagued her for months. The culture of Roe Head had changed since Charlotte had spent her happy school days there. Charlotte and Anne had both become very troubled at school, caused by no less a crisis than fear for their own souls. Two of the five Wooler sisters had married strict Calvinist clerics who had involved themselves in the affairs of the school. Charlotte and Anne were both confused and fearful due to the clerics' judgmental and threatening warnings, so unlike their father's teachings.

Charlotte had been exposed to frightening sermons and literature at Cowan Bridge, but seventeen-year-old Anne had not, and she was filled with guilt and fear that she was an unredeemable sinner, with no hope of heaven. The Calvinists taught that only a few—the elect—were predestined to find salvation. She wisely did not confide her anxieties to the churchmen who had frightened her at the school but, instead, asked to see a kind cleric from another denomination. He was able to ease some of the anxieties of the very ill and troubled teenager. Anne's father would have been shocked by the cause of suffering of the sweetest and most spiritual of his children. It's not known if she ever confided her fears to him.

Charlotte was suffering from the same fears, and her spiritual crisis continued to be made worse by Ellen, who had greatly influenced Charlotte's complicated feelings. Charlotte wrote Ellen, "What am I compared to you I feel my own utter worthlessness when I make the comparison."[19] Apparently Ellen was not frightened by Calvinist doctrines.

Charlotte believed Ellen was a model of piety. Her own thoughts were more often on her stories and on the fascinating, sensual heroes she had created than on religion. Charlotte feared she had exchanged her worship of God for making idols of her fictional characters. She wrote to Ellen: "If you knew my thoughts, the dreams that absorb me, and the fiery imagination that at times eats me up, and makes me feel society, as it is, wretchedly insipid, you would pity and I dare say despise me."[20] Self-worth-destroying criticism was encouraged. Impossible perfection was their goal.

Charlotte was alarmed by Anne's illness, and she could only think of taking her sister home. She endangered her friendship with her mentor, Miss Wooler, resulting in arguments and tears. The older woman believed there was no necessity to remove Anne from school. But Charlotte was adamant. Miss Wooler and Charlotte both wrote emotional letters to Mr. Brontë. He settled the issue by calling both his daughters home. Anne would recover at the parsonage, and would not return. Her only formal education was at an end. Charlotte, however, would return to Roe Head alone, still troubled, still wishing only to write.

New Ventures

My health and spirits had utterly failed me.

Though Charlotte and Miss Wooler had put their argument aside, Charlotte was particularly anxious to return home for Christmas, and when the holiday ended, she felt only dread about returning to teaching. It wasn't only her usual reluctance to leave her home and family, however, that made her departure more difficult than usual. Continuous snow had fallen for a week, and Miss Wooler would soon be relocating her school to a smaller house several miles beyond Roe Head. The move would undoubtedly involve all of the staff. Heald's House was closer to the headmistress's ailing father and her extended family, who lived in Dewsbury Moor. The new school was a pleasant brick house set among gardens and, as with Roe Head, was well placed on a hill above the smoke of the many mills in the area. Still, Charlotte was not comfortable there. She felt like a prisoner.

At home that cold winter, Anne and Emily were writing some of their most evocative poetry, including Emily's celebration of imagination and her ability to lose herself in the "unseen land of thought."

> I'm happiest now when most away
>   I can tear my soul from its mould of clay.
> On a windy night when the moon is bright,
>   And my eye can wander through worlds of light.

> When I am not, and none beside,
>   Nor earth, nor sea, nor cloudless sky,
> But only spirit wandering wide
>   Through infinite immensity.[1]

Mr. Brontë was trying to determine suitable employment for Branwell, as his career as a professional painter was looking doubtful. He wrote to a merchant banking acquaintance in Manchester, seeking a position for his son. He confided that he had thought of sending Branwell to university, but the expenses would be very high and his son would then not be earning a living for four or five *more* years. It was necessary for Branwell to have a paying job—soon. Mr. Brontë had decided a position as a clerk in a bank would be best for his son. He thought working away from home and seeing a little more of the world—Liverpool, Manchester, or London—would be beneficial for Branwell. It was time for his son to grow up—to be a responsible young man.

It was hard to give up the dream shared by the whole family that Branwell would go to London to study and become a great painter who could take care of his sisters when Mr. Brontë died. It was time for the plan to be altered. Branwell, however, was never going to be employed as a bank clerk in Manchester; no job materialized.

There has been confusion as to whether Branwell ever did visit London. He was, of course, a storyteller with a talent for tall tales. The owner of the Black Bull sometimes sent a servant to the parsonage to ask Branwell to come and entertain guests at the tavern. He shared clever quips and entertaining tales, including his supposed knowledge of the capital city. Branwell had studied London maps thoroughly, and Mr. Brontë had once hand-drawn a map of the area of the city where he had stayed as a young man on visits from university. Branwell was able to go on at length about alleys, shortcuts, and back streets, as though he was very familiar with the great city. Then he paused—and announced dramatically to his audience that he had never been to London in his life!

At Heald's House, Charlotte, unsurprisingly, suffered from nervous depression. The religious fears she had experienced at Roe Head still haunted her and left her in a constant state of anxiety. The dreary atmosphere of the new location was even worse than Roe Head. Kind and sensible Miss Wooler, seemingly oblivious to the grim new state of her school, spent a great deal of her time with her family, leaving Charlotte in charge of the school. Charlotte felt overworked and overwhelmed with responsibility. Alone for more than two weeks over the Easter holiday, isolation and her morbid thoughts overcame her.

By June, an ailing Charlotte was home again. "My health and spirits had utterly failed me, and the medical man whom I consulted enjoined me, if I valued my life, to go home. So home I went; the change has at once roused and soothed me, and I am now, I trust, fairly in the way to be myself again."[2] There were lingering religious fears, but her physical health was soon fine. Her fear, and dislike of her job, had made her ill. Returning home was usually enough to dispel the depression and anxiety she and her sisters fought all their lives.

Her quick recovery was aided by the lively company of Mary and Martha Taylor, whose visit she described in a letter to Ellen Nussey. "They are making such a noise about me I cannot write any more. Mary is playing on the piano; Martha is chattering as fast as her little tongue can run; and Branwell is standing before her, laughing at her vivacity."[3]

A decision was made about Branwell's painting career. He would have been pleased and the rest of the family hopeful—the twenty-one-year-old would move to the growing city of Bradford and open a proper portrait studio. He found a pleasant, respectable lodging house, where he both lived and had his studio. He was popular with his landlord and landlady, Mr. and Mrs. Kirby. Branwell was charming and gregarious and made a good impression on everyone he met. He soon had a new circle of friends—talented young artists and writers, some already successful in their careers—who met regularly at the George Hotel for spirits and conversation.

Branwell painted one of his best portraits of the Kirbys' pretty, dark-eyed, thirteen-year-old niece, Margaret Hartley. Years later she remembered the young painter, who was short and "slight in build, though well-proportioned." She recalled Charlotte visiting him, just for the day, and remarked on her "sisterly ways." She also remembered: "It was young Mr. Brontë's practice to go home at each weekend and . . . while sometimes he took the coach . . . he on other occasions walked to Haworth across the moors," twelve miles each way. "He was a very steady young gentleman, his conduct was exemplary and we liked him very much."[4]

During the first months in his new studio, Branwell painted several portraits of local ladies and gentlemen, as well as wealthy clerics who were friends of his father. Even so, he could barely cover his expenses with what he earned, and it was becoming more difficult to attract new customers. He may not have shared with his father his concerns that there were many more experienced painters competing for commissions in Bradford, and still more in nearby towns.

At home, Emily and Anne were busy studying on their own and writing romantic poetry and stories. Emily was working on a translation from the original Latin of Virgil's *Aeneid*. Anne, too, was occupied with improving her education. Charlotte began to write again, obsessively trying to recover from her miserable time at Dewsbury Moor. But by August, she had returned to the school.

In September, twenty-year-old Emily steeled herself to become a teacher. There was not a position available for her to join Charlotte at Heald's House, so with determination she set about finding employment herself.

Though she had not been able to make it through school at Roe Head and had little formal education, Emily bravely secured a post at a school east of Halifax—Miss Patchett's, at Law Hill. The three-story house was advertised as a boarding academy. High on a windy hill, it was built of dark sandstone and appeared from the outside to be a very austere establishment. A converted barn was used for the schoolroom for the forty students, a combination of day students and boarders. Emily, however, would have appreciated the beautiful view of moors, fields, and woods she could see from the house. There was a garden in front, with trees that shaded the house.

The well-established school must have seemed very different to Emily from Roe Head, and forty-two-year-old Elizabeth Patchett, who ran the school, seemed very different from Miss Wooler. There were conflicting opinions about the schoolmistress. Some said she was dignified, remote, and demanding. Others described her as a kind and popular woman who loved teaching. All agreed Miss Patchett was very beautiful, and a skillful horsewoman.

The nearness of Halifax was an attractive feature of the location. As a teacher chaperoning her students, Emily had quite likely been able to visit museums, concerts, and theaters in Halifax. She wrote to Charlotte, however, that her duties at Law Hill included working from six in the morning to eleven at night, with a half hour of exercise. Charlotte did not think her sister would be able to manage the harsh regimen. Emily was one of only three teachers for the forty students, ages eight to fifteen, half of whom were boarders who slept in five bedrooms on the ground floor of the house. Emily took charge of the younger children. It was due to the boarders that there was such an added workload. Emily was not a quick worker, and was still reserved and difficult to get to know. Not surprisingly, she had befriended the house dog, and was devoted to it. Years later one of her young students remembered Emily informing her class that the dog was dearer to her than they were. Despite the harsh-sounding remark, there were no indications from any former student that Emily was unkind or disliked at Law Hill. The seriousness or tone of her comment cannot be known.

Surprisingly, during her first months at the school, Emily may not have been as unhappy as she had been at Roe Head. As a teacher she may have had some privacy, and would not have been bullied or laughed at. She produced a number of poems—both Gondal and personal poetry—including some of her best work. She had somehow found time to write. Although Emily was homesick, she was never reported as being ill at Law Hill, and she would have enjoyed exploring the area around the school.

Like her sisters, she found inspiration for stories from tales she heard. The novel she would write years later benefited greatly from her time spent at Law Hill, which was a working farm as well as a school. Emily may have learned details about farming, which she would include in *Wuthering Heights*, as she envisioned it as an old farmstead in the novel. Emily was told the history of the house, which was built by a vengeful scoundrel who was involved in stealing an inheritance and wreaking havoc on his adoptive family. These gothic touches, plus the appearance of the façade of a nearby half-ruined house, apparently contributed to the plot and the visual depiction of Wuthering Heights itself, which included "a quantity of grotesque carving lavished over the front and . . . a wilderness of crumbling griffins and shameless little boys."[5]

In December, Emily was thinking of home. Excited about the coming holiday she wrote a new poem, which includes:

> There is a spot, 'mid barren hills,
>> Where winter howls, and driving rain;
> But, if the dreary tempest chills,
>> There is a light that warms again.

The house is old, the trees are bare,
  Moonless above bends twilight's dome;
But what on earth is half so dear,
  So longed for, as the hearth of home?
The mute bird sitting on the stone,
  The dank moss dripping from the wall,
The thorn-trees gaunt, the walks o'ergrown,
  I love them—how I love them all![6]

All the siblings were home for Christmas. The parsonage and the snow-covered moors—even in their wintry setting—were a welcome sight. Mr. Brontë had had a stressful year and was not feeling well, but was heartened when Emily and Branwell both told him they were fine and managing as well as they could in their respective first jobs. Charlotte, however, home from Dewsbury Moor, announced she had told Miss Wooler she would be leaving her position in the New Year.

Charlotte did not resign her position due to ill health. She was cheerful, explaining that Miss Wooler had been relying more and more on her to help with the young and old members of her family as well as her teaching duties. When she found the school was being turned over to Miss Wooler's sister Eliza, to whom Charlotte felt no loyalty, she had given her notice and would return home. The news would have been worrisome to her father, who had to constantly be aware of family finances. Aunt Branwell, in charge of meal planning and household management, would have to consider another family member at home again.

Mr. Brontë's relief that Branwell and Emily were settling into the routine of their jobs was short lived.

Branwell's former teacher, William Robinson, died suddenly at age thirty-nine, leaving a wife and six children destitute. Branwell would have had to face the uncertainties and difficulties that lay ahead of him if he continued his career as a painter. If William Robinson—experienced and well known—had not prospered, how could he? The truth of his situation was so unlike the rosy future he and his family had foreseen for him that he made the decision to close his studio.

Branwell did have talent. Did he possess the facility of catching true likenesses, or were his paintings only vague resemblances? The subjects of his portraits—including those of his sisters—even when poorly executed are distinctive from one another and express diverse personalities. With discipline, dedication, and better training, he might have had success as a portraitist. There were many painters no better or worse than Branwell at the time. Today there are collectors who appreciate such paintings for their almost naive folk art quality. He and his family, however, had always felt he would be a master painter, famed for his talent like Sir Thomas Lawrence. To be fair, Branwell's struggle to succeed as a portrait painter coincided with the development of the new process of photography, which would soon be a commonplace method of having a portrait made, making it even more difficult to succeed in the profession.

Arriving home, Branwell seemed to suffer no disappointment or guilt concerning the failure of his long-planned career. He quickly changed his focus. His first love may have always been writing. He had the strong belief he would achieve greatness as a poet and novelist. But he had to find work soon. Branwell and his father agreed it was time to plan a new way forward.

It was decided Mr. Brontë would give Branwell a thorough refresher course in the classical education he'd given him as a boy, so he could pursue a career as a teacher as his sisters were doing. Branwell agreed. He believed he could begin his writing career while he worked as a tutor. He was a very good student, and he particularly enjoyed translating ancient Greek and Latin works. He and his father read the first six books of *The Aeneid* in Latin, and the first four chapters of the Gospel of St. Matthew, in Greek. Though Branwell had previously hated (and done a poor job of) teaching Sunday school classes to the groups of restless local boys, he expected he would succeed as a tutor to one or two boys in their home. He continued to submit poetry to local papers, and repeated his request to be hired for his dream job at *Blackwood's Magazine*. As usual, there was no reply to his letter.

Emily had returned to Law Hill after Christmas, but the winter weather probably brought the usual colds, asthmatic attacks, depression, and homesickness. There may no longer have been fine weather to explore the area, intriguing ideas for poems, or diverting dreams of Gondal. By spring, Emily returned to Haworth, after six months at Law Hill. No evidence of the reason for her sudden departure has survived.

While Branwell was studying with his father in anticipation of his finding work as a tutor, his sisters sewed new shirts and collars for him. Charlotte,

Emily, and Branwell had all returned home within a three-month period. Mr. Brontë again was patient with his children and, perhaps, overly lenient. When Charlotte had a prospect of employment, her father thought she should wait a while longer before finding a new post. He must, however, have been very concerned about his children's future.

11

Proposals

I leave you to guess what my answer would be . . .

Charlotte and Branwell were, once again, writing on the same story—a long tale, "Henry Hastings," about a disreputable brother and his loyal sister who tried to prevent his coming to a bad end. For Charlotte, it was also a love story, whose central character was different from Charlotte's usual aristocratic beauties. Elizabeth Hastings was a more interesting and realistic character. She was small, witty, and clever. She was very like Charlotte, and also an early version of Jane Eyre. She was a young woman who longed to be loved by someone of equal intellect and passion. Charlotte wrote that her heroine "thought she had not met with a single individual equal to herself in mind, & therefore not one whom she could love."[1] "She was always burning for warmer, closer attachment. She couldn't live without it, but the feeling never woke and never was reciprocated."[2]

As Charlotte was thinking of an ideal husband for Elizabeth Hastings, she received an unexpected letter. It was a marriage proposal from Ellen's brother, the Reverend Henry Nussey. The twenty-seven-year-old curate, who had dreams of being a missionary, had decided the time had come to marry. Charlotte had probably met him at the Nussey family home, or in Mirfield when he was a cleric there and she was at Roe Head. Ellen may have suggested he propose to Charlotte when she learned he was seeking a wife.

Henry Nussey's letter to Charlotte has not survived, but it seems he was very matter of fact and direct in his wording, though he surely did not tell her she was his second choice. The first, he recorded in his diary, was "a steady, intelligent, sensible and, I trust, good girl."[3] When that young lady refused him, he made a short unemotional comment in his diary.

Charlotte wrote to Ellen that her brother's proposal was a surprise, and she had not intended to share the news except that Ellen inquired about it. "Henry says he is comfortably settled . . . that his health is much improved." (He had fallen off a horse years before, suffering a brain injury that affected his nerves and speech the rest of his life.) Charlotte added, "it is his intention to take pupils. . . . He then intimates that in due time he should want a wife to take care of his pupils, and frankly asks me to be that wife."[4]

Though it's hard to believe Charlotte's romantic nature would have reacted well to the curate's letter, the honesty and pragmatism of his letter did appeal to her. She realized marriage would be a solution to her problems, and she thought the cleric's proposal was probably the only one she would ever receive. She had told Henry Nussey she had "no personal repugnance to the idea of a union"[5] with him—a frank and personal remark, which did not seem to shock him. A husband would take care of her. She would not have to live and teach in other people's houses or schools. She would have her own school, and Ellen could live with them. And her father would no longer have to worry about her future.

The romantic side of her nature won out. Charlotte thought a great deal about love—and passion. She wanted what her latest heroine wanted: to love her husband, and be loved in return. As she wrote to Ellen, "I had not, and could not have, that intense attachment which would make me willing to die for him; and, if ever I marry, it must be in that light of adoration that I will regard my husband."[6] Her answer to the proposal was a definite "no."

She answered Henry's letter with an explanation. "I am not the serious, grave, cool-headed individual you suppose. You would think me romantic and eccentric. You would say I was satirical and severe. . . . I will never, for the sake of attaining the distinction of matrimony and escaping the stigma of an old maid, take a worthy man whom I am conscious I cannot render happy."[7]

Henry Nussey wrote in his diary, "Received an unfavourable reply from 'C. B.' The will of the Lord be done."[8] After another refused proposal, he would become engaged to his fourth choice for a wife, who met his qualifications and was also wealthy.

Charlotte did not regret her refusal. She could create in her writing the kind of romance she craved. Surely it was Charlotte's experience of Henry Nussey's proposal that inspired the memorable character of St John Rivers in her novel *Jane Eyre*. The dispassionate cleric, who wished to be a missionary, wanted Jane Eyre to marry him, primarily to aid him in his work. Such a suitor would never be acceptable to Jane Eyre—or to Charlotte Brontë. It was a fortunate decision as well, for Henry Nussey's future would be a sad one. His future marriage would not be happy, and he would give up his curacy and his dreams of being a missionary due to ill health. Three of Ellen's brothers, including Henry, George (her favorite brother), and John (the respected and successful court physician to Queen Victoria), would die in mental asylums.

With all the young Brontës at home and unemployed, nineteen-year-old Anne decided it was time to seek employment. It would be her first job—and she very efficiently found it on her own. Anne's new position was governess to the wealthy Ingham family at Blake Hall, Mirfield. The Inghams' house— a large, three-story, eighteenth-century mansion with a grand façade—was close to Roe Head, so at least Anne was familiar with the area. The coach ride to Mirfield was the same route she had taken to Miss Wooler's school.

Though it could be a mistake to assume a work of fiction has been taken exactly from the author's life, the Brontë sisters did use experiences from their lives in their novels. In Anne's first novel, *Agnes Grey*, her heroine contemplates becoming a governess, with high hopes. It seems very possible that Agnes's experiences and emotions are the same as Anne's own first venture into the world as a governess. After her sheltered life as the baby of the family, she may have felt she suffered from not being taken seriously. She may have wanted to be seen as an adult.

In Agnes's words: "How delightful it would be to be a governess! To go out into the world; to enter upon a new life; to act for myself; to exercise my unused faculties; to try my unknown powers; to earn my own maintenance, and something to comfort and help my father . . . to show papa what his little Agnes could do . . . that I was not quite the helpless, thoughtless being they supposed."[9]

Before she embarks on her new adventure, Agnes—seeming very like Anne—takes a last walk on the moors with her sister, feeds her pet birds and kisses them goodbye, plays a last tune on their piano, and mourns leaving her kitten.

Charlotte wrote to Ellen about Anne's departure, "no one went with her; it was her own wish that she might be allowed to go alone, as she thought she could manage better and summon more courage if thrown entirely upon her own resources." Showing what would be a life-long lack of belief in the abilities of her youngest sister, Charlotte wrote, "I hope she'll do. You would be astonished what a sensible, clever letter she writes; it is only the talking part that I fear. . . . I do seriously apprehend that Mrs. Ingham will sometimes conclude that she has a natural impediment of speech."[10] Since all three sisters had trouble speaking due to shyness, this is an odd comment.

If Anne had dreams of finding well-behaved children with a desire to learn at her destination, she was soon disillusioned. It was clear that Anne's task of teaching six-year-old Cunliffe and five-year-old Mary Ingham would be very difficult. The younger Ingham children were fortunately in the nursery maid's care. Anne soon described her charges to her sisters as "desperate little dunces" and was surprised that they could not read, and seemed to "sometimes . . . profess a profound ignorance of their alphabet."[11] The children were overindulged, wild, and uncontrollable. Anne was not allowed to correct them, and was told to deliver her complaints about their behavior to their mother. She wrote that if she did that she would be making complaints constantly, from morning till night.

The children Anne described in *Agnes Grey* were apparently inspired by the Ingham children. Family legends told by descendants of the family include a story about the children's behavior to Anne that is very similar to a scene in *Agnes Grey*. Cunliffe and Mary, in new red cloaks, ran outside shrieking that they were devils. Anne, who could not make them return to their studies, went to their mother in tears. Her inability to teach the children made her desperate, resulting in the disturbing and out-of-character occasion of Anne tying the children to a table leg to make them sit still and listen. Similar measures by teachers at that time were not unusual but was a surprising solution for Anne to try. And it didn't work. The children were beyond her ability to control.

Since her younger sister had found employment so easily, a reluctant Charlotte began seeking a new position. A post, only a dozen miles from Haworth, was soon located. The position was only for two months, while the regular governess was away, and Charlotte chose it for that reason. She also thought that since Mrs. Sidgwick, her new employer, was raised in Keighley and her sister was married to a friend of Mr. Brontë there was a connection that would confirm her equal social standing with Mrs. Sidgwick.

The Sidgwick family spent the summer months at their house, Stonegappe, in Lothersdale. The house was on a hillside, with a view of a wide river valley. Charlotte thought the large three-story house and the surrounding grounds and woods were delightful. But she quickly grew to resent Mrs. Sidgwick and to realize that being a private governess was no improvement over teaching in a school. Charlotte expected familiarity and respect, but she was treated as a governess—an almost-servant. She never would adapt to the strange, painful, in-between position of being a governess.

Charlotte's charges—Matilda, age seven, and John Benson, four—were as unmanageable as Anne's charges were. And just as Anne had been told at Blake Hall, Charlotte was not allowed to correct the children's behavior. They could do anything they pleased, she wrote to Emily. Adding to her grievances, Charlotte, who had never enjoyed sewing, was given "oceans of needlework, yards of cambric to hem, muslin nightcaps to make, and, above all things, dolls to dress."[12] She considered she was being given menial tasks to do. She had many of the duties of a nursemaid, which she did not believe should be required of her.

Always quick to feel slighted, Charlotte was discontented and depressed. Realizing her letters to Emily expressed her resentment, Charlotte told her sister she should not share her constant complaints with their father and aunt—only with Branwell, because he wouldn't judge her.

There were outings, such as a visit to a nearby house—Norton Conyers— where Charlotte heard the story of a madwoman who had been confined to the attic. She had heard other such tales, as asylums were so terrible that mentally ill family members were sometimes kept at home to be cared for—or hidden away. Charlotte didn't forget the tale, or the attic space she had seen, when she wrote her novel, *Jane Eyre*.

In June, Charlotte accompanied the Sidgwicks to the summer home of Mrs. Sidgwick's father. Despite beautiful surroundings, Charlotte felt she had been thrown into an even more uncomfortable setting. Her employer's large, wealthy family was gathered together with their friends for a happy summer visit. Charlotte, shy of strangers, felt burdened with the care of the spoiled and rowdy children. She was astonished when a stern Mrs. Sidgwick complained of her behavior. Charlotte cried and felt misunderstood. She considered giving her notice, but decided against it.

Mrs. Sidgwick did have valid complaints. She was soon to have her fifth child, and was occupied with the care of her invalid father. She claimed Charlotte often stayed in bed all day, suffering from depression, leaving the care of the two children to her. Charlotte was described as taking offense when no offense was intended. If she was invited to walk to church with the family, she felt she was being ordered. If not invited, she felt left out.

Charlotte also had cause for complaint. Little John Benson—who would grow up to be a vicar—threw a Bible at her in a burst of temper. He also threw rocks at her when she tried to get him to leave the stable yard, where the children were forbidden to go. John Benson had been egged on by his older brother. The two boys were frightened when one of the rocks hit Charlotte. But when Mrs. Sidgwick asked about Charlotte's injured forehead, she did not tell her about their bad behavior—she said that her injury was an accident. The boys were grateful, and were better behaved after the incident. When four-year-old John Benson put his hand in Charlotte's and said, "I love 'ou, Miss Brontë," his mother exclaimed in astonishment—in front of all the children— "Love the *governess*, my dear!"[13] as though that were a ridiculous statement.

In July, Charlotte's unhappy experience with the Sidgwick family ended. It seems very likely they were as relieved as Charlotte when the regular governess returned.

Charlotte, happy to be home from her job at Stonegappe, was excited when Ellen suggested they travel to the seashore together, but Mr. Brontë and Aunt Branwell had other plans. They wanted the whole family to take their first-ever trip together, and had chosen Liverpool as their destination. Liverpool at the time was a very popular vacation choice with much to see and do. The young people had suffered from various ailments in the previous months, and Mr. Brontë and Aunt Branwell, especially, wanted to treat Anne to a real holiday. Anne was home from Blake Hall for her summer break but would soon be returning. Since a new assistant curate was due to arrive, Mr. Brontë was looking forward to a rare, much-needed holiday himself.

It's unknown why the planned family excursion was abandoned, but Aunt Branwell had organized trips in the past and later changed her mind, finding reasons to cancel the proposed excursions. Branwell, however, decided to travel to Liverpool, with friends, promising his father he would report back on a sermon to be given by a famed preacher Mr. Brontë had hoped to hear speak. During the trip, Branwell suffered from a severe form of neuralgia, which caused a muscle spasm in his face. To alleviate the pain he took opium, which, at the time, was used for medical purposes and was not illegal. A liquid form—laudanum—was readily available from apothecary shops (pharmacists) and probably a doctor's prescription was not even required. Laudanum, however, would prove to be an unfortunate choice of remedy for Branwell.

Charlotte, still wishing to see the sea, was determined to have her holiday with Ellen, but before they left in September she had a surprising experience. She wrote to Ellen about "an odd circumstance. . . . This is not like one of my adventures, is it? It more nearly resembles Martha's," she wrote, referring to Mary Taylor's charming, outgoing younger sister. A former assistant curate of Mr. Brontë had come to spend the day and had brought his own assistant with him. Charlotte had apparently enjoyed the company of the young Irish clergyman, David Pryce, even flirting with him. She reported that "after the manner of his countrymen, he soon made himself at home. His character quickly appeared in his conversation; witty, lively, ardent, clever too; but deficient in the dignity and discretion of an Englishman. At home, you know, I talk with ease, and am never shy—never weighed down and oppressed by that miserable *mauvaise honte* [shyness] which torments and constrains me elsewhere. So I conversed with this Irishman, and laughed at his jests; and, though I saw faults in his character, excused them because of the amusement his originality afforded. I cooled a little, indeed, and drew in towards the latter part of the evening . . . they went away, and no more was thought about them."[14]

A few days later Charlotte received a letter that "proved to be a declaration of attachment and proposal of matrimony. . . . Well! thought I, I have heard of love at first sight, but this beats all! I leave you to guess what my answer would be, convinced that you will not do me the injustice of guessing wrong." In a more serious note, Charlotte wrote, "I am certainly doomed to be an old maid. Never mind. I made up my mind to that fate ever since I was twelve years old."[15] Though Charlotte and Ellen laughed about the proposal, and Charlotte never considered it seriously, it was her second chance to escape the life of a governess—just as with Henry Nussey. It was, however, fortunate that she did not marry this young curate either. He died less than six months later. When Charlotte heard the news, she wrote to Ellen: "I confess, when I suddenly heard he was dead, I felt both shocked and saddened: it was no shame to feel so, was it?"[16]

Charlotte, as the oldest daughter, was given the respectful title of Miss Brontë. Her younger sisters were addressed as Miss Emily and Miss Anne. As her father's hostess, Charlotte met more visitors than her sisters, who were apparently allowed to make themselves scarce. Tiny, plain, short-sighted Charlotte would receive four proposals of marriage in her lifetime. Mr. Brontë certainly considered marriage a possibility for all his daughters as shown by his attempts at vigilance when Charlotte and Emily went to Roe Head in 1835. The sisters all yearned to be loved, as indicated by their reading choices as well as by their poetry and later novels, though they each envisioned love and romance in their novels in their own way. There is no reason to believe Charlotte's sisters would not have received proposals of marriage (either for convenience or from love) had they been less shy and more willing to be known for themselves.

In addition to her housekeeping duties, Emily spent the autumn writing. Since her return from Law Hill in March, she had been absorbed in composing Gondal poetry about a doomed man—an early version of her troubled and troubling character, Heathcliff, in her future novel *Wuthering Heights*. A poem she wrote began:

> I am the only being whose doom
>   No tongue would ask, no eye would mourn;
> I've never caused a thought of gloom,
>   A smile of joy, since I was born.
>
> In secret pleasure, secret tears,
>   This changeful life has slipped away,
> As friendless after eighteen years,
>   As lone as on my natal day . . .[17]

Emily wrote another powerful poem showing sympathy for the disturbing character.

Well, some may hate, and some may scorn,
    And some may quite forget thy name;
But my sad heart must ever mourn
    Thy ruined hopes, thy blighted fame!
'Twas thus I thought, an hour ago,
    Even weeping o'er that wretch's woe;
One word turned back my gushing tears,
    And lit my altered eye with sneers.
Then, "Bless the friendly dust," I said,
    "That hides thy unlamented head!
Vain as thou wert, and weak as vain,
    The slave of Falsehood, Pride, and Pain—
My heart has nought akin to thine;
    Thy soul is powerless over mine."
But these were thoughts that vanished too;
    Unwise, unholy, and untrue:
Do I despise the timid deer,
    Because his limbs are fleet with fear?
Or, would I mock the wolf's death-howl,
    Because his form is gaunt and foul?
Or, hear with joy the leveret's cry,
    Because it cannot bravely die?
No! Then above his memory
    Let Pity's heart as tender be;
Say, "Earth, lie lightly on that breast,
    And, kind Heaven, grant that spirit rest!"[18]

At the end of November, Tabby made the decision that she should stay with her sister. Her leg, injured by the fall on the ice three years before, had become ulcerated. She was lame and needed to keep off her feet. The plan was for her to return when she was healed, and her "childer" would be able to visit her until then. While she was away, Charlotte and Emily would stay home to take over her duties, aided by eleven-year-old Martha Brown. She was one of John Brown's daughters—a pretty child, with dark hair and eyes.

The Brontë family had known Martha all her life. Charlotte or Anne had probably taught her in Sunday school. She had previously run errands for them, but she was too young to take on much of the work of the household. Leaving home at eleven—a common fate for working-class girls—would surely have been painless in Martha's case, as her parents were only a few steps away in the sexton's house. She would also later write about her life with the family. "From my first entering the house . . . I was always recognised and treated as a member of the family, although by outsiders I was spoken of as 'the servant girl.'"[19]

Charlotte and Emily were happy to take charge. "We are such odd animals, that we prefer this mode of contrivance to having a new face among us." They were also confident Tabby would return, "and she shall not be supplanted by a stranger in her absence." Charlotte took over the ironing and house cleaning, and Emily, who had always been happy working in the kitchen, cooked their meals and baked their bread. "I excited aunt's wrath very much by burning the clothes, the first time I attempted to iron; but I do better now. Human feelings are queer things; I am much happier black-leading the stoves, making the beds, and sweeping the floors at home, than I should be living like a fine lady anywhere else."[20]

Mrs. Gaskell included many sensationalized, unconfirmed, and even erroneous anecdotes in her biography of Charlotte (and the Brontë family). She wrote that Emily had badly beaten her beloved dog, Keeper, for sleeping on a clean bedcover and then treated the dog's injuries tenderly. Still, Keeper remained devoted to her for the rest of her life. When asked about the often-repeated tale, Martha Brown said she had no memory of the event, though she would have been there at the time. Apparently she did not believe the story. Emily loved Keeper. She could often be found sitting on the rug, reading, with her large dog sprawled next to her, sleeping, and her hand resting on his furry back. Emily would be young Martha's favorite of the Brontë sisters. She thought Emily was "the best-looking, the cleverest, and the bravest-spirited of the three" and "the very embodiment of truth and honour."[21]

If they wished for more help, they soon received it. Anne arrived home for Christmas, and she would not be returning to Blake Hall. She had been dismissed. Despite her sincere efforts, the Inghams saw no improvement in their unruly children, who had successfully resisted all Anne's efforts to teach them. Their parents blamed Anne. Years later Mrs. Ingham wrote she had at one time employed a very unsuitable governess named Miss Brontë.

Mr. Brontë's adult children were all home again for the holidays—and none of them had jobs to which they would be returning.

Hope, Love, and Resolution

We thank you for the fun . . .

For months, Branwell had no success in finding a post as a tutor. Then, in December, there was an advertisement in the *Leeds Intelligencer* that seemed perfect. A tutor was required, to teach young boys basic subjects with an emphasis on grammar, plus Greek and Latin. Branwell believed the location was ideal—the Lake District, famed for many of the poets and writers that Branwell and his sisters had admired since childhood.

He secured the post and, on the last day of the year 1839, the twenty-three-year-old set off confidently for his new job. (Presumably his grammar had improved since childhood.) He was to be tutor to the two sons of Robert Postlethwaite in Broughton-in-Furness, on the edge of the Lake District. He expected to find inspiration for his writing in the lovely countryside where William Wordsworth wrote his beautiful poetry. Charlotte worried about her brother's suitability. "How he will . . . settle remains yet to be seen; at present he is full of hope and resolution."[1]

Branwell traveled by stagecoach from Keighley, stopping for the night in Kirkby Lonsdale (only two miles southeast from the site of his sisters' old school at Cowan Bridge, which had since moved to a new location). There he claimed, in a letter to his friend John Brown, to have become very drunk with others at the Royal Hotel, and engaged in a brawl. Branwell often exaggerated; the tale may have been true, though it sounded very much like one of his Angrian stories. He continued his coach journey the next morning—thirty miles bumping along on mountain roads to Ulverston. He then traveled another ten miles in a one-horse, two-wheel conveyance to his destination at Broughton-in-Furness.

The little town, amid the fells and forest-covered hills close to the Duddon River Estuary, had been founded in the eleventh century. It had thrived in the 1600s and 1700s. In those days, the large, cobbled market square was the site of cattle and wool markets. Tall merchant houses, only one room wide, surrounded the square.

It wasn't the town Branwell found interesting, however, but the fact that William Wordsworth had composed poetry about the nearby river and Black Combe Mountain. From the hills, Branwell could see across the fells to the area where several of his favorite poets lived. He took idyllic walks, observing a variety of birds and plants that would have reminded him of childhood pastimes with his sisters.

Branwell found lodgings on the very edge of town. He rented a tiny, cramped room in the hundred-year-old High Syke House, a two-story, low-ceilinged farmhouse whose timbers were salvaged from old sailing ships. The house still stands, as do several of the same name in the area. The name means "house by a stream." Branwell's Syke House gave him a view from his window of fields and a twelfth-century church, as well as the estuary and a far-away glimpse of the Irish Sea. His landlord was a surgeon who enjoyed his ale. The landlord's wife was a cheerful, kind lady who liked to chat. They had a pretty eighteen-year-old daughter and two younger children.

Branwell was happy to be in Broughton and wished to make a good impression on his employers. In a letter to John Brown, he again wrote about himself as though he were a character in one of his stories. "Well, what am I? That is, what do they think I am? A most calm, sedate, sober, abstemious, patient, mild-hearted, virtuous, gentlemanly philosopher,—the picture of good works, and the treasure-house of righteous thoughts. . . . I dress in black, and smile like a saint or martyr. Everybody says, 'what a good young gentleman is Mr Postlethwaite's tutor!'"[2]

Robert Postlethwaite was a prosperous landowner and retired county magistrate. He was a genial and generous man with a quiet, pleasant wife. Branwell's students—John, age twelve, and William, eleven—were "two fine, spirited lads"[3] according to their tutor. They lived in the large, starkly plain, three-story Broughton House, in the center of town.

Branwell's sisters, working and living in the homes of their employers, had little free time, but Branwell only worked a few hours a day teaching the two young boys. The rest of his time was his own, and he could take long rambles in the area, a copy of Wordsworth's sonnets in his pocket for perusal among the poet's famed haunts.

Being in the countryside made famous by Wordsworth and Samuel Taylor Coleridge inspired Branwell to labor happily on his own sonnet about Black Combe. He also sent a letter, asking advice, to poet Samuel Coleridge's son Hartley (himself a writer and poet) who lived in a cottage northeast of Broughton. Branwell enclosed one of his older long poems as well as translations from classical Latin. He must have been thrilled when Coleridge replied to his letter, with an invitation to visit him in his home, Nab Cottage. The sixteenth-century cottage had once been the home of poet Thomas de Quincey as well as Hartley's father. Branwell would have been excited about the setting. A walk along the lake edge would have taken him to two other cottages that had belonged to William Wordsworth, and to Wordsworth's favorite vantage point to enjoy the view over the water.

Branwell spent a delightful day with the poet, discussing and reading each other's translations. He decided to do another version of Horace's *Odes*, and Coleridge promised to read it and discuss it with him afterward. Before he could finish the translation, however, he was dismissed from his position. He had only been there for six months. The reason for his firing is not known. Branwell may have spent too much time on his own projects, walking through the countryside, or in the local tavern. A story circulated that a servant, possibly in the Postlethwaite household, had a child believed to be Branwell's. The child, a girl, later died. One of his later poems was titled "Epistle from a Father on Earth to His Child in Her Grave."

Branwell returned home in summer 1840. Despite his dismissal, he arrived at the parsonage heartened by his experience with Coleridge and his renewed belief in the possibility of literary success. Charlotte, perhaps envious of Branwell's experience with Coleridge, sent one of her stories to the famed writer for advice. He responded, but was not encouraging. Branwell quickly finished the translations he had promised to send to Coleridge in great anticipation of hearing back from him. Branwell's translations were some of his best pieces, and might have been publishable. Coleridge began the draft of a very complimentary and encouraging letter in response. He wrote of Branwell's masterful skill, great promise, and fine scholarship.

The unfinished letter was later found among Coleridge's papers. Had it been sent, it would have been very encouraging to the intense young poet.

In February 1840, Mr. Brontë's new curate, William Weightman, set off walking across the cold, wind-whipped moors from Haworth to Bradford to mail four mysterious sealed envelopes. Each one was addressed to a different young lady and contained a valentine, complete with a flowery message, but was unsigned. The valentines were meant to surprise and hopefully bring a smile to the faces of his friends, the daughters of the Reverend Brontë. He had recently learned none of them had ever received a valentine. Neither Mr. Brontë nor the sisters' strict aunt knew of his plan—the girls deserved a secret of their own. The ten-mile walk (each way) to mail the cards was worth it to him to see their reactions.

The cards were soon delivered and were met with surprise and laughter, as well as excitement, as the recipients read the verses: "Soul divine," "Away fond love," and even one for Ellen Nussey, "Fair Ellen, Fair Ellen."[4] The sisters were pleased and also touched, but there was no mystery—they knew the valentines were sent by the cheerful, kind young man who had arrived the summer before to assist their father in his work. They quickly began writing a playful message to thank him:

> A Roland for your Oliver
>   We think you've justly earned;
> You sent us such a valentine,
>   Your gift is now returned.
> We cannot write or talk like you;
>   We're plain folks every one;
> You've played a clever jest on us,
>   We thank you for the fun.[5]

Mr. Brontë had many assistant curates over the years, and his three daughters hadn't liked any of them—until Mr. Weightman's arrival. Haworth was the twenty-six-year-old's first curacy. He quickly became a favorite and was on unusually intimate terms with the parson's entire household. His lodgings

AWAY FOND LOVE!

WILLIAM WEIGHTMAN

were nearby, and in his free time, according to Ellen, he made "frequent and agreeable visits" to spend time with the young people. Everyone he met liked him. He teased Aunt Branwell, which she apparently enjoyed, and flirted with the three Brontë sisters and their friend Ellen.

He was handsome, with blue eyes and auburn hair, and the girls (certainly Charlotte) had fallen under his spell. He had qualities Charlotte admired—qualities her two recently rejected suitors had lacked. She managed to spend time with Mr. Weightman by having him pose for her while she sketched an excellent portrait of him, possibly in preparation for a painting. Ellen believed "the sittings became alarming for length of time required."[6] Charlotte mentioned the young man repeatedly in letters to Ellen. She shared almost his every comment and activity, even those related to church business—which had never interested her before—causing Ellen to gossip about her to the Taylor sisters.

Charlotte had coined the nickname "Miss Celia Amelia" for Mr. Weightman—probably a subconscious way to avoid impropriety for herself and her sisters. The young Victorian spinsters could then spend time with him in a playful manner while allowing his surprising familiarity and pleasant attentions. Hearing the laughter of young people in the often-silent house would surely have been appreciated by their father. Mr. Weightman may have been the only young man they ever knew besides their brother with whom they shared such an enjoyable and comfortable relationship. And neither their father nor aunt disapproved.

Typical of the young cleric was his wish to give the girls a special outing. He had been invited to give a lecture in neighboring Keighley. He arranged for the girls to be properly chaperoned by a friend—a married clergyman—who sent them an invitation to tea and to the lecture. Mr. Weightman and his very respectable friend would soberly accompany them home after the lecture. The young people returned home in high spirits, at midnight, to be met with their aunt's annoyance. The hour was late, and she had prepared refreshments—but not enough for the entire happy group, and Mr. Weightman pretended to be very thirsty. Before the night was over, he had probably teased Aunt Branwell out of her bad mood. (It was a talent he shared with Branwell.)

By June, more flirtations followed. Mary Taylor was visiting, and Mr. Weightman and she played games of chess, with the loser pretending to pout.

The young people were enjoying themselves until Branwell—recently re-turned from Broughton-in-Furness—flirted outrageously with Mary, whom Miss Wooler had described as "too pretty to live."[7] She may have been in love with Branwell for some time. They were both lively and intelligent, and had a love of music in common. She responded to his attentions, taking him seriously. Branwell backed off. His rejection of her was cruel and contemptu-ous. He was offensive, and Mary—out of character—became very emotional, perhaps even hysterical, showing how much she cared. Charlotte was embar-rassed. Mr. Weightman was shocked. It's likely that the usually strong and independent—but actually very sensitive—Mary vowed never to be so vul-nerable again. Charlotte confided to Ellen that she didn't believe their friend would ever marry—which would turn out to be true. The party was over.

Mary would write a book, published many years later, titled *Miss Miles: A Tale of Yorkshire Life Sixty Years Ago*. It's the story of four young women in 1830s Yorkshire and their struggle against the many financial, social, and po-litical inequalities at the time. Had the novel been published earlier, it might have been included as an important radical feminine testament in conjunc-tion with her friends, the Brontë sisters.

The Branwell Brontë Mary knew was surely the inspiration for Sydney Wynde in the novel. Though not a principal character, Mary created a complex, contradictory, and very human version of Branwell. Along with a physical resemblance, he shared his qualities of charm, talent, wittiness, and kindness. He was also sexist, superficial, and weak. He didn't mean to disappoint, but he did. Mary was a clear-eyed writer and friend. Perhaps in memory of once caring for Branwell, she treated the character of Sydney with kindness and forgiveness, showing his virtues as well as his faults. In *Miss Miles*, Sydney does not come to a bad end.

Charlotte began to realize Mr. Weightman had not given her more atten-tion than he had given her sisters and her friends, and that they, too, had all been thrilled and pleased by his attention. It's not hard to imagine that none of the sisters would have been immune to the charms of a handsome and kind young man in their midst. Even Emily did not avoid his company. Charlotte had given Emily the title of "The Major" for her supposedly militant chaperoning of Ellen when Mr. Weightman seemed to be too attentive and flirtatious with her friend. It was all in good fun. After watching the hand-some curate with Anne in church one day, Charlotte thought he might be in love with her youngest sister. She wrote to Ellen, "He sits opposite to Anne at church, sighing softly, and looking out of the corners of his eyes to win her attention, and Anne is so quiet, her look so downcast, they are a picture."[8]

The lighthearted young man who appeared to fall a little in love with every girl he met appeared to have actually fallen seriously in love with a girl while on a visit to his hometown. When Charlotte learned of this, her praise of him turned spiteful and disparaging. She warned her sisters and friends he was "a thorough male-flirt"[9] and they must ignore his attentions. She later wrote Ellen, emphatically and unkindly, that the young cleric "ought not to have been a parson; certainly he ought not,"[10] as though he were unworthy of the position.

Charlotte would eventually admit, however, she had judged him unfairly. He took on a great deal of her father's exhausting duties. Mr. Brontë thought extremely highly of him. He was helping him in his longtime effort to improve the lives of the townspeople. Seeing Mr. Weightman depressed one evening, she listened in to his explanation to her father. He was upset about a young parishioner who was dying. Charlotte then learned from the sick girl's family of his visits, and his kindness and compassion to her. He had a mischievous side, but he was clearly a sincere and dedicated clergyman and sincerely fond of the entire Brontë family. She had badly misjudged him.

Charlotte had been home for ten months, but it was Anne who found a post first. It's been suggested that Anne would not have left Haworth if she had been in love with her father's handsome young curate. But Anne was not Charlotte or Emily, and she had an unbending sense of duty, probably made stronger by her firm belief in religious teachings of self-sacrifice. She always seemed most aware that it was a financial hardship on their father when all his children were home. In May, surely reluctantly, she left the carefree company of young people and the sense of fun that had been introduced by William Weightman. She had taken a position with the family of the Reverend Edmund Robinson, who resided at a large estate in a rural area ten miles from York. The exhausting trip from Haworth to the estate would have involved both coach and rail.

If Blake Hall had seemed large and comfortable, Thorp Green would have been extremely impressive to twenty-year-old Anne. Though its Viking name meant "farm"—one of the many words that found their way into the language due to the long-ago invasion of England—the Georgian mansion was a great estate. It was twice the size of Blake Hall. It boasted a conservatory, a library, and its own dairy, and it was staffed by three male and seven female servants—and herself. It was surrounded by eleven acres of parkland and woods, and there was stabling for more than a dozen horses. Mr. Robinson owned most of the land in the area and was Lord of the Manor of Little Ouse-burn, the nearest village to Thorp Green.

Anne's experiences of being away from home had not been pleasant, and despite her first sense of lovely surroundings, she was homesick again, missing her family and the fun at home. There is no mention of Anne in Charlotte's letters to Ellen for months, so there is no record of her reaction to her new post, but she would have been anxious and determined to do better than in her last position. The oldest girls were only a few years younger than Anne. She would be in charge of four of the five Robinson children: Lydia, fourteen; Elizabeth, thirteen; Mary, twelve; and Edmund, eight. There was a baby—still in the nursery, and not in her care—who sadly would die within the year. Because of the ages of her pupils, she believed they would be less trouble than younger children, who required constant attention. But she found her four charges to still be difficult, spoiled, and demanding.

Anne's invalid employer, the Reverend Edmund Robinson, did not often officiate as a clergyman, due to ill health. He was a generous man, especially to his wife, Lydia. She was a small woman—lively, dark haired, and more charming and charismatic than pretty.

All the rooms—the spacious drawing room, library, and dining room—were luxuriously furnished, and there were many valuable paintings. The schoolroom, where Anne would spend so much of her time, had received less attention. But even though it had old, shabby furnishings, there were many fine paintings, and the bookshelves were filled with classical literature. Perhaps it was being surrounded by so many works of art that inspired her to bring out her own paint box to entertain herself in her free time, to paint and draw the house and surroundings of Thorp Green.

Considering how all the sisters complained of the brief time they had for themselves when working in other people's houses, Anne's choice of spending precious free time painting and drawing, as well as writing, makes it clear she loved the activity as much as her siblings.

In the summer, Anne accompanied the Robinson family to Scarborough—a seaside town originally built by Viking raiders as a stronghold. She traveled to the coast with the Robinsons in one of their carriages as the railroad was not yet connected to the town. Her job was still to look after her charges (probably keeping them out of the way of the adults) but she was able to see the sights and enjoy the visit. The Robinson party stayed at the fashionable Woods Lodgings on the top of St. Nicholas Cliff, overlooking the bay. From their windows they could see the harbor, beaches, and the ruins of an imposing medieval castle on the headland.

Their apartment was large and comfortable, but it was meant to be occupied by more than one family. Shy Anne would have had to adjust to the arrangement. Their fellow renters, however, only shared space with the Robinson party in the dining room. This detail about Anne's time away from home shows that, in addition to the Robinsons, Anne could observe wealthy and even titled people. Such experience helped make her depiction of characters in her second novel, *The Tenant of Wildfell Hall*, vivid and memorable.

Woods Lodgings was only minutes from the popular Theatre Royal. The Roxby family owned and ran the theater, and the Robinson party would have enjoyed seeing concerts and even comedy performances as the owner, Robert Roxby, was a famous comedian. Unfortunately, the Robinsons would later regret they had ever frequented the Theatre Royal.

Anne fell in love with the sea, the town, and the beaches. Scarborough was a town that withstood three hundred years of sieges, and with the discovery of health-giving springs, it now had to withstand the seasonal invasion of masses of fashionable, health-conscious visitors. The sea air was also considered to have healing properties. Hopefully those weeks in summer were a real vacation for Anne, and an escape from her classroom duties.

Anne's activities in the beach town give a rare glimpse of her interests. She was intelligent and curious. Like her father, she found the field of scientific inquiry interesting, especially as it concerned nature. Her godmother, Elizabeth Firth Franks, may have shown Anne and her siblings her collection of gemstones, purchased or collected on beaches visited in her youth.

In Scarborough, Anne might have remembered those stones as she visited the beach below the apartments. It could be reached by taking paths snaking their way down the cliffside. Information about the tides, which could rush in quickly over the beach, would have been shared with the guests. The best time to visit during Anne's summers there was early morning. She would later include in her novel, *Agnes Grey*, an important morning walk on a beach very much like South Sands Beach. She may have found most of the sea-smoothed, deep-red carnelians; yellow jasper; and gray agates there. She kept them in her velvet-lined writing box.

At first glance, the stones appear to be merely simple, easy-to-find souvenirs of happy holidays at the beaches of Scarborough. Perhaps they were touchstones and holding them calmed or cheered Anne. The stones, however, were also well chosen. Public interest in the natural sciences was at a high point in the 1840s, and discoveries and many advances in knowledge were being made. In Scarborough, there were shops to buy stones, lapidaries to polish them, and a museum in which to gain knowledge about them. Perhaps Anne could be found leaning over the glass cases in the museum or in one of the busy shops in town, studying the stones—seizing a moment for her own interests while her teenaged charges urged her away for more frivolous pursuits.

Anne loved her summers by the sea, and returning to Thorp Green may have been a letdown. In August of that first year, she wrote a poem purported to be part of the Gondal saga. It may also have been an expression of her personal feelings. If one is among those who believe it possible that Anne was in love with Mr. Weightman, the detail that the young curate was in the area at the time will be of interest. Might she have wished he would stop by to see her?

> Oh, I am very weary,
>   Though tears no longer flow;
> My eyes are tired of weeping,
>   My heart is sick of woe;
>
> .   .   .   .
>
> Oh didst thou know my longings
>   For thee, from day to day,
> My hopes, so often blighted,
>   Thou wouldst not thus delay![11]

There was a large library in the house, with many books, to which Anne would surely have had access. She would not be happy at Thorp Green, but at least she had books, pencils, paint, and pens. Though her surroundings were so unlike Haworth, flat and with no hills in sight, she could still take pleasant walks. And clearly she could still be diverted and filled with joy by the beauty of nature. Anne wrote one of her finest poems at Thorp Green when, walking in the woods north of the house, she scribbled down "Lines Composed in a Wood on a Windy Day."

> My soul is awakened, my spirit is soaring
> And carried aloft on the wings of the breeze;
> For above and around me the wild wind is roaring,
> Arousing to rapture the earth and the seas.
>
> The long withered grass in the sunshine is glancing,
> The bare trees are tossing their branches on high;
> The dead leaves, beneath them, are merrily dancing,
> The white clouds are scudding across the blue sky.
>
> I wish I could see how the ocean is lashing
> The foam of its billows to whirlwinds of spray;
> I wish I could see how its proud waves are dashing,
> And hear the wild roar of their thunder to-day![12]

Anne began writing an early draft of a manuscript, which would be her first published novel—the tale of a plain governess, living and working in a house and setting very much like Thorp Green. Perhaps the reason so many have believed Anne felt more than friendship for William Weightman was the plot of her first novel. Her heroine, Agnes Grey, was lonely and pined for the love of a young assistant curate who, though more sober than lighthearted William Weightman, was also kind and considerate, and visited with the sick and troubled poor in his parish. Agnes would be separated from him and wonder if he cared for her, and if she would ever see him again. The novel is given a happy ending. Agnes does meet the young curate again on a familiar-seeming beach, and the governess and the curate look forward to a happy future together.

In Haworth, the excitement of the railroad coming to Yorkshire had attracted the interest of newly unemployed and footloose Branwell Brontë. A new railway linking Leeds with Manchester was being built. The section between Leeds and the town of Hebdon Bridge, to the west, was soon to be completed. Beyond Hebdon Bridge, a mountainous portion of the route to Manchester was being excavated to create a tunnel. The entire country was infected with railroad fever, and so was Branwell.

After hearing stories about new opportunities working for the railroad, Branwell was happy to secure a job with the Leeds and Manchester Railway. Charlotte disapproved, and let her brother know of her opinion on his choice of employment. Perhaps having believed all her life that Branwell would achieve greatness, she couldn't believe he would settle for being a lowly clerk. She should have appreciated that he had found a job. She had not even been looking for a new post.

Although his salary was less than he'd made as a tutor, the clerk's job included yearly raises and opportunities for advancement. His father and aunt approved of his decision and were willing to stand surety for him. This served as a guarantee against loss or damage if Branwell failed to perform his duties as stationmaster—and the amount of the surety was more than a year's income for Mr. Brontë. Branwell's destination was the new station at Sowerby Bridge, a small town four miles from Halifax. Branwell was to be assistant clerk-in-charge.

In early October, Branwell was already at his post in time for the official grand opening of the newly completed section of the railway line between Leeds and Hebdon Bridge. The station was still in a temporary building, but it was festooned with banners and bunting. There was a festive holiday atmosphere and a great deal of excitement. Thousands of spectators, lining the tracks to witness the passing of the first train, cheered and waved flags. With more passengers than could be accommodated inside the train, many climbed atop the carriages. Some even stood, and were forced to duck as the train passed through arches and tunnels.

Branwell undoubtedly enjoyed the celebration, and thought it was a great beginning to his job. His duties at the station were to keep track of the trains and their cargos, oversee the loading and unloading of the railway cars, and make sure the passengers were kept safe. Until the Summit Tunnel (roughly twenty-seven miles by rail to the west of Sowerby Bridge) was completed, there would be only three trains daily, each way. Travelers from nearby Halifax who wanted to take one of those trains, however, had to take a wild ride up the steep hill to Sowerby Bridge. Omnibuses were provided by competing inns, and drivers raced to make it to the train on time and ahead of their rivals. The omnibuses were four-wheeled, horse-drawn coaches that could carry up to twenty-eight people, inside and on top of the vehicle. Pulled by four horses, the omnibus could cover more than eight miles an hour, when racing! This dangerous daily drama would have supplied a sense of excitement to the town.

Sowerby Bridge was a bustling and prosperous textile and market town. Branwell rented rooms in the home of a respectable family, as he had done in Bradford and Broughton-in-Furness. The town was close to Halifax, a cultural hub where Branwell could meet writers and artists and attend lectures and concerts. His friend in Halifax—sculptor Joseph Bentley Leyland—visited Branwell at Sowerby Bridge, bringing along his brother Francis, an antiquarian bookseller. Francis later wrote of his impressions of Branwell:

"The young railway clerk was of gentleman-like appearance, and seemed to be qualified for a much better position than the one he had chosen . . . the expression of his face . . . [was] lightsome and cheerful. His voice had a ringing sweetness, and the utterance and use of his English were perfect. Branwell appeared to be in excellent spirits, and showed none of those traces of intemperance with which some writers have unjustly credited him about this period of his life.

"My brother had often spoken to me of Branwell's poetical abilities, his conversational powers, and the polish of his education; and, on a personal acquaintance, I found nothing to question in this estimate of his mental gifts, and of his literary attainments."[13]

The longest railway tunnel in the world at that time (1.6 miles), the Summit Tunnel was built at the highest section of the Leeds and Manchester Railway and was a critical part of the line. Boring beneath the Pennines, the excavation proved more difficult than expected. A major engineering challenge, it cost more to build than planned, utilizing up to 1,250 men and boys, one hundred horses, and millions of handmade bricks. As many as sixty thousand of the bricks were installed in a day, by candle- or torchlight, to line the tunnel's walls and arched ceiling. Tragically, men's lives were lost during the tunnel's construction.

The Summit Tunnel was officially opened amid an even greater celebration than the one at Sowerby Bridge. It had taken more than two years to complete. One of the engineers predicted the tunnel would withstand storm, fire, wartime, and the ravages of age. It is still in use today.[14]

Branwell's employers were pleased with his work. Rail traffic quickly increased after the grand opening of the Summit Tunnel. Within six months of the station opening, there were twenty-four trains (twelve in each direction) passing through Sowerby Bridge—and everything was running smoothly.

Branwell had pleased his father and aunt by doing very well in his new job. Charlotte, however, so close to her brother all their lives, still felt he was wasting his talents. She also worried about his past inability to keep a job and feared his present success would not last.

13

Bold Plans

We are all separated now,
and winning our bread amongst strangers

Though she had refused Henry Nussey's proposal and he was finally engaged to be married, he seemed to be more interested in Charlotte than ever. He still wished them to be friends and had become a regular correspondent. In one letter, he sent her a poem and asked her to send him one in return. She replied that she had written poetry when she was a teenager, but she was now at the advanced age of twenty-four. "I have not written poetry for a long while."[1]

It was true—Charlotte had not had a desire to write for months, since she sent the story to Hartley Coleridge, which had failed to impress him. Even Angria seemed finally to be losing its magic appeal.

Mary and Martha Taylor's father died at the beginning of the new year, and Charlotte predicted "a dissolution and dispersion of the family."[2] There had been financial problems for years, and she wondered if Mary and Martha would be forced to become governesses.

Charlotte, feeling trapped in the role society dictated for her, finally accepted a position in February (after a year and a half at home). Her new employer, John White, was a merchant in Bradford. He and his wife had three children. Charlotte was to be governess for eight-year-old Sarah and six-year-old Jasper. Upperwood House, in Rawdon, was a comfortable hillside house, with beautiful extensive grounds. It was only a few miles from Leeds and—especially appealing—not far from where Ellen was now living, at Brookroyd. Though Charlotte was a more experienced teacher with more education than her younger sister, her salary was half of what Anne was earning at Thorp Green.

It was only a matter of time before Charlotte began to judge her employers and their children for faults real and suspected. "I find it so difficult to ask either servants or mistress for anything I want. . . . It is less pain to me to endure the greatest inconvenience than to request its removal. I am a fool. Heaven knows I cannot help it!"[3] She complained to Ellen that she was kept so busy that she even had to sew in the evenings, but she admitted the White family was preferable to the Sidgwicks. She liked hospitable Mr. White, and made an effort to like his wife. "The children are not such little devils incarnate as the Sidgwicks,'"[4] she wrote Ellen. She even grew fond of the fat, cheerful baby, Arthur, until she became critical of the way she believed his mother was spoiling him. She was even finding the baby annoying.

Charlotte was amused by Mrs. White's pretensions about her family, but believed she became coarse and unladylike when angry, and had been offensive to Charlotte. She also disliked Mrs. White's incorrect grammar, and resented working for people she believed to be her inferiors. She chose to forget her own very ordinary background—her grandfathers were an Irish farmer and a Cornish merchant. Charlotte was following her usual pattern that was guaranteed to end in an unhappy departure.

When Henry heard from his sister Ellen that Charlotte was unhappy at Upperwood House, he wrote to her expressing his understanding that it was hard for her to be away from home. She agreed, writing that her home "contains what I shall find nowhere else in the world—the profound, the intense affection which brothers and sisters feel for each other when their minds are cast in the same mould, their ideas drawn from the same source—when they have clung to each other from childhood, and when disputes have never sprung up to divide them. We are all separated now, and winning our bread amongst strangers."[5] Charlotte was homesick, and missing her family.

The Whites were very good to Charlotte. They were happy that the children were doing well in their lessons with their governess. They went out of their way to be considerate. They allowed her to lengthen a visit home to three weeks instead of one. They let her visit Ellen at Brookroyd. They even invited

Mr. Brontë to come and visit them for a week (a remarkable kindness to a governess), which Charlotte resented. She was suspicious of their motives, thinking she would be under obligation to them.

Charlotte learned Mary Taylor and her brother, Waring, were taking extreme measures to solve the financial problems that had arisen from their father's death. They were planning to immigrate to the fairly new settlement at Port Nicholson, on the north island of New Zealand. "Mary has made up her mind she can not and will not be a governess, a teacher, a milliner, a bonnet-maker nor housemaid. She sees no means of obtaining employment she would like in England, so she is leaving it."[6] She wrote of her friend: "It is vain to limit a character like hers within ordinary boundaries—she will overstep them. I am morally certain Mary will establish her own landmarks."[7]

Charlotte must have been filled with envy for Mary's ability to stand up for her beliefs and her refusal to conform to society's expectations of women. Mary's decision made Charlotte even more discontented, and fed her sense of injustice. She began to think of the possibility of opening a school with her sisters—a school where they would not have to be subservient to anyone.

In her friendship with Ellen Nussey and Mary Taylor, Charlotte was responding to qualities she shared with both young women. She was docile, domestic, and conventional—as was Ellen. Charlotte found Ellen restful and uncomplicated. She would write that her friend was "a conscientious, observant, calm, well-bred Yorkshire girl . . . and I love her."[8]

Independent Mary Taylor encouraged Charlotte to be bold in pursuing her desires. She shared qualities of rebelliousness, intellectual curiosity, and courage. Charlotte wrote, "Mary alone has more energy and power in her nature than any ten men you can pick out,"[9] and "Mary's price is above rubies."[10]

Emily, at home in Haworth, was celebrating its calm and peace. "It is Friday evening, near 9 o'clock—wild rainy weather. I am seated in the diningroom, having just concluded tidying our desk-boxes, writing this document. Papa is in the parlour—aunt upstairs in her room. She has been reading *Blackwood's Magazine* to papa. Victoria and Adelaide are ensconced in the peat-house. Keeper is in the kitchen—Nero in his cage. We are all stout and hearty, [meaning healthy, not fat] as I hope is the case with Charlotte, Branwell, and Anne."[11] Branwell was content in his job at Sowerby Bridge, her sisters less so in their places of employment.

In addition to her household tasks, Emily was deeply involved in advancing the plot of the Gondal saga—including composing poetry that accompanied the prose narration. In the spring, she had written a Gondal poem expressing a love of the earth and a desire for a heaven that was as much like the earth as possible. She repeated the recurring theme in her Gondal writings years before she wrote her novel *Wuthering Heights*.

> Shall Earth no more inspire thee,
>   Thou lonely dreamer now?
> Since passion may not fire thee,
>   Shall nature cease to bow?
>
> Thy mind is ever moving,
>   In regions dark to thee;
> Recall its useless roving,
>   Come back, and dwell with me.
>
> I know my mountain breezes
>   Enchant and soothe thee still,
> I know my sunshine pleases,
>   Despite thy wayward will.
>
> . . . .
> Few hearts to mortals given,
>   On earth so wildly pine;
> Yet none would ask a heaven
>   More like this earth than thine.
>
> Then let my winds caress thee;
>   Thy comrade let me be:
> Since nought beside can bless thee,
>   Return—and dwell with me.[12]

In *Wuthering Heights*, her character Cathy confides: "If I were in heaven . . . I should be extremely miserable. . . . I dreamt once that I was there . . . heaven did not seem to be my home; and I broke my heart with weeping to come back to earth; and the angels were so angry that they flung me out into the middle of the heath on the top of Wuthering Heights; where I woke sobbing for joy."[13]

Emily did not want to return to teaching in a school or in a stranger's house. The dreary prospect of a lifetime of working in conditions they disliked hung over all the sisters. Emily and Anne often expressed favorite themes of liberty and captivity in their poetry, both personal and Gondal related. Emily, deeply involved in writing new poetry, composed what would be one of her most famous poems, expressing her deep love of freedom.

> Riches I hold in light esteem;
>   And Love I laugh to scorn;
> And lust of fame was but a dream
>   That vanished with the morn;
>
> And if I pray, the only prayer
>   That moves my lips for me
> Is, "Leave the heart that now I bear,
>   And give me liberty!"
>
> Yes, as my swift days near their goal,
>   'Tis all that I implore;
> In life and death, a chainless soul,
>   With courage to endure.[14]

Despite the reference to a short life, Emily always wrote in the diary papers about a long, hopeful, and happy future. Charlotte, Emily, and Anne had been discussing ideas about how their lives could be improved. They all still hoped, as they had as children, to one day be published, but in summer 1841, they were dreaming of teaching in more favorable circumstances than they had encountered previously. They were trying to be practical. Emily wrote, "A scheme is at present in agitation for setting us up in a school of our own; as yet nothing is determined, but I hope and trust it may go on and prosper and answer our highest expectations."[15]

She pictured herself four years in the future when she, Anne, and Charlotte would be "all merrily seated in our own sitting-room in some pleasant and flourishing seminary, having just gathered in for the midsummer ladyday [a religious holiday]. Our debts will be paid off, and we shall have cash in hand to a considerable amount."[16] Perhaps there would be a happy visit from her father, aunt, and brother to their successful school. She envisioned a fine, warm summer night when she and Anne would step out into their garden to read their diaries. "I hope either this or something better will be the case." Perhaps having careers as writers? Emily closed her entry sending "courage, to exiled and harassed Anne, wishing she was here."[17]

Miles away, in the Scarborough apartment of the Robinson family, and perhaps at the same rainy hour, Anne sat at her writing box. She was wondering about the location of family members as well as the dog, the cat, the hawk, and the geese—and the latest adventures in the secret world of Gondal. She wrote: "We are now all separate and not likely to meet again for many a weary week, but we are none of us ill that I know of and all are doing something for our own livelihood except Emily, who, however, is as busy as any of us, and in reality earns her food and raiment as much as we do. . . . What will the next four years bring forth? Providence only knows." Referring to her diary paper from four years earlier: "I have the same faults that I had then, only I have more wisdom and experience, and a little more self-possession than I then enjoyed."[18] And, as Emily had written, Anne wrote of the three sisters' goal of "a school of our own."[19]

Charlotte continued to build on her resentments of the Whites at Upperwood House. She had been there only four months and might never find better employers, but she was already thinking of escape. It was only a matter of time before she gave notice.

Branwell, working in Sowerby Bridge, was doubtless enjoying nature walks and writing poetry.

He was hopeful for a successful future on the railroad while he pursued his literary career. He scribbled poetry when there were lulls between the trains. He was happy to be proving his skeptical sister Charlotte wrong, especially in the spring when, after only six months, he was promoted to be clerk-in-charge at Luddendenfoot, the next station up the line, and was given a substantial raise. He would be making more than his good friend, William Weightman. Charlotte, when she heard the news, remained unimpressed. She was apparently disillusioned about her brother's inability to stay with any endeavor, not seeing any similarity in their lack of effort to succeed in their work. She wrote to Emily, "It is to be hoped that his removal to another station will turn out for the best. As you say, it *looks* like getting on at any rate."[20]

Branwell's failure as a painter and a teacher had caused Charlotte's bitterness about the differences in his life and her own (and her sisters). Since boyhood, Branwell had been their father's and aunt's favorite—and may have been Charlotte's as well when they were happy, creative children. He had been allowed more freedom, had every advantage possible—still he had failed. Had the thought come to the three sisters yet that, perhaps, the whole family had expected too much of him? And yet their father's preference for Branwell was clear, and it was painful to Charlotte.

Despite her quiet, lady-like demeanor, Miss Brontë, the curate's daughter, was angry about the unfairness of her life and that of her sisters.

Luddendenfoot was a small community located at the foot of the Ludden-den Valley where it opened into the Calder Valley. Steep, forested hills rose on both sides of the narrow valley where the railway ran alongside the river. Branwell undoubtedly loved the beauty of the area, with its pastures, wild moors, and—in springtime—carpets of bluebells on both the hillsides and the valley floor. He took rooms at Brearley Hall, a seventeenth-century farm-house, which was only a half-mile walk across the fields to his new station.

Local legend claims Branwell belonged to the Luddenden Reading Soci-ety, which met at the Lord Nelson inn and alehouse. There may have been a lending library in the inn, but perhaps the title was meant to be amusing. The group included local weavers, mill owners, and fellow employees of the railroad. Branwell admitted in his notebook he was sometimes quarrelsome—probably after visiting the pub. He didn't seem to hold grudges, however, and wrote of becoming friends with a fellow reveler he had scuffled with. He also became friends with a newly ordained young curate who often visited him in the station to chat. With much in common, curate Sutcliffe Sowden and Branwell took long hikes, enjoying the beauty of the local countryside.

As an employee of the railway company, Branwell could travel free of charge. He could quickly get to any of the nearby towns and cities when he had time off. Branwell wrote a note to himself about the details of an upcom-ing choral recital in Halifax of Haydn's sacred music, which he may have attended. There was also a Christmas concert of Handel's Messiah in Halifax. The great pianist Franz Liszt also gave a concert there to rapturous encores. It's quite possible Branwell attended the acclaimed concert and others, as he had become friends with the concert organizer.

There were also many libraries and bookstores in Halifax. As well as finding new books to read, Branwell—outgoing, articulate, and personable—became friends with well-respected and successful writers, artists, and musicians. He reunited with an old artist friend from his portrait-painting days in Bradford and his sculptor friend Joseph Leyland, as well as a friend of his father's (a poet) who knew Branwell when he was a child. The group of friends, new and old, enjoyed visiting together. Branwell was liked and admired by them all.

A poet friend, William Heaton, wrote of Branwell: "He was . . . blithe and gay, but at times appeared downcast and sad; yet, if the subject were some topic that he was acquainted with, or some author he loved, he would rise from his seat, and, in beautiful language, describe the author's character, with a zeal and fluency I had never heard equalled. His talents were of a very exalted kind, . . . I had written many pieces [poems], but they had never seen the light; and, on a certain occasion, I showed him one, which he pronounced very good. He lent me books which I had never seen before, and was ever ready to give me information. His temper was always mild towards me. I shall never forget his love for the sublime and beautiful works of Nature."[21]

This was an important time for Branwell. He received encouragement and the helpful criticism he was always seeking. The friends met at various pubs in Luddendenfoot, as well as others in Halifax and Bradford. They even traveled to the Black Bull in Haworth, and to the Cross Roads pub between Haworth and Keighley. Aside from being pleasant gatherings of friends, the meetings were an opportunity for the writers and poets in the group to read aloud and critique each other's latest manuscripts and poetry.

Branwell listened to his friends' advice. He kept a personal notebook—a mix of poetry, drawings, and scribbles related to his job as clerk. He made constant changes and revisions to his poetry, working patiently to improve what he had written, which he had rarely done with his childhood and teenage stories and poems. He had dreamed of being published all his life. His friends encouraged him, as did the example they set. He had only been at Luddendenfoot a month when his first poem, "Heaven and Earth," was published in the *Halifax Guardian*. The newspaper was known for having a high standard for acceptance. They welcomed the fresh, original work of new poets as well as the works of famous poets of the day. He must have been thrilled to finally see his work in print. It was what he had always wanted. He and his sisters scribbling their thousands of words throughout their childhood had led to this moment. He was a published poet!

> In *Heaven* a thousand worlds of light
>   Revolving through the gloom of night
> O'er endless pathways rove.
>   While daylight shews this little Earth
> It hides the mighty Heaven,

> And, but by night, a visible birth
>   To all its stars is given;
> And, fast as fades departing day,
>   When silent marsh or moorland grey
>
> Mid evening's mist declines,
>   Then, slowly stealing, star on star,
> As night sweeps forward, from afar,
>   More clear and countless shines.[22]

The *Halifax Guardian* would publish twelve more of Branwell's poems in the next six years. The twenty-four-year-old seems to have been finally growing up, becoming more reflective about himself, and recognizing he was not fulfilling his potential. Sitting in his rooms in Brearley Hall, he wrote:

> When I look back on former life
>   I scarcely know what I have been
> So swift the change from strife to strife
>   That passes o'er the wildering scene
> I only feel that every power—
>   And thou hadst given much to me
> Was spent upon the present hour
>   Was never turned My God to thee[23]

Charlotte had shown a sarcastic lack of belief in her brother that must have hurt his pride. There had been a habit since childhood of desiring each other's approval. Branwell had had periodic bouts of depression in his year at Luddendenfoot, but in early spring 1842, he was full of energy and optimism that he could still achieve the greatness he and his family had expected of him all his life. He felt his future looked bright.

At the end of March 1842, Branwell was dismissed from the Leeds and Manchester Railway. The company had conducted an audit of the messy and confusing ledgers. There was a discrepancy in the accounts, and Branwell, as clerk-in-charge, was responsible. Either his assistant clerk (who also lived in Brearley Hall) or the railway porter had most likely taken the missing money. Still, Branwell was held responsible for the shortfall. Though the amount was deducted from his quarterly salary, he was still discharged due to carelessness.

He was humiliated but not suspected of theft. Luckily, the surety his father and aunt had posted was not at issue.

To be fair, Branwell had been a hard worker—at Christmas he had even elected to stay in Luddendenfoot because he was needed. His overall carelessness and lack of discipline, however, had caused him to fail again. His friends—perhaps including those from the Luddenden Reading Society, mill owners, merchants, his young curate friend Sutcliffe Sowden, even weavers and factory workers he had met—tried to have him reinstated by signing a petition testifying to his good character. They were unsuccessful. The railway company was known for its strict rules. They didn't hesitate to have employees arrested and prosecuted if they considered the offense serious enough. Branwell was merely let go, and he was left with the impression that he might be reemployed sometime in the future.

Feeling ill and anxious, Branwell returned home to inform his father and aunt of the loss of his position at Luddendenfoot. He may have been glad he did not have to confront his sister Charlotte, who was not at home. Soon, however, Branwell was occupied with new projects, as well as spending time with William Weightman. (Mr. Brontë was happy about his son's friendship with the responsible young curate, considering him a good influence.)

Branwell continued to celebrate his first literary successes. A new poem he had written at Luddendenfoot was published in the *Bradford Herald*. Soon several more poems were published in Leeds, Halifax, and Bradford newspapers. He was also trying to find another post on the railroad, even considering looking in France. He was unlikely, however, to be given another chance on the English railways so soon, if at all, or to be given recommendations from his previous employers. Branwell renewed his efforts to be published by *Blackwood's Magazine*. He had finally learned to send a well-written submission letter, without arrogance. But he received no response.

All the siblings had benefited from their father's liberal education, but Branwell had been allowed too much freedom, and not enough discipline. His father may have believed his son was more like he, himself, had been as a boy and young man—ambitious and self-motivated. Both Charlotte and Anne had expressed similar opinions about boys' education. Charlotte shared with Miss Wooler her opinion that boys were "not half sufficiently guarded from temptations. Girls are protected as if they were something very frail and silly indeed, while boys are turned loose on the world as if they, of all beings in existence, were the wisest and the least liable to be led astray."[24] The Brontë sisters had, in varying degrees, learned good habits of discipline, fortitude, and patience. They had worked long hours, receiving little respect—the fate of working women at the time. Anne was doing well at Thorp Green. Charlotte and Emily were embarking on a new adventure, which also required the qualities their brother lacked.

14

An Education Abroad

. . . a wild and ambitious scheme . . .

Charlotte and her sisters had been intrigued for months by the idea of having a school of their own, instead of working for demanding and condescending employers in private homes. They were trying to figure out details when Charlotte received a letter from Mary Taylor, who had changed her plans to immigrate to New Zealand and instead had taken a tour of the Continent with her brother. She now planned to join her younger sister Martha studying in Belgium, where schools were less expensive than in England.

Charlotte was overcome with a desire to join them, writing that she had "such a strong wish for wings . . . such an urgent thirst to see, to know, to learn" that she was "tantalised by the consciousness of faculties unexercised."[1] It would be education combined with travel and an experience of living abroad! Charlotte was thrilled and excited by the prospect, and quickly devised a plan. She was determined now to study on the Continent herself, whatever it took.

Charlotte knew Aunt Branwell would never let her go abroad alone. She wanted Emily to go with her. She outlined the merits of her plan to her sister, arguing that more education and travel to the places they had read about in their father's books would increase their success as teachers. Perhaps she even mentioned that they would gather impressions and ideas that would inspire new stories. The truth, of course, was that Charlotte did not want to teach at all, and neither did Emily.

Charlotte wrote a carefully worded letter to Aunt Branwell, asking her to agree to finance the new venture. Their aunt had already agreed to supply the funds to rent a building for a school. Miss Wooler had also made a very good offer for Charlotte to take over Heald's House, in Dewsbury Moor—she would even lend the furniture for the school. Charlotte had considered the offer, not telling Anne and Emily that it was only for her, and there was no place for her sisters. But studying in Brussels was what Charlotte wanted, and surprisingly Emily agreed. (Perhaps her thirst for knowledge, and her childhood desire to see foreign places, won over her usual wish to remain at home.) In Charlotte's letter to her aunt, she wrote: "Papa will, perhaps, think it a wild and ambitious scheme; but who ever rose in the world without ambition?"[2]

Charlotte presented her case to her father and aunt in a long, persuasive, and determined letter. If she and Emily perfected their French it would be a plus in advertising the school they wished to open later. Perhaps they would make useful connections abroad for gaining foreign students. Mr. Brontë and Aunt Branwell agreed Emily and Charlotte could go to Brussels for six months. Steady, responsible Anne would remain at Thorp Green.

Anne may have been the logical choice to accompany Charlotte to the Continent, benefiting from further education that would give her more credentials for teaching. Reclusive, home-loving Emily might not be able to stand the stress of being so far from home. But though twenty-one-year-old Anne was unhappy at Thorp Green and yearning to leave, she had a stable, paid position. At least she could comfort herself with her summer vacation at the seaside in Scarborough. Charlotte was always more impressed with Branwell's and Emily's talent and intelligence than with her youngest sister. She wanted Emily's company in Belgium, and she also had a plan other than the one she expressed to her aunt and father.

Probably very happy for the chance to travel to the Continent, too, and with the intention of visiting the battlefield at Waterloo, Mr. Brontë had created his own small, hand-stitched book of repurposed paper, similar to the small books his children once made. He filled it with useful French phrases he would use while in Belgium and on a side trip he planned to take to France before returning home. He felt confident in leaving his curacy in the capable hands of William Weightman.

ANNE BRONTË

Charlotte, Emily, Mr. Brontë, the Taylor girls, and their brother Joe took the 9 a.m. train from Leeds to Euston Station in London. An excited Charlotte, insistent that they see as much as possible during their brief stopover, exhausted herself and her fellow travelers during three days of sightseeing. At London Bridge Wharf, they boarded the steam packet *Earl of Liverpool*, which carried passengers, mail, and goods to Ostend, Belgium. From Ostend, they traveled by horse-drawn diligence (stagecoach) to Brussels.

It was dark when the exhausted travelers arrived in Brussels, where they stayed overnight at a hotel close to the diligence terminus. The next morning the Brontës and Taylors made their way to their respective schools. Mr. Brontë, Charlotte, and Emily passed the quays, markets, and tall, ancient houses crowded together in the old part of the city on their way to the Pensionnat Heger. The Educational Establishment for Young Ladies was more affordable for them than the school the Taylor girls had chosen. Charlotte and Emily had been given a lowered tuition after Charlotte wrote a letter expressing their eagerness to learn and their cleric father's moderate means. The extra fees for bedding, French-language lessons, and music and drawing classes were even waived.

Mr. Brontë stayed a week in Brussels to make sure Charlotte and Emily were settled and, perhaps, to convince himself they were safe to leave in a foreign country. He then traveled on, to the highlight of his trip—the battlefield of Waterloo. There the Duke of Wellington and British forces, in conjunction with European armies, had defeated Napoleon and determined the fate of Europe. Perhaps Patrick Brontë reminisced about being a young student in the militia, training to save England from invasion. He traveled home through the Netherlands and France, crossing the Channel from Calais. For years, he would happily repeat the story of his visit to the battlefield at Waterloo to any captive audience.

The Pensionnat Heger, on narrow rue d'Isabelle, occupied a long, low building with a severely plain frontage. Inside, however, the two-story school was attractive and spacious. There were classrooms, dormitories, dining rooms, and private areas for the large number of boarders, family, teachers, and servants. Two of Charlotte's future novels, *The Professor* and *Villette*, would be set in schools based on the Pensionnat Heger, and apparently she described the school quite accurately, just as she would accurately portray the school at Cowan Bridge in *Jane Eyre*.

The Belgian school was advertised as being run with the comfort and well-being of the students in mind. The young ladies were not overloaded with too much schoolwork. There was exercise to keep them healthy, and food was plentiful and nutritious. Holidays were celebrated, and outings to the countryside were organized. The girls were given privileges, and nothing was rushed. Charlotte, however, soon believed the directress had a policy of intrusive watchfulness of the students and teachers. This was said to be common in Continental schools, but it annoyed the privacy-loving Brontë sisters.

Classes were separated by age, and Charlotte (at twenty-five) and Emily (twenty-three) were the oldest students at the school. Since they were not native French speakers, they were given the privilege of private lessons with Monsieur Heger, the husband of the directress. Charlotte wrote that the private lessons "have . . . excited much spite and jealousy in the school."[3] The sisters also attended regular class sessions with the other students, who were not very friendly. Charlotte disliked their classmates as much as Emily did.

As foreign Protestants in a Catholic country and not yet fluent in French, Charlotte and Emily were made very aware of their differences—including being given their own curtained-off sleeping area at the end of the large dormitory. Charlotte wrote in a letter to Ellen, "We are completely isolated in the midst of numbers," which they did not seem to mind. "Yet I think I am never unhappy; my present life is so delightful, so congenial to my own nature, compared with that of a governess."[4]

Surprisingly, considering the first impression the school's plain frontage made from the street, there was a large, delightful walled garden behind the school. In fine weather, the students spent a great deal of time under a large vine-covered arbor where classes were held, lectures given, meals taken, and holidays celebrated. The enclosed garden was filled with roses, jasmine, nasturtiums, and fruit and acacia trees, including an ancient, partially dead pear tree that reportedly still produced honey-sweet fruit. There was even a resident ghost who haunted the grounds. Though it was in the center of the city, the garden felt hidden, private, and secluded. From their dormitory's large casement window, however, the sisters could see the city beyond the garden and hear band music from the nearby park or the palace square, or bells from Brussels' churches. They must have felt a sense of the life and energy of the great city all around them.

The directress of the school was aloof and dignified Madame Clair Zoë Heger, pregnant with her fourth child. (Ultimately the Hegers would have six children.) Madame Heger was thirty-eight and attractive, with auburn hair and blue eyes, and was said to be beloved by her family and students. Her youngest son would later describe her as one who wished all those around her to be happy. Charlotte originally liked her, considering her kind, pleasant, and cultured.

Monsieur Constantin Heger, five years younger than his wife, taught literature and rhetoric at his wife's school. He also was the director of a boys' school across the alley behind the garden of the girls' school. He was dark haired, dark eyed, and short in stature. Though not handsome, he made an impression with his animated and passionate lectures. As a teenager in Paris, he was paid to applaud appreciatively in the audience of the Comédie Française. After seeing the productions there, he may have discovered in himself a talent for entertainment, which he would later find useful in his teaching, readings, and lectures.

Monsieur Heger had also shown a passion for freedom when, at age twenty-one, he had fought at the barricades against the Dutch in a successful struggle for Belgian liberty. The drama and romance of his earlier life would have appealed to the sisters who had created Angria and Gondal. He was an excellent teacher, and like their father, he believed fervently in the importance of education—even for girls.

The professor was described by some as mild and kind, but perhaps more often as irritable, excitable, impatient, and perhaps even domineering. Charlotte's first impression of him was dislike. She had been reduced to tears by his criticism during one of his early lectures.

Soon, however, her opinion of him changed. She realized the professor appreciated the sisters' love for learning and their perseverance in their studies. He recognized their talent and, along with their private lessons with him, suggested useful, well-chosen, books for them to read and offered them excellent advice on improving their writing skills.

Monsieur Heger was most impressed with Emily. He knew Emily had known very little French when she arrived. All their lessons were taught in that language, and Emily worked very hard to catch up, learning quickly while at the same time studying the more difficult German. Monsieur Heger also admired her superior ability to reason and express herself. The girl who

couldn't, or wouldn't, speak easily to most people she encountered, spoke
spiritedly to Monsieur Heger. Sometimes he couldn't get her to stop arguing
her opinions. Both Emily and Charlotte showed passion, strong will, temper,
and a penchant for arguing their beliefs. According to Charlotte's biographer,
Elizabeth Gaskell, Monsieur Heger believed Emily's genius was "even higher
than Charlotte's" and that "Emily had a head for logic, and a capability of
argument, unusual in a man, and rare indeed in a woman. . . . Impairing the
force of this gift, was a stubborn tenacity of will, which rendered her obtuse to
all reasoning where her own wishes, or her own sense of right was concerned.
'She should have been a man—a great navigator,' said Monsieur Heger in
speaking of her. 'Her powerful reason would have deduced new spheres of
discovery from the knowledge of the old; and her strong imperious will would
never have been daunted by opposition or difficulty; never have given way
but with life.'"[5]

Not knowing Emily's history of illness when she was too long away from
home, Monsieur Heger commented to Mrs. Gaskell on Charlotte's solicitude
for Emily, saying that "in the anxiety of the elder to make her younger sister
contented she allowed her to exercise a kind of unconscious tyranny over
her."[6] In all probability, however, Charlotte feared that if Emily became so
ill she needed to return to Haworth Charlotte would be told to return home,
too. Emily had felt ill at first, but managed to overcome her usual depression.
Perhaps she dreamed of a future with their own school, and a time when she
would not have to work in strangers' homes or schools.

Charlotte was grateful for the professor's guidance and the discipline she
learned, which resulted in a new way of writing for her—clear and to the
point without the extensive flowery, descriptive passages she had always lovingly included in her stories. Emily disliked the professor's method of teaching, which was to study various French authors and write essays in that same
author's style.

Emily believed in the importance of originality and wished to only write in
her own style, but her compositions also improved under his tutelage.

There was a family of young English sisters at the school. The eldest was
fourteen-year-old Laetitia Wheelwright, who became a friend of Charlotte's,
but who would later report that she "simply disliked [Emily] from the first."
She complained disapprovingly that Emily was "ungainly" and "ill-dressed."[7]
She was critical of Emily's out-of-fashion dresses, with their large sleeves and

limp skirts. Ellen Nussey had described Emily as graceful and lithesome only a few years before. Other classmates at the Pensionnat also made fun of Emily's appearance (Laetitia called it their "jokes"),[8] causing her to stubbornly respond, "I wish to be as God made me."[9]

Emily's reaction seems understandable. Perhaps she had memories of being laughed at and bullied when she was a seventeen-year-old student at Roe Head. Though the three Brontë sisters were described as dressing alike, it was Emily who was always described as being badly dressed. This may be because she didn't wear the then-fashionable full, cumbersome petticoats under her dresses. She had frequently exhibited a lack of patience for what she considered unnecessary or ridiculous. For the sake of comfort, did she also eliminate the uncomfortable—and unhealthy—corset from her wardrobe? With little evidence, much has been made of Emily's entire character on the basis of schoolgirl comments at the Pensionnat.

Charlotte was usually more liked than Emily, but neither sister liked most of their fellow students, whom they considered foolish and flighty. One exception was a young girl who befriended Emily. Louise de Bassompierre preferred Emily to Charlotte, considering the younger sister kinder and easier to talk to. Biographers usually emphasize that Emily had no friends. Perhaps Louise was kind and made an effort to be a friend to Emily. They exchanged letters after Emily returned home. She even gave Louise one of her sketches, which the younger girl had admired and reportedly treasured into old age.

Both sisters were still reserved, and their usual discomfort with the other students and teachers had not improved. They were invited regularly to visit the English family of the British embassy chaplain who had helped in finding the Brontë sisters an appropriate school in Brussels. The Jenkins family soon realized, however, that their guests felt "more pain than pleasure" from such visits. Emily barely spoke, and although Charlotte made an effort at conversation, she behaved in an even more eccentric manner than Emily. Charlotte "had a habit of gradually wheeling round on her chair, so as almost to conceal her face from the person to whom she was speaking."[10] There were also ongoing invitations from the English Dixon family, who were cousins of the Taylor sisters.

As Charlotte had told Emily before they left Haworth, she was not ready to go home after the six months Aunt Branwell had agreed to and determinedly, even ruthlessly, intended to stay abroad at least a year. She asked Madame

Heger if she and Emily could stay longer—teaching, in exchange for further tuition and board. The directress agreed to her request. Charlotte would teach English, and Emily would give piano lessons. Charlotte wrote to their father and aunt that the professor and Madame Heger had suggested they remain, and that they wished to accept. Emily was managing well and doing very well in French, German, music, and drawing. Their health was good, and they both felt hopeful about their plans—content, and even happy, as Mary Taylor had reported to Ellen. Emily, however, did not do well as a teacher, angering Laetitia Wheelwright by scheduling her piano classes with Laetitia's little sisters during their free time.

Professor Heger's belief in their talent encouraged and gratified Charlotte, and perhaps even Emily. Charlotte believed she and the professor shared a special relationship. She respected and admired him and was happy she and Emily would be staying in Brussels. But soon there was shocking, unhappy news from home. In September, their kind young friend—William Weightman—had died of cholera, which he contracted while visiting an ill parishioner, a practice the siblings had admired.

Branwell was extremely upset by the loss of his friend. Their father felt the young curate was like a son to him. He'd had an impact on the people of Haworth, who raised money for a monument to his memory. In Brussels, Charlotte, Emily, and the Taylor sisters were saddened and depressed by the loss of their cheerful, fun-loving friend. Anne, far from home at Thorp Green, mourned his passing alone.

Anne may have known Mr. Weightman better than is usually asserted. At home during her summer break from Thorp Green that year, she may well have had the opportunity to spend time with her brother and the young curate, even taking part in enjoyable conversations and outings. The speculation that Anne was in love with her father's curate stems from several poignant, sorrow-filled love poems Anne was to write soon after Mr. Weightman's death. A romance between the two is believed to be unlikely, but Anne may well have suffered the sorrow of unrequited love.

More tragedy was to follow. In mid-October, Martha Taylor (Mary's mischievous younger sister, nicknamed "Miss Boisterous" by her school friends) died suddenly of cholera. The Brontë sisters had been especially fond of the vivacious young chatterbox, who was only twenty-three years old, and tried to comfort her devastated older sister. Soon there was a third shock.

A second letter arrived from Haworth. Aunt Branwell was very ill and not expected to live. Before Charlotte and Emily left for home on the Sunday packet boat, they learned she had died. They arrived too late to attend her funeral. Aunt Branwell had chosen to be buried beside her sister in the family vault beneath the floor of St. Michael and All Saints Church. She may have ultimately embraced Mr. Brontë's religious beliefs, convinced by all those lively discussions with her brother-in-law. Or perhaps she found it comforting to be buried beside those she had shared her life with for so many years.

Anne and Branwell, their aunt's favorites, were able to attend the service. Anne was given permission by her employers to spend a few weeks at home. She took on the housekeeping tasks, but she willingly turned over the duties of running the house to Emily when she arrived home.

Mr. Brontë was greatly saddened by the death of Elizabeth Branwell, whose aid in the raising of his children he had greatly appreciated, and whose companionship he would miss. It was difficult for the family, including Tabby and Martha, to believe she was gone.

In addition to the loss of their aunt, Emily and Anne were also unhappy to learn several of their pets had disappeared. It was likely that Aunt Branwell had taken the opportunity, while the sisters were away from home, to remove them from the household. Emily searched for days for her pet hawk, Nero, whose beautiful portrait she had painted years before. The neighbors had not seen or heard word of him—Emily and Anne believed Nero and the two pet geese, Victoria and Adelaide, must be dead.

The siblings were home together again, but Branwell suffered from severe depression. He had devotedly nursed both his aunt and his friend, but he had helplessly watched them die. He could not contain his sorrow. He wrote to his friend, Francis Grundy, about his aunt, saying that she had been "for twenty years as my mother. . . . I have now lost the guide and director of all the happy days connected with my childhood."[11]

Anne wrote a poem believed to be about William Weightman, expressing love and sorrow, before her return to Thorp Green.

> I will not mourn thee, lovely one,
> Though thou art torn away.

> And yet I cannot check my sighs,
> Thou wert so young and fair,
> More bright than summer morning skies,
> But stern death would not spare;
>
> He would not pass our darling by
> Nor grant one hour's delay,
> But rudely closed his shining eye
> And frowned his smile away,
>
> That angel smile that late so much
> Could my fond heart rejoice;
> And he has silenced by his touch
> The music of thy voice.
>
> I'll weep no more thine early doom,
> But O! I still must mourn . . .[12]

Depressed and unhappy, Anne wished to find other employment but dutifully returned to Thorp Green. She asked her employers to consider her brother as tutor for their son, Edmund, who had outgrown the need for a governess. They agreed, and Branwell—who had made himself ill with grief—recovered his emotional and physical health enough to join Anne at Thorp Green. His family would all later regret the decision that Branwell join the Robinsons' household.

Aunt Branwell left equal shares in her estate to Charlotte, Emily, Anne, and a female cousin in Cornwall. Though their shares were not huge, the sisters' worries about immediate hardship, should their father die, were eased. Their aunt had believed her nieces were more in need than Branwell, who had more opportunities for financial success. He was left a special keepsake, as were each of his sisters. Emily took up the task of handling the railroad shares. She would manage them well, though Charlotte believed she herself should take over decisions on their handling. Anne backed up Emily, and Emily stayed in charge.

Charlotte had not been as close to her aunt as the rest of the family had been, and she was in a good mood by Christmas. She had made up her mind to return to the Pensionnat Heger. Monsieur Heger, wishing Charlotte and Emily would return to school, had written their father a letter that he must have been gratified to receive. "I have a feeling of profound admiration for you, for in judging the father of a family by his children one cannot be mistaken and in this respect the education and sentiments that we have found in your daughters can only give us a very high idea of your worth and of your character. . . . We did not have to teach them the value of time and instruction."[13] The professor was hopeful both young women would return to Pensionnat Heger. As an added incentive, he wrote that if Emily would return she could have lessons with an acclaimed piano teacher.

15

Charlotte Alone

. . . he has . . . withdrawn the light of his countenance.

Charlotte was disappointed, but probably not surprised, when Emily did not wish to return to Brussels with her. Emily had taken over Aunt Branwell's duties as housekeeper. Charlotte, however, was determined to resume her studies with Monsieur Heger, and her position as teacher at his wife's school.

Aunt Branwell would have forbidden Charlotte's traveling alone to Brussels. Charlotte believed she could convince her father to let her go—and she was right. Knowing how important the return to the school was to her, as well as Monsieur Heger's glowing letter and mention of her teaching position, he reluctantly agreed. He was surely never told of her experience when she arrived in London, however. It was late on a cold January night, and she immediately took a horse cab from the train station to London Bridge Wharf. The driver left her with her luggage on the wharf, by the *Earl of Liverpool*. It was not a place for a woman alone. Told it was against the company's rules to board before morning, stubborn and persuasive Charlotte won the battle with the captain of the vessel and spent the night aboard. The next day she continued her journey across the Channel to Ostend, the Pensionnat Heger, and the professor she had missed so much.

Mary Taylor had followed the plan she made before Martha died, and traveled to Germany to teach in a boys' school. She had received a letter from

Charlotte in Brussels and reported to Ellen a prediction that Charlotte would be lonely without Emily, saying, "she seems *content* . . . but [I] fear her sister's absence will have a bad effect."[1]

"Mademoiselle" Charlotte resumed teaching English. At first she was treated well by both the Hegers, having tea in their parlor and private lessons with Monsieur Heger. She also began teaching English to the professor and his brother-in-law. Though Charlotte had initially liked Madame Heger, her feelings had changed. Just as she had done with all her former employers, she found fault with the older woman.

Her feelings for Monsieur Heger had also changed—to an obsessive desire for his attention and approval. When he left books in her desk she was thrilled. She knew when he had been there by the lingering scent of his cigar. Outside her family circle she had always felt misunderstood and undervalued, but in Monsieur Heger, she felt she had finally found someone who was equal (or superior) to herself in intelligence. She believed she possessed genius, and wrote several essays as assignments for the professor as a way to discuss the subject of genius. He did not disagree with her opinion of herself, but he stressed that it would take study and hard work, combined with genius, to develop her talent. She came around to his thinking after repeated discussions. She was thrilled to be understood and appreciated. She had finally met her intellectual equal—someone she could love.

At the same time, in England, Branwell had fallen in love with someone equally inappropriate—and also married.

Soon Madame Heger realized the depth of Charlotte's affection for her husband. There were no more private lessons, no more invitations to spend evenings with the couple, and the English classes with Monsieur Heger were cancelled. He lectured Charlotte on making friends with the other teachers. Charlotte did not like the teachers. She believed one fellow teacher, Mademoiselle Marie, was "talented and original, but of repulsive and arbitrary manners, which . . . made the whole school . . . her bitter enemies."[2] Mademoiselle Marie and Mademoiselle Blanche (another teacher) "hate each other like two cats . . . on a system of war without quarter."[3] Regarding Monsieur Heger, Charlotte wrote miserably to Emily, "I fancy he has taken to considering me as a person to be let alone—left to the error of her ways; and consequently he has in a great measure withdrawn the light of his countenance."[4]

Madame Heger also advised Charlotte to make an effort to socialize with the other teachers. Charlotte did not wish to even try. She still wondered if the directress had a policy of surveillance in the Pensionnat. Her distrust of the older woman, who had become even colder and more reserved toward Charlotte, grew. Charlotte became convinced Madame Heger was spying on her, and that she was devious and sly.

When the Hegers, teachers, and students all left the school during the August school holiday, Charlotte was left alone. She had written to Branwell at Thorp Green. "It is a curious metaphysical fact that always in the evening when I am in the great dormitory alone, having no other company than a number of beds with white curtains, I always recur as fanatically as ever to the old ideas, the old faces, and the old scenes in the world below."[5] (The "world below" was how they had referred to their imaginary worlds since childhood.) But still she did not resume writing. She could not even bring herself to make the effort, though she had so often been helped by the process of writing.

The English friends Charlotte had met through the Taylor sisters and the cleric friend of her father had left Brussels. Martha Taylor was dead, and Mary Taylor remained in Germany. Charlotte was lonely and miserable.

In the silent school, thinking longingly of home, Charlotte wrote to Emily: "I should like uncommonly to be in the dining-room at home, or in the kitchen. . . . I should like even to be cutting up the hash . . . and you standing by, watching that I put enough flour, not too much pepper, and, above all, that I save the best pieces of the leg of mutton for Tiger [the cat] and Keeper [the dog], the first of which personages would be jumping about the dish and carving-knife, and the latter standing like a devouring flame on the kitchen-floor. To complete the picture, Tabby blowing the fire, in order to boil the potatoes to a sort of vegetable glue! How divine are these recollections to me at this moment!"[6]

At Thorp Green, Anne was also unhappy, writing poetry expressing yearning for home. Charlotte was in love; Branwell was in love. Anne had written seven love poems that did not belong to the Gondal saga.

> Farewell to thee! but not farewell
>   To all my fondest thoughts of thee:
> Within my heart they still shall dwell;
>   And they shall cheer and comfort me.

> If I may ne'er behold again
> That form and face so dear to me,
>   Nor hear thy voice, still would I fain
> Preserve for aye their memory.
>
>   That voice, the magic of whose tone
> Can wake an echo in my breast,
>   Creating feelings that, alone,
> Can make my trancèd spirit blest.
>
>   That laughing eye, whose sunny beam
> My memory would not cherish less;—
>   And oh, that smile! whose joyous gleam
> No mortal language can express . . .[7]

As Charlotte imagined, Emily was contentedly following the routine that she found made her most happy.

Martha Brown later said "Many's the time that I have seen Miss Emily put down the 'tally iron' as she was ironing the clothes to scribble something on a piece of paper. Whatever she was doing, ironing or baking, she had her pencil and paper by her."[8] Ellen Nussey had also described Emily in the kitchen, mixing dough for making bread while studying a German grammar book propped up in front of her on the table. She was continuing to advance her German studies so she could read the grim, gothic German novels she had learned to appreciate in Brussels. They would influence the writing of her novel.

Charlotte may have wished her family would ask her to come home, but they did not. She confided her unhappiness to Mary Taylor, who seems to have been the only one to offer advice. Mary believed Charlotte should leave the school, where she had become so unhappy, and join her in Germany. She generously offered to share her students with her friend so Charlotte would have an income. Charlotte said no, though she appreciated the offer. She didn't tell Mary the truth was that the conventional side of her nature dictated that she not teach boys (or young men) as "opinion and custom run so strongly against" it.[9] (Ellen Nussey would have agreed with her decision.) Mary continued to advise Charlotte to be bold. She should leave Brussels, but she should also not spend the rest of her life in Haworth.

In the five weeks of the summer school closure, a lonely Charlotte aimlessly wandered through the streets of Brussels seeking distraction. On one of her walks along the busy rue Royale, she was diverted by the sight of a carriage pulled by six horses and surrounded by soldiers. Inside was a plump, vivacious young lady, laughing and chattering gaily to a fellow passenger. Charlotte recognized her. It was the English queen, Victoria, plainly dressed and seeming very unpretentious. Charlotte had read that the queen was, for the most part, well liked by the Belgians, and that she enlivened their King Leopold's somber court. Charlotte knew that Anne and Emily would enjoy the story, remembering their interest in the young queen when they were teenagers.

Charlotte and Emily, together, had happily visited all the art museums and noteworthy sights in Brussels. Now miserably alone, Charlotte walked over treeless and depressing fields to the Protestant cemetery to visit the grave of her vibrant young friend Martha, knowing it would worsen her mood even more. As further proof of her unhappiness, this daughter of a Church of England curate went to confession at the Catholic Church of Ste. Gudule. (Did she confess her feelings for her married teacher?) She even let the priest believe she might discuss conversion to Catholicism. Her father would have been shocked. She confided her secret to Emily, but told her not to tell their father.

Finally, with too much time to think and unable to fight her depression, Charlotte decided to go home to Haworth. She half-heartedly gave her notice to Madame Heger that she would be leaving the school, but Monsieur Heger vehemently told her she must stay. He renewed his lessons with her, but Charlotte was to find that her time in Brussels was not improved. She wrote in her diary in October, "First class—I am very cold—there is no fire—I wish I were at home with Papa—Branwell—Emily—Anne & Tabby—I am tired of being amongst foreigners it is a dreary life—especially as there is only one person in this house worthy of being liked"[10]—the professor, of course.

By the end of the year, she again decided to go home. When Monsieur Heger repeated his desire for her to stay at the school, she declined. As a last kindness, he offered to send one of his daughters to the school she and Emily had told him they planned to open. Charlotte rejected the offer, feeling Madame Heger would be unwilling to agree to the arrangement.

In December, the directress—probably pleased with Charlotte's decision—escorted her to Antwerp and the steamship *Wilberforce*. Charlotte returned home with a diploma as proof of her teaching credentials. This had been the original reason for the time spent in school in Brussels, but an unhappy Charlotte arrived at the parsonage depressed, confused, and anxious about the future.

Charlotte was reluctant to even think of opening a school or finding work as a teacher. She delayed making any effort to plan her next step, using her father's deteriorating health as a reason to remain at home though she was not needed there. Emily was very capably managing the household, assisting her father, and even prolifically producing poetry related to the Gondal saga.

Charlotte was predictably obsessed with her regrets at leaving Professor Heger. She nursed a secret desire to return to Brussels even as she and Emily finally began to discuss the opening of a boarding school in the parsonage. The small inheritance Aunt Branwell had left each of the girls meant they could now do so. Charlotte and Emily thought five or six students could sleep in Branwell's and Anne's rooms, since both were away working. Charlotte would teach, and Emily would continue as housekeeper. The plan really only benefited Charlotte, enabling her to remain at home while still earning her keep. Emily's job would entail much more work, Mr. Brontë would be inconvenienced, and again Anne had been left out of the plan entirely. Still, Mr. Brontë agreed to the venture, and Charlotte, perhaps without a great deal of enthusiasm herself, had cards printed, and wrote letters to acquaintances informing them of the Misses Brontë's Establishment.

"Board and Education" were offered for "a limited number of young ladies" at the parsonage in Haworth. Included were "Writing, Arithmetic, History, Grammar, Geography, and Needle Work." French, German, Latin, music, drawing, use of a pianoforte and washing were offered for extra fees. Arithmetic and Latin were subjects usually reserved for boys' education. German was generally only desired by "bookish" girls, but offering it would show their superiority as a school. Additionally "Each Young Lady to be provided with One Pair of Sheets, Pillow Cases, Four Towels, a Dessert and Tea Spoon."[11]

In addition to their own efforts, Ellen tried to help them find students among her wider circle of acquaintances, but there was not even one inquiry. The parsonage was too isolated. They were forced to give up all plans for a school. The truth was that all three sisters had lost interest in running a school, at home or elsewhere. Mr. Brontë and Emily were probably relieved to not have the quiet of the parsonage disturbed. The school plan was abandoned.

Charlotte was happy to be reunited with her friend Mary Taylor in the new year, but Mary had distressing news. Her youngest brother, Waring, had already immigrated to New Zealand, and Mary was going to join him. After their father's death, the Taylors had moved from the Red House to a more modest home next to their mills. Visiting her friend there, Charlotte couldn't even pretend to be anything but a depressing presence amid the gay and lively Taylors, who were apparently making a valiant effort to celebrate their loved one before she set off on her potentially dangerous new adventure. Mary tried to convince Charlotte to leave Haworth, telling her that if she spent the next five years at home, alone and in ill health, it would ruin her. She believed Charlotte would never recover. "Think of what you'll be five years hence!" Mary told her. Charlotte, upset, pacing the floor, but using her affectionate name for Mary, answered, "But I intend to stay, Polly."[12]

Mary sailed for New Zealand on the ship *Louisa Campbell* in March, arriving in Wellington in late July. "To me it is something as if a great planet fell out of the sky,"[13] Charlotte wrote about the loss of Mary's companionship. The friends would write, but they never saw each other again.

Charlotte had been in low spirits even before she heard Mary's news, of course. She continued to dwell on thoughts of Monsieur Heger, and her regret over her abrupt exit. She wrote letters to him obsessively for months, twice a week at first. She was frantic in her desire to hear from him. He seems only to have written an occasional letter in response.

Monsieur Heger's letter to Mr. Brontë expressing admiration for the sisters' talents and qualities as dedicated students was kept, but none of his letters to Charlotte have been found. It's tempting to speculate on their fate. The most likely answer is Charlotte burned them. A more dramatic and less likely answer is found in one of Charlotte's novels.

Readers of *Villette* have always believed the heroine, Lucy Snow, to be Charlotte herself. And when Lucy decides to hide special letters she had received from a man she loved, she confesses that she "made a little roll of my letters, wrapped them in oiled silk, bound them with twine. . . . I knew there was . . . a hollow, hidden partly by ivy and creepers . . . and there I meditated hiding my treasure. But I was not only going to hide a treasure—I meant also to bury a grief. That grief over which I had lately been weeping, as I wrapped it in its winding sheet, must be interred. I rested, leaning against the tree; lingering, like any other mourner, beside a newly sodded grave."[14]

Bruxelles
Belgique

M. HEGER

MME HEGER

It's not known if Monsieur Heger ever encouraged Charlotte's attraction to him, but it seemed unlikely to those who knew him. Years later a friend of the professor commented on his relationship with Charlotte: "He made much of her, & drew her out, & petted her, & won her love. . . . He was a worshipper of intellect & he worshipped Charlotte Brontë thus far & no further."[15] The professor had exchanged letters with other former students, however, and continued to do so in later years. In his letter to "L," he expressed affection in a surprisingly intimate manner. "I only have to think of you to see you. I often give myself the pleasure when my duties are over, when the light fades. I postpone lighting the gas lamp in my library, I sit down, smoking my cigar, and with a hearty will I evoke your image—and you come (without wishing to, I dare say) but I see you, I talk with you—you, with that little air, affectionate undoubtedly, but independent and resolute, firmly determined not to allow any opinion without being previously convinced, demanding to be convinced before allowing yourself to submit—in fact, just as I knew you, my dear L—, and as I have esteemed and loved you."[16] A letter such as this, had Charlotte received it, could easily have been misunderstood by her—a passionate young woman in love.

Charlotte's letters became more agitated. She wrote in French, which seems to have made her bolder. "Day and night I find neither rest nor peace. If I sleep I am disturbed by tormenting dreams in which I see you, always severe, always grave, always incensed against me," she wrote in one letter, begging him to answer. "I know that you will be irritated when you read this letter. You will say . . . that I am hysterical . . . that I have black thoughts, etc. So be it, Monsieur. . . . All that I know is, that I cannot, that I will not, resign myself to lose wholly the friendship of my master. I would rather suffer the greatest physical pain than always have my heart lacerated by smarting regrets. If my master withdraws his friendship from me entirely I shall be altogether without hope; if he gives me a little—just a little—I shall be satisfied—happy; I shall have a reason for living . . . for working."[17]

Her behavior seemed not unlike that of the dramatic romantic and submissive heroines of her Angrian stories. Even her frequent references to him as "master" is not entirely intended as "Master of Instruction" as used in a school setting. Charlotte wrote a poignant poem around this time that seems likely to have been inspired by her love for Monsieur Heger. It begins:

> If thou be in a lonely place,
>   If one hour's calm be thine,
> As Evening bends her placid face
>   O'er this sweet day's decline;
> If all the earth and all the heaven
>   Now look serene to thee,
> As o'er them shuts the summer even,
>   One moment—think of me![18]

Charlotte suspected Madame Heger of reading her letters—and she was right. Though he had not immediately destroyed them, the professor, aware of Charlotte's infatuation, eventually discarded them. A suspicious Madame Heger, however, retrieved the torn pieces, painstakingly sewing their ripped edges together so she could read and preserve them. Her motive may have been curiosity, anger, or distrust. She wished to be able to prove the improper nature of Charlotte's letters, if necessary, to protect her husband's and her school's reputations. The sensational letters to her husband shocked Madame Heger. She insisted her husband only answer Charlotte's letters every six months, if at all.

In the spring Arthur Bell Nicholls, a young Irishman, arrived at the parsonage to introduce himself as Mr. Brontë's new assistant curate. The first service he conducted in the church caused Charlotte to take note of him as a respectable man who read well and, she hoped, would turn out to be satisfactory.

16

At Thorp Green

. . . wondrously valued . . .

Branwell had spent his childhood writing and dreaming about wealthy and powerful people in grand houses and palaces. He had been raised to believe he would achieve great things, which he may have thought included a privileged lifestyle. At fifteen, he had raved about Ellen Nussey's house, Rydings, calling it "paradise!" Thorp Green, however, might have been the most impressive establishment Branwell had ever seen. He would have been thrilled by the beauty of the house and grounds that belonged to the Lord of the Manor of Little Ouseborn. He was not, however, installed in the great house as Anne was. He was lodged in the nearby Old Hall, a brick house built in the seventeenth century as part of a working farm.

It was difficult for Branwell to adjust to working again as a tutor. He had enjoyed a sense of freedom and importance while in charge of his own railway station at Luddendenfoot. He was still depressed and grieving the loss of his aunt and William Weightman. He also still missed his friends in Halifax, and their literary meetings. Though impressed with his surroundings, a homesick Branwell, turning inward, picked up his pen and wrote.

> I sit this evening far away
>> From all I used to know
> And nought reminds my soul to day
>> Of happy long ago
>
> Unwelcome cares unthought of fears
>> Around my room arise
> I seek for suns of former years
>> But clouds oercast my skies[1]

At first Branwell seemed to have made himself ill with unhappiness, and his father, who had business in nearby York, was worried enough to visit his son to assure himself of his well-being.

All the siblings seem to have had moments of yearning for the happy period of their childhood. Cathy, in *Wuthering Heights*, may have expressed Emily's and her sisters' feelings and memories of playing on the moors as children when she wrote, "I wish I were a girl again, half savage and hardy and free. . . . I'm sure I should be myself were I once among the heather on those hills."[2]

Anne had also suffered a great deal at Thorp Green from depression, loneliness, and homesickness. She still had recurrences of religious anxieties, but her unhappiness may have been eased by the presence of her older brother nearby. She had also rejected the Calvinist teachings, which had disturbed her so much at Roe Head, in favor of her own (unusual at the time) brave belief in universal salvation. She wrote a strongly worded poem expressing her feelings about the Calvinist dogma. It begins:

> You may rejoice to think *yourselves* secure;
> You may be grateful for the gift divine—
> That grace unsought, which made your black hearts pure,
> And fits your earth-born souls in Heaven to shine.
>
> But is it sweet to look around, and view
> Thousands excluded from that happiness
> Which they deserved, at least, as much as you,—
> Their faults not greater, nor their virtues less? . . .[3]

Emily would later express her feelings about religion in another bold poem:

No coward soul is mine
No trembler in the world's storm-troubled sphere
I see Heaven's glories shine
And Faith shines equal arming me from Fear

. . . .

Vain are the thousand creeds
That move men's hearts, unutterably vain,
Worthless as withered weeds
Or idlest froth amid the boundless main

. . . .

With wide-embracing love
Thy spirit animates eternal years
Pervades and broods above,
Changes, sustains, dissolves, creates, and rears.

Though Earth and moon were gone
And suns and universes ceased to be
And thou wert left alone
Every Existence would exist in thee

There is not room for Death
Nor atom that his might could render void
Since thou art Being and Breath
And what thou art may never be destroyed.[4]

It was only a few months after Branwell's arrival at Thorp Green that he wrote John Brown to say he was living in a "palace" and announced, "I am the favourite of all the household."[5] He always enjoyed attention and opportunities to brag about himself to his friends and family. When Mrs. Robinson gave the young man gifts and kept questioning Anne about her brother, she believed her employer was simply happy at how well young Edmund was advancing in his studies with his tutor. Anne probably didn't realize for months that her brother had a secret.

The Robinson girls, despite their spoiled and frivolous natures, were very fond of their serious, book-loving governess; they gave Anne a silky, curly haired, black-and-white King Charles spaniel named Flossy, which became her devoted companion. The dog, with his fancy name, was a breed generally owned by the wealthy, but the lively, happy dog was as spoiled and coddled in the parsonage as it would have been in any nobleman's estate. He was given a brass collar that he is shown wearing in a charming portrait Emily painted of him, perhaps as a gift for Anne. Emily and Anne both made several sketches of the beloved dog.

By their Christmas break, Charlotte, still at home, was able to half-jealously write to Ellen that Branwell and Anne were home from Thorp Green, and that they were, according to Branwell, "both wondrously valued in their situations."[6] The brother and sister were working hard with their charges and deserved the praise they received.

Anne had begun teaching the girls German and Latin, and Branwell was attempting to instruct young Edmund in classical languages as well. On visits home, however, Branwell's behavior was distracted, restless, and erratic. He did not mind when his holidays were over, seeming eager to return.

Charlotte continued to suffer obsessively from her unrequited love for Monsieur Heger. She wrote poetry that reflected her yearning for a romantic relationship with a dominant figure—her "master." Charlotte would later be famous for bringing to life independent-minded heroines who demanded equality. But she had always been attracted to the dominating heroes of the Silver Fork, Romantic and Gothic stories she had read, and written herself, since childhood.

Though no one at the parsonage suspected all was not well at Thorp Green, Anne unexpectedly gave her notice to Mr. Robinson and returned home. After five years, she had finally left Thorp Green for good. On a rainy July evening in what was proving to be a cold, dreary summer, Anne was sitting in a rocking chair before the fire in the dining room, with her feet on the fender. She was writing in her diary that since her last entry, four years before, "I have had some very unpleasant and undreamt-of experience of human nature," which she was "now . . . just escaped from."[7]

Anne and Emily had decided to celebrate Anne's "escape" from Thorp Green by taking a short trip to York—their first ever vacation together. On the train, the sisters (Emily, soon to be twenty-seven, and Anne, twenty-five) pretended to be characters from their Gondal stories—a proven method since childhood to distract themselves from anxiety. It worked for Emily, who was still deeply involved in Gondal. But Anne, troubled by her exit from Thorp Green, was not finding the long-continuing saga as diverting and absorbing as she once had.

There was a reason for depression and anxiety in the parsonage. Anne may not have mentioned to her father the real reason for leaving her employment after five years. It is likely she left due to embarrassment at her brother's behavior with their employer's wife. She would have confided in Emily, but Charlotte was away, visiting Ellen Nussey. Branwell was due home soon for his summer break.

Charlotte returned from Ellen's after Branwell had arrived home, and she soon realized he was ill. Charlotte confided in a letter to Ellen that a few days after Branwell's return a note had come from Mr. Robinson. In it he sternly dismissed Branwell, indicating that "he had discovered his (Branwell's) proceedings, which he characterized as bad beyond expression, and charging him on pain of exposure to break off instantly and for ever all communication with every member of his family. We have had sad work with Branwell since." Though the young man had rarely drunk to excess until he left Thorp Green, Charlotte wrote, "He thought of nothing but stunning or drowning his distress of mind. No one in the house could have rest."[8]

Branwell had been uncertain whether to embark on the dangerous affair with Mrs. Robinson, and had written to his friend and confidant, John Brown, for advice. Branwell's letters to his more worldly friend, who had a reputation as a philanderer himself, still took the same swaggering tone as his Angrian stories, and never showed him at his best. John Brown's answering letter has been lost, but whatever advice he gave, Branwell made the wrong choice, becoming disastrously involved with his employer's wife.

The scandal of an adulterous affair in Victorian England was shocking—and would have been especially so when the son of a clergyman was involved.

Both Anne and Emily were making an effort to hold on to normalcy, and wrote their diaries in their usual calm manner. Branwell was not at home, so it was a quiet evening. But in Anne's post, there is an undercurrent of anxiety. She wrote that Charlotte "is now sitting sewing in the dining-room Emily is ironing upstairs . . . Papa is in the parlour. Tabby and Martha are, I think, in the kitchen. Keeper and Flossy are, I do not know where. Little Dick [the canary] is hopping in his cage . . . Charlotte is thinking about getting another situation. She wishes to go to Paris. Will she go? She has let Flossy in, by-the-by, and he is now lying on the sofa. Emily is engaged in writing the Emperor Julius's life She has read some of it, and I want very much to hear the rest. She is writing some poetry, too. I wonder what it is about? . . . E. and I have a

BRANWELL BRONTË

LYDIA ROBINSON

great deal of work (plain sewing) to do. When shall we sensibly diminish it? I want to get a habit of early rising. Shall I succeed? We have not yet finished our Gondal Chronicles that we began three years and a half ago. When will they be done? . . . I for my part cannot well be flatter or older in mind than I am now."[9] Anne, understandably, was still upset from her often troubling time at Thorp Green, her disquiet over Branwell, and the worry and dread of finding a new position as governess.

Though Anne's diary ended on a depressed note, Emily—celebrating her twenty-seventh birthday—seemed to feel more hopeful about the many family problems that summer. Perhaps she was less shocked by the histrionics of her brother, though his dismissal from Thorp Green seemed far more serious than his past errors and indiscretions. Emily was content with her quiet life and happy that her writing was going well. She mentioned the Gondal scenes she and Anne had acted out during their holiday. "The Gondals still flourish bright as ever. . . . We intend sticking firm by the rascals as long as they delight us, which I am glad to say they do at present."[10] Though seeming somewhat oblivious to the concerns of her family, Emily may have used the usual method of escaping reality and finding comfort in her imaginary world. This was a habit she had retained more determinedly than her siblings. Her deep involvement in her writing seems to have again buffered her from the anxiety, humiliation, and disgust felt by the rest of the family.

"We are all in decent health, only that papa has a complaint in his eyes, and with the exception of B., who, I hope, will be better and do better hereafter. I am quite contented for myself: not as idle as formerly, altogether as hearty, and having learnt to make the most of the present and long for the future with the fidgetiness that I cannot do all I wish; seldom or ever troubled with nothing to do, and merely desiring that everybody could be as comfortable as myself and as undesponding, and then we should have a very tolerable world of it . . .

"We are now all at home, and likely to be there some time . . . Tabby has just been teasing me to turn as formerly to 'Pilloputate.' Anne and I should have picked the black currants if it had been fine and sunshiny. I must hurry off now to my turning (taking apart worn clothing to turn the unfaded side to the outside, to make clothes last longer) and ironing. I have plenty of work on hand, and writing, and am altogether full of business. With best wishes for the whole house till 1848, July 30th, and as much longer as may be,—I conclude."[11]

Mr. Brontë had sent Branwell on a trip to Liverpool and the coast of Wales—with John Brown to look after him. He hoped the trip would calm and distract his son. While there, Branwell wrote to Charlotte to express "some sense of contrition for his frantic folly." He promised her he would behave better when he returned home, but Charlotte believed that, as long as he remained at home, there was unlikely to be peace in the parsonage. "We must all, I fear, prepare for a season of distress and disquietude."[12] Charlotte's worries were justified.

Home again, Branwell was by turns hopeful and distraught. He wrote to an old friend from his railroad days, telling him his life had become a disaster. He indicated Mr. Robinson, his employer at Thorp Green, had not liked him, but his wife had shown him kindness that had developed into "declarations of more than ordinary feeling." He admired Lydia Robinson's "mental and personal attractions . . . unselfish sincerity, her sweet temper, and unwearied care for others."[13] Though she was seventeen years older than Branwell, he had fallen in love with her and was surprised when the feeling was reciprocated.

He wrote that he had been dismissed, and about the "furious letter from my employer, threatening to shoot me if I returned from my vacation . . . and letters from her (Lydia Robinson's) lady's-maid and physician informed me of the outbreak, only checked by her firm courage and resolution that whatever harm came to her, none should come to me."[14]

Unable to cope with his misery, Branwell obtained money from his father under false pretenses and spent it in the nearby taverns. His sisters were disillusioned by his behavior and said he was "a hopeless being." Charlotte wrote to Ellen, "In his present state, it is scarcely possible to stay in the room where he is. What the future has in store I do not know."[15]

While Charlotte found her brother's behavior and lack of control reprehensible, she failed to see any similarities to her own obsession and despair concerning Monsieur Heger. She had written to Ellen, "I suffered much before I left Brussels. I think, however long I live, I shall not forget what the parting with M. Heger cost me."[16] All the drama and passion of Charlotte and Branwell's Angrian fantasies were to be found in their choices of, and reactions to, their first loves. Charlotte, however, judged her brother harshly. She seemed to think her secrecy about her suffering hopeless love for a married man bore no similarity to her brother's louder misery over his love for a married woman.

She continued to write frantic, passionate letters to the professor. In one, she wrote she intended to see him again, even briefly, once she had money for the trip to Brussels. Later she declared, "I have forbidden myself completely the pleasure of speaking about you—even to Emily, but I cannot conquer . . . my regrets . . . and that is humiliating—not to be master of one's own thoughts, to be slave to a regret, a memory."[17]

Branwell tried to recover his equilibrium. He made an effort to fight off his despair by a method that had always worked in the past. He began a new novel, but by using his romance with Mrs. Robinson as its inspiration, he constantly dwelt on his sorrow. Branwell tried to find work with the railroad company that had fired him, but without success. His misery and self-pity continued. He did not suffer silently, and continued to make the lives of those around him difficult and distressing.

He considered trying to find a post abroad. He complained of the "quietude of home, and the inability to make my family aware of the nature of most of my sufferings."[18] On a trip to Halifax he visited with his friend, Joseph Bentley Leyland, a talented sculptor who had been a rising star in the same Leeds exhibition the year Charlotte showed her drawings. The two young men made a friendly agreement to trade their work. Leyland requested Branwell compose an epic poem about his ancestors' home—Morley Hall, in Lancashire—which should have been a diverting and important project for Branwell. In exchange, Leyland was to create a portrait medallion of Branwell's aristocratic profile. The impressive medallion is Branwell's only portrait, except for rough sketches he made of himself. There are enough similarities to believe the medallion is a fine likeness. Apparently Branwell never finished the epic poem, but Leyland gave Branwell the medallion anyway. Father and son were proud of the portrait, which was given a place of honor in the parsonage.

Branwell apparently did not finish his novel. He did not find another job, but he did write more poetry.

A Book of Poetry

. . . wild, melancholy, and elevating.

On an autumn day in 1845, Charlotte, curious about what Emily was writing, went into her room and lifted the lid of her sister's portable lap desk. There she found in the mauve velvet interior two notebooks of carefully transcribed poems. One contained Emily's personal, autobiographical work, and the other held poetry from the Gondal saga. What she surreptitiously read surprised and impressed Charlotte—her younger sister possessed great talent. Charlotte later described them as "vigorous and genuine. To my ear they had also a peculiar music, wild, melancholy, and elevating."[1]

Emily was furious at what could only be described as Charlotte's snooping. Her private work had been read without her permission. It was a betrayal of trust—in a house so crowded with family and servants, privacy was important, especially to reticent Emily. By that time, she may not have even been sharing her work with Anne, though they often wrote Gondal poems on the same theme.

It took days for Emily to forgive her and for Charlotte to convince her sister of her admiration for her work. She told Emily and Anne that the excellence of Emily's writing had given her an idea. Branwell's poetry had already been published in several newspapers, which had probably made competitive Charlotte jealous. What if a collection of the sisters' poems could be compiled in a manuscript? Hadn't they always wanted to see their work in print, ever since they were children, reading their father's published books and pretending to be authors and poets themselves? The dream had not died. There were published women poets—though not many.

Charlotte shared with her sisters a selection of her own work, and Anne brought out a bundle of her poetry tucked away in her own lap desk. Finally Emily agreed, but only if they could remain anonymous. Though she had so often expressed angry disregard of others' opinions of her, apparently where her work was concerned she *did* care what people thought. The more they talked the more real the idea became. Privacy was important to Charlotte as well, though she *had* always wanted to be famous. But she agreed.

They decided that if their work was believed to be written by men they were more likely to be read, and to be reviewed by critics—men's work was taken more seriously than women's. It was unfair, but true. Emily wanted their pen names to keep the same initials as their actual names. They decided to call themselves Currer, Ellis, and Acton Bell.

Perhaps the name "Bell" came to mind as it was the middle name of their father's latest assistant, curate Arthur Bell Nicholls, who had arrived just prior to Anne leaving Thorp Green. He had stayed despite Branwell's histrionics, which he could not have avoided observing. The reserved, strongly built, young man was not handsome, but he had an interesting face. His hair was very black, and his angular face was lengthened even more by his impressively long sideburns. His best features were his eyes, which were beautiful and expressive. Though born in Scotland, he had been raised in Ireland. The sisters all thought he was far too conservative and boring, though he was very passionate and outspoken about his opinions. He was strongly opposed to Dissenters—Methodists and Baptists. The young man also willingly walked the dogs, gave sweets to the schoolchildren (who loved him), and liked to wade up and down moorland streams, "tickling" trout (catching fish by hand).

The choice of the name Bell for the sisters seems odd, however, as a few months earlier Ellen had told Charlotte there were rumors among their friends that Charlotte was going to marry her father's curate. Charlotte hated that she was being gossiped about, and demanded to know details of the chatter. She informed Ellen "never was rumour more unfounded. A cold far-away sort of civility are the only terms on which I have ever been with Mr. Nicholls. I could by no means think of mentioning such a rumour to him even as a joke.

It would make me the laughing-stock of himself and his fellow curates for half a year to come." She added that the curates "regard me as an old maid, and I regard them, one and all, as highly uninteresting, narrow, and unattractive specimens."[2] Mr. Nicholls, however, would play an important part in Charlotte's life, and her father's as well.

For Charlotte, especially, the plan for publication gave her new hope and a sense of purpose after the misery of the previous months of obsessing about Monsieur Heger and the constant worries about Branwell. She was excited, and enthusiastically took charge of the hunt for publishers. The sisters chose a collection of sixty-one of their poems to submit for publication. Surely there was exhilaration, anxiety, and hopefulness—would they soon be published poets? They probably agonized over their choices. Some had to be rewritten to take away references to Gondal or Angria. Next they named them, which they had not done before.

The poems selected ranged in subject matter from the joy they found in nature to love, faith, sorrow, longing, and loss. Emily chose one of her most haunting Gondal poems, "Remembrance," to include.

> Cold in the earth—and the deep snow piled above thee,
> Far, far, removed, cold in the dreary grave!
> Have I forgot, my only Love, to love thee,
> Severed at last by Time's all-severing wave?
>
> Now, when alone, do my thoughts no longer hover
> Over the mountains, on that northern shore,
> Resting their wings where heath and fern-leaves cover
> Thy noble heart for ever, ever more?
>
> Cold in the earth—and fifteen wild Decembers,
> From those brown hills, have melted into spring:
> Faithful, indeed, is the spirit that remembers
> After such years of change and suffering!
>
> Sweet Love of youth, forgive, if I forget thee,
> While the world's tide is bearing me along;
> Other desires and other hopes beset me,
> Hopes which obscure, but cannot do thee wrong!
>
> No later light has lightened up my heaven,
> No second morn has ever shone for me;
> All my life's bliss from thy dear life was given,
> All my life's bliss is in the grave with thee . . .[3]

Anne also had a poem of loss and remembrance—"A Reminiscence"—believed to be about young Mr. Weightman, buried in a vault beneath the floor of St. Michael's, and so remembered for his winning smile.

> Yes, thou art gone! and never more
> Thy sunny smile shall gladden me;
> But I may pass the old church door,
> And pace the floor that covers thee,
>
> May stand upon the cold, damp stone,
> And think that, frozen, lies below
> The lightest heart that I have known,
> The kindest I shall ever know.
>
> Yet, though I cannot see thee more,
> 'Tis still a comfort to have seen;
> And though thy transient life is o'er,
> 'Tis sweet to think that thou hast been;
>
> To think a soul so near divine,
> Within a form, so angel fair,
> United to a heart like thine,
> Has gladdened once our humble sphere.[4]

Charlotte would prove to be better known as a novelist than as a poet, but her poem titled "Passion" is one of her most evocative.

> Some have won a wild delight,
>   By daring wilder sorrow;
> Could I gain thy love to-night,
>   I'd hazard death tomorrow.
>
> Could the battle-struggle earn
>   One kind glance from thine eye,
> How this withering heart would burn,
>   The heady fight to try! . . .[5]

Finally research of publishers and the choice of poetry were completed. The sisters wanted to keep the project secret—especially from Branwell. They didn't want to include him, but they also did not want to hurt him. "We could not tell him of our efforts for fear of causing him too deep a pang of remorse for his own time misspent, and talents misapplied."[6]

The packet of poems was sent, but only rejection letters were returned until one company offered to publish their poetry collection. They must, however, bear the expense of publishing their own book, and printing would cost them the same as a year's earnings working as a governess. There must have been long discussions before they made the decision to go forward. Dreams and ambitions, however, would have made up a large part of their conversation. As with self-published writers before and since, they decided to gamble. If they thought spending money on the project was irresponsible, it was also a chance to be recognized as poets and hopefully could lead to recognition and even to earning their living as writers. In March, with nervous anticipation, they sent the payment, and their directions for the book design. They paid for it out of the legacies left them by Aunt Branwell. Probably they justified it as an investment in their future.

Did the sisters ever give a thought to the source of their Grandfather Branwell's fortune? Author Sharon Wright, researching her very interesting book *Mother of the Brontës*, discovered intriguing information concerning the Branwell grandfather. It may be that Thomas Branwell was involved in business dealings with murderous smugglers in Penzance, forty years before Charlotte's birth. (Cornwall was famous in the eighteenth century for the smuggling of goods from abroad in an attempt to avoid high taxation.) Mr. Branwell—an astute, respected merchant and banker—did have an encounter with customs officers and the law. He was part owner, in 1795, of a known smuggling vessel, the *Liberty*. It was the legacy left by Grandfather Branwell to his children, including his daughter Elizabeth (Aunt Branwell), that paid for the publication of the poetry book. Had their father or they, themselves, known, would they have been shocked? As children, they had loved thrilling news stories. Reportedly, grave robbers had once stolen bodies from their own graveyard to sell to doctors for research. The little girls and their brother, who gleefully wrote stories inspired by them, and other articles about miscreants, might have been thrilled by tales of criminal smugglers (and their own grandfather!) in Penzance. It's been argued, however, that there were two ships called *Liberty* sailing in Cornish waters. Which one was associated with Thomas Branwell?

It was perhaps cruel to have omitted their brother from a project that might have distracted him from his painful obsession. Though they made an effort to keep their publication secret, Branwell most likely came to know about the book. In such a small house—with letters, packets of proofs, and boxes of advance copies for Currer Bell arriving from a publishing house—it's sadly likely that Branwell was not oblivious to his sisters' activities. And being left out of what once would have involved all four "geniuses" may have sunk him further into despair.

His three sisters were undoubtedly excited and pleased when they actually saw their own slim volume of verse. The publisher, Aylott & Jones, made mistakes in the printing, however, and did not follow all of Charlotte's directions—such as her choice of quality paper, for which they had probably paid extra. The cost of the book, printed right on the green leather cover, was less than the agreed-upon amount, and they had not wished the price to spoil the beauty of the cover in such a tasteless, commercial manner. Still, the pleasure of holding their own professionally bound little book (first imagined years before, in their tiny handmade "publications") made up for any dissatisfaction about its production.

They had been anxious about the opinions of the critics, but the little book received good reviews. Annoyingly, however, some critics were also intrigued by the identity of the unknown, mysterious poet brothers, for the very reason that they were anonymous. They had attracted more curiosity from the press than if their real names had been given. Emily's poetry, especially, was praised by critics. One, writing in the *Athenaeum*, particularly admired the talent of Ellis Bell, who "may have things to speak that men will be glad to hear,—and an evident power of wing that may reach heights not here attempted."[7] Their best review, in the *Critic*, was highly appreciative. The reviewer wrote, "it is long since we have enjoyed a volume of such genuine poetry. . . . Here we have good, wholesome, refreshing, vigorous poetry . . . original thoughts expressed in the true language of poetry . . . they have chosen subjects that have freshness in them, and their handling is after a fashion of their own."[8]

Still, they may have been relieved to think that their brother, father, and friends did not know of its existence.

The book sold only two copies. The young poets decided the books would not be wasted, however. They sent some of the unsold books to famous writers they admired, hoping to receive helpful critiques of their work. They refused to be discouraged. The poetry book would not be their last publication, they decided. The small, handsome volume made them want to see more of their work published. Novels were more popular with the public. Seeing their work in print had strengthened their ambition, given them confidence, and encouraged them to finish manuscripts they had already begun.

Why not novels? In their childhood, they had written many novels. In fact, for Charlotte and Emily favorite themes and characters would appear again in their adult books.

Soon after the poetry book was published, Edmund Robinson died at Thorp Green. When Branwell heard the news, he was ecstatic and expectant that all his dreams could now come true. He believed Lydia Robinson would soon summon him to her side, and that "ere very long I should be the husband of a Lady whom I loved best in the world, and with whom, in more than competence, I might live at leisure to try to make myself a name in the world of posterity, without being pestered by the small but countless botherments . . . of work-day toil."[9]

He would be a gentleman of leisure, could seriously pursue his literary career, and no longer be a failure in the eyes of his family. His desire for wealth was not just for himself. He could end his father's anxiety for his children's futures, and take care of his sisters, which had been his family's hope when they all had believed in the likelihood of a glorious career for him.

He had, however, misjudged Mrs. Robinson's devotion to him—she would never consider marrying the son of a poor clergyman who was penniless, unemployed, and years younger than herself, no matter what she may have said to him. She instead involved her maid, her doctor, and her coachman in an elaborate plan to rid herself of the now-inconvenient Branwell Brontë.

It is unknown how the affair had been discovered. It's speculated that the gardener at Thorp Green had observed them together in the boathouse on the river that flowed through the property, and told Mr. Robinson. It's also possible that an incriminating poem Branwell gave to Mrs. Robinson fell into the wrong hands. Branwell had kept a notebook of his poems, which he may have treated carelessly.

Ann Marshall, lady's maid and confidante of Mrs. Robinson, had originally been the children's nurse and probably knew many secrets of the household. Branwell claimed she knew about the affair. The Robinson family physician, Dr. John Crosby (whom Branwell believed to be his friend), also knew their secret. So did the coachman, who was sent to Haworth by Mrs. Robinson to meet with Branwell at the Black Bull. When the coachman left, Branwell was discovered collapsed from the news he had received.

The tale Mrs. Robinson had invented to disentangle herself from Branwell was dramatic—and untrue. Charlotte wrote to Ellen that news had come that "Mr. Robinson had altered his will before he died and effectually prevented all chance of a marriage between his widow and Branwell, by stipulating that she should not have a shilling if she ever ventured to reopen any communication with him. Of course, Branwell then became intolerable. To papa he allows rest neither day nor night."[10]

At the beginning of the year, Mr. Robinson had made a new will, but it made no reference to Branwell Brontë. Mrs. Robinson would have a large income from her husband's estate and continue as one of the trustees, executor, and guardian of the children unless she remarried. This was usual at the time, before the Married Women's Property Act of 1870 would finally give wives the right to keep their own wages or inheritance. If Mrs. Robinson married again she would undoubtedly do as she had directed her daughters to do—marry for wealth and status. By law, she would lose all rights to her deceased husband's money if she remarried.

The actual purpose of Mr. Robinson's new legal document was to cut his eldest daughter, Lydia—named after her mother—out of his will. The twenty year old, whose education Anne had taken charge of five years before, had eloped with penniless actor Henry Roxby (son of the comedian and owner of the Theater Royal in Scarborough). Young Lydia had somehow met him at one of the teas, concerts, balls, or cliff-side strolls in the seaside town. Lydia had several broken engagements behind her, but this time she eloped to Gretna Green, in Scotland, where she and Henry could wed without parental consent as she was underage. Mrs. Robinson followed her husband's lead, and cut her daughter out of her own will.

Mrs. Robinson used the story of the will in her plot to end any hope Branwell might have of their being together. Branwell believed Mr. Robinson was very angry with his wife, but in fact she had blamed Branwell for unwanted advances and her husband had believed her.

The Robinsons' doctor wrote to Branwell, claiming the widow was suffering from grief and guilt. Branwell was led to believe that Mrs. Robinson was now insane, owing to remorse for her conduct toward her husband, which she supposedly believed hastened his death. The doctor reported that Mrs. Robinson fainted upon mention of Branwell's name. She spoke of her "inextinguishable love" for him and "her horror at having been the first to delude" him "into wretchedness." Dr. Crosby ended his report saying that she "wandered into talking of entering a nunnery."[11] Branwell was told he must not disturb her. They must never see one another again.

The doctor had lied about Lydia Robinson being on the brink of madness, but Branwell was emotionally overcome and unable to eat or sleep for days. He was again drinking and taking laudanum. Mrs. Robinson continued to manipulate Branwell. She also sent him money, which enabled him to set about his own self-destruction even more determinedly in the taverns of Haworth and Halifax. He felt there was an atmosphere of judgement surrounding him at home.

Both Mrs. Robinson's maid and doctor continued to keep in touch with Branwell. They also continued to prevent him from seeing Lydia Robinson. It was a melodrama worthy of one of Branwell's own youthful stories. His excitable imagination and the wild tales he had concocted in childhood enabled him to believe the overwrought explanation of the end of their affair. Victorian entertainments were also known for their overly dramatic productions, and may have contributed to his unwavering belief in her story. His family blamed Mrs. Robinson for everything that had happened, while also despairing of Branwell's actions and weaknesses.

If widely known, however, the affair would be a scandal. Mrs. Robinson and her oldest daughter weren't the only members of the family to be guilty of scandalous behavior, by the standards of the day, and probably contributed to Anne's exit from Thorp Green.

When she wrote in her diary the previous summer about the unpleasant situation she had escaped when she left Thorp Green, she may have also been thinking of the Robinson girls. They were reportedly great flirts, likely to follow their mother's and sister's examples.

Anne had tried to guide, influence, and advise the Robinson girls when she was their governess. Her experiences with them inspired her novel *Agnes Grey*. In her first novel, the young governess tries to convince her charges to marry kind, respectable men they loved rather than choosing wealthy husbands—regardless of their bad qualities or behavior—or attractive scoundrels for their charm.

18

Being Anonymous

They too will have their troubles.

The three sisters' novels were finished and mailed together to a London publisher. They were wrapped in paper much like what they had used to make their tiny books when they were imaginative, creative children. The sisters expressed their desire that the books be published as a three-volume set, which was popular with both publishers and libraries. Money from renting sets was how libraries were funded. They were not free. It was disheartening and frustrating when the novels were rejected by one publisher after another throughout winter and spring 1846. The sisters were determined to be published, however, and as each manuscript was returned, it was then sent to the next publisher on the list Charlotte had compiled.

There were more serious worries—Mr. Brontë was almost blind. All his life he had been zealous on behalf of the poor and working class, and now his work was curtailed. He had been in Haworth more than twenty years and had been active and energetic in accomplishing many of his aims. Along with finding funds for the Sunday school, the organ, and bells for the church—all requiring large sums of money—he had given political lectures and been active and outspoken in reform movements. He was known for his high principles and courage.

The *Times* of London covered a meeting where Mr. Brontë had attacked the new Poor Law Act, which contributed to social unrest in Yorkshire and elsewhere. The law determined that relief would only be given to the poor if they lived in workhouses, where conditions were such that none but the most desperate would seek aid there, and it was difficult to ever leave. The crowd that came to hear him speak was so large the event had to be held outdoors. The meeting ended with three rousing cheers for Mr. Brontë's speech. Years later, after the Brontës were long gone, Nancy Garrs would die in a workhouse in Bradford.

Mr. Brontë also wrote many letters and articles that were published in local papers. In one, he advocated that fire-safe clothing (silk or wool) be worn to prevent injuries and death from open fires, lamps, and candles used for cooking, heating, and lighting. He wrote that in his years in Haworth he had performed funeral services for ninety to a hundred children who had burned to death wearing cotton or linen clothing. He ensured his own household only wore the most flame-resistant fabrics. There were no drapes, few rugs, and a bucket of water had always been kept on the stair landing.

Unlike the head of the Cowan Bridge School and many others of his day, he realized it was not God who set children's clothes on fire to punish them for their "sins," and that steps could be taken to prevent great suffering.

Mr. Brontë's church duties were more and more difficult. He could deliver his sermons but had to be assisted up and down from the high three-decker pulpit. As his eyesight grew worse, he had to rely more and more on his curate, Arthur Nicholls. Mr. Brontë was relieved that Mr. Nicholls was so able and responsible, and could take on all of his parish work when needed. He also relied on his daughters to be his eyes, helping him walk, writing what he dictated, and reading to him. Cruel gossips in the village spread a rumor he had taken to drink, since his eye lotion was alcohol based and presumably smelled strongly of spirits. His condition had reached a point where he must have an operation or go totally blind.

Charlotte and Emily traveled to the busy cotton manufacturing city of Manchester to find a doctor, arrange for the operation, and find suitable accommodations. Charlotte, however, would be alone in running their household and arranging for provisions for their lodgings. She was very anxious and felt "excessively ignorant" about what supplies to order for meals. She asked advice of Ellen and Ellen's sister Ann. "For ourselves I could contrive

... but there will be a nurse coming . . . and I am afraid of not having things good enough for her . . . a nurse will probably expect to live much better."[1]

Charlotte and her father would have to stay in Manchester for a month at least. "It will be dreary. I wonder how poor Emily and Anne will get on at home with Branwell? They too will have their troubles,"[2] she wrote to Ellen.

Mr. Brontë was, understandably, frightened by the prospect of the operation. He was sixty-nine years old, and the very human thought that he might not survive the ordeal caused his fear that "I shall never feel Keeper's paws on my knees again!"[3]

The procedure—cataract surgery—is quickly and painlessly done today, but was an ordeal for Mr. Brontë. He was awake throughout the fifteen-minute operation, without anesthesia. Fortunately the acute pain was short. The surgeon was perhaps impressed with Mr. Brontë's patience and courage. Her father did request Charlotte stay in the room with him during the operation, which was very likely distressing for her but would have comforted him. On the day of the operation, Charlotte was disheartened to receive her manuscript, *The Professor*, back for the sixth time.

Charlotte, too, suffered physical pain during the stay in Manchester, apparently unable to get treatment for a very bad toothache. She sat with her father for weeks. He had to remain in bed, in a quiet, darkened room, unmoving, for four days without speaking. He was confined—on his back—for a month. The nurse stayed with him day and night. He was bled with leeches (blood-sucking worms) twice. Bloodletting was believed to remove poisons, prevent inflammation, and help many medical problems. It was used for two thousand years, even into the twentieth century. Mr. Brontë later recorded his experience in the margins of his much-used and scribbled-in copy of Graham's *Domestic Medicine*.

Charlotte managed well in their lodgings, though she did not like her father's nurse. To pass the time, she began to write a new novel she called *Jane Eyre*.

Mr. Brontë's operation was a success, but his recovery was slow and would require even more rest for his eyes when they returned home. He would, however, be able to read, write, and find his way without a guide. He was gratified to realize he would be able to resume his church work. Mr. Nicholls could then leave for a three-week vacation with his relatives in Ireland. Charlotte was pleased and excited at the ease with which she was progressing on her work-in-progress, *Jane Eyre*. Her new manuscript was about a girl who suffered cruelly in a charity school (much like Cowan Bridge) and became a governess when she grew up. The book also included a difficult but intriguing gentleman, named Mr. Rochester, with whom the girl falls in love. Mr. Rochester was very much like the heroes Charlotte had created in her Angrian tales—masterful and a little wicked.

Father and daughter returned home in good spirits. When they reached the parsonage, they found Branwell had continued to deteriorate and had fallen deeper into debt and depression and his addictions to alcohol and laudanum. By December, Mr. Brontë had to pay his son's outstanding debts to keep him out of debtors' prison.

Charlotte, Emily, and Anne probably felt alternating disappointment and hope as the packet containing their manuscripts were mailed to publishers, and returned—rejected. Each time, Charlotte merely crossed out the old address and added the next one from the list she had compiled. She was giving away the fact to each publishing house that no other recipient had wanted their novels. Each time their manuscripts were returned it must have been more difficult to feel their work would ever be accepted for publication. At stake were not only a lifetime of dreams but also their intention to never work as governesses again.

Finally, in July 1847 a letter arrived from London publisher Thomas Cautley Newby, agreeing to accept Anne's *Agnes Grey* and Emily's *Wuthering Heights*. Emily and Anne were thrilled at first, but then read further. They were required to pay £50 for a print run of 350 books, which amount they would only get back if a sufficient number of the books were sold. (Only 250 of the promised copies were actually printed at that time.) Their excitement was tempered by the harsh terms as well as the fact that Charlotte's manuscript, *The Professor*, was rejected again. Charlotte was quite likely shocked, surprised, and jealous that her younger sisters' manuscripts were worthy of publishing, but not hers. Emily and Anne decided to accept the terms, but it soon became apparent that once he was paid Mr. Newby was in no hurry to actually publish their books.

The seventh publisher to receive Charlotte's novel *The Professor* was Smith, Elder, in London. They also rejected the manuscript, probably resulting in the usual frustration until she read further in the letter. This rejection was different. The reader at the publishing house believed its author showed talent, and asked if there was a longer work of fiction they could consider. Thrilled and hopeful, Charlotte quickly finished her new novel, *Jane Eyre*, and submitted it to the publishing house. William Smith Williams, who first read the manuscript, strongly recommended that publisher George Smith read it. The publisher was so intrigued by the manuscript he read it nonstop in one day—cancelling plans, and even eating at his desk, in order to finish it. He then quickly wrote to the unknown gentleman, Currer Bell, about his desire to publish it. Charlotte immediately agreed, but it would not have surprised anyone who knew her when she refused to rewrite any portion of her novel, even when the young publisher feared some scenes would offend readers.

This was in August—*Jane Eyre* was published in October. Emily's and Anne's books would not be published until December, despite having been sold first. The success of Currer Bell's *Jane Eyre* encouraged Mr. Newby to publish the other Bell brothers' work.

Charlotte was gratified to receive her first of many favorable reviews for *Jane Eyre*. Emily and Anne were relieved their books were finally going to be published. The sisters were feeling excited and hopeful that all their novels would soon meet with success. Branwell had gone to Halifax, giving the household welcome relief from his distressing behavior. Even Mr. Brontë, so anxious about his son and unaware of his daughters' literary ventures, was in a good mood. Inspired by his curate's ongoing battle with local housewives, he engaged in a bit of lighthearted creative writing himself.

Though his new curate, Arthur Bell Nicholls, did not have the charm and amiability of Mr. Brontë's favorite assistant, William Weightman, he was steady, reliable, and dedicated to his work. The serious young curate had been shocked since his arrival at the impropriety of a Haworth custom that Mr. Brontë himself had long tried to stop. The neighborhood women brought their laundry to spread over the tombstones to dry on Monday washdays, if there was even a hint of sun. Mr. Nicholls took on the fight with such determination that Mr. Brontë found the battles funny. When the young curate finally declared victory over the washerwomen, Mr. Brontë wrote a bit of affectionate light verse for the occasion, which reads in part:

> The females all routed have fled with their clothes
> To stackyards, and backyards, and where no one knows,
> And loudly [have sworn] by the suds which they swim in,

They'll wring off his head, for his warring *with women*.
Whilst their husbands combine & roar out in their fury,
They'll *Lynch* him at once, without trial by Jury.
But saddest of all, the fair maidens declare,
Of marriage or love, he must ever despair.[4]

It's likely that Mr. Nicholls laughed heartily at the verse, as he is known to have had a good sense of humor regarding himself. He kept the clever verse Mr. Brontë had given him.

Jane Eyre was an immediate success and quickly went into second and third printings. It was considered an unusual book. Plain, impoverished female protagonists were never written about. Jane Eyre was not the usual Victorian heroine—a blushing, weak beauty in an often sentimental romance. Charlotte's Jane was strong, brave, and outspoken. Charlotte was given credit for having created such an unusual heroine, and later told her friends she'd had to convince her sisters of the good idea she had come up with—a plain heroine. The protagonist Anne had created in *Agnes Grey*, however, had the same qualities—and Anne's book was written, though not published, first. *Agnes Grey* suffered by the comparison and was critiqued as a copy of *Jane Eyre*, which must have been painful to Anne. One reviewer described Agnes as "a sort of younger sister to *Jane Eyre*; but inferior to her in every way."[5]

Some critics called *Jane Eyre* the best book of the year. Queen Victoria was reported to have read it avidly. Renowned author William Makepeace Thackeray, among other famous writers, reportedly said he was unable to put it down. He guessed that the writer was a woman, writing, "if a woman she knows her language better than most ladies do, or has had a 'classical' education. . . . Some of the love passages made me cry."[6] Many readers were impressed with the realism of the book, though later that very realism would be attacked.

One critic, reviewing *Jane Eyre*, said, "The story is . . . unlike all that we have read . . . for power of thought and expression, we do not know its rival."[7] *Fraser's Magazine* claimed, "This, indeed, is a book after our own heart . . . no such book has gladdened our eyes for a long while." The author "has perception of character . . . passion . . . knowledge of life."[8]

Charlotte decided to dedicate the second edition of *Jane Eyre* to one of her literary idols, William Thackeray. She did not realize, however, that

Thackeray's wife had been committed to an insane asylum, or that his novel, *Vanity Fair*, was about a governess who married her employer. The correlation with the plot of *Jane Eyre* and Thackeray's wife's illness caused gossip. Thackeray politely thanked Currer Bell for the compliment of the dedication. The gossip lessened, but Charlotte was horrified by her blunder and the accompanying scandalous rumors.

Charlotte's outspoken picture of the lives of real women was upsetting to many readers. The novel has been called one of the first feminist novels. Jane Eyre is speaking out for women everywhere when she tells Mr. Rochester, "I am no bird; and no net ensnares me; I am a free human being with an independent will."[9] Through Jane she could express her firm belief that "women feel just as men feel; they need exercise for their faculties, and a field for their efforts, as much as their brothers do; they suffer from too rigid a restraint, too absolute a stagnation, precisely as men would suffer."[10]

The critics' reviews began to attack the novel for its perceived unsuitability for women and young people, as women should not be depicted as being independent. Words like *coarse* and *immoral* were used to discuss the book. But it continued to sell (perhaps even more), and new editions continued to be printed. The harsh reviews also continued. Astonishingly, one critic wrote, "*Jane Eyre* is pre-eminently an anti-Christian composition. There is throughout it a murmuring against the comforts of the rich and the privations of the poor, which . . . is a murmuring against God's appointment. . . . We do not hesitate to say that the tone of mind and thought which has overthrown authority and violated every code—human and divine—abroad, and fostered . . . rebellion at home, is the same which has written *Jane Eyre*."[11]

In Yorkshire, *Jane Eyre*'s Lowood School was recognized as Charlotte's childhood school at Cowan Bridge. Written about with such authenticity, the school and its harsh headmaster were easily identified. This troubled Charlotte, who worried she would lose her anonymity. She also worried her father would learn of the book from others, so she made the decision, with Emily and Anne, to tell him about *Jane Eyre*. She also hoped knowledge of her accomplishment would raise his spirits, as he was depressed about the death of an old friend. When she showed him a copy of *Jane Eyre*, she was gratified he was pleased, if also surprised, that his oldest daughter was a successful, published writer. He had educated his daughters almost as thoroughly as his son, and he took pride in all his daughters becoming published writers, as

Charlotte told him about their books, too. He was most pleased about *Jane Eyre*, perhaps due to its initial critical and popular success.

Charlotte wrote to her trusted friend Mary Taylor in New Zealand, telling her about *Jane Eyre*. She also sent her Emily's and Anne's books. She must have had their permission to do so, indicating their trust in Mary, and even friendship. Charlotte still had not told Ellen that she had written the book everyone was talking about, perhaps because she feared she could not keep the secret of the author's identity. She even denied the fact to Ellen, more than once, when confronted by her suspicious friend. All three sisters still wished to be anonymous authors, sharing their very personal lives as writers only with one another, their father, and trustworthy Mary Taylor.

Wuthering Heights was considered even more frank, shocking, and unusual for the times than *Jane Eyre*. The siblings' childhood appreciation of their father's and Tabby's shivery Yorkshire tales and the gothic novels (both English and German) she had read had strongly influenced Emily's novel. *Wuthering Heights*—with its chilling plot of obsessive love, hate, and revenge—originally attracted attention because it was thought to be written by the author of *Jane Eyre*, but it soon became talked about in its own right.

A reviewer wrote that it "is a strange sort of book, baffling all regular criticism; yet, it is impossible to begin and not finish it; and quite as impossible to lay it aside afterwards and say nothing about it."[12] Another had described it as "next in merit to Shakespeare for depth of insight and dramatic power."[13] When Emily's Cathy says "I've dreamt in my life dreams that have stayed with me ever after, and changed my ideas; they've gone through and through me, like wine through water, and altered the colour of my mind,"[14] she turned prose into poetry.

But the novel received even more harsh reviews than positive ones. A reviewer in America wrote, "If we did not know that this book has been read by thousands of young ladies in the country, we should esteem it our first duty to caution them against it simply on account of the coarseness of the style."[15]

Emily was surprised and unhappy at the extreme reaction to *Wuthering Heights*. The sisters laughed about some of the reviews, but the harsh ones were upsetting. Emily saved five, however, and put them away in her desk box.

Anne's book had no omens or ghosts, as did *Wuthering Heights* and *Jane Eyre*, but it did include disagreeable characters and issues. Many of her Victorian readers did not wish to know about the difficult lives of governesses and other working women. *Agnes Grey* was the least controversial of the three books and was mostly overlooked at the time, but even Anne's book shocked readers. *Agnes Grey* was a very different book from her sisters' and didn't benefit from being compared to them. It should never have been coupled in a set with *Wuthering Heights*. Anne had used her own experience to make a braver, more powerful statement than *Jane Eyre* against the casual cruelty of the upper classes and their treatment of governesses.

Agnes Grey, quiet and undramatic, did not receive as much attention from the critics as her sisters' books. Sometimes there would only be a few words added at the end of a review of *Wuthering Heights*. One reviewer did write that the novel was "a tale well worth the writing and the reading."[16] Another felt that the book was a "tale of every day life . . . not wholly free from exaggeration (there are some detestable young ladies in it)." The young ladies were inspired by the Robinson girls and, according to Anne, had not been exaggerated at all. The critic felt that the novel, "though lacking the power and originality of *Wuthering Heights*, is infinitely more agreeable. It leaves no painful impression on the mind—some may think it leaves no impression at all."[17]

Anne's books have actually run the gamut of criticism and praise, but it wasn't until the twentieth century that they would be fully appreciated. One avid admirer wrote, "if Anne Brontë had lived ten years longer she would have taken a place beside Jane Austen, perhaps even a higher place."[18] He felt that "her first story, *Agnes Grey*, is the most perfect prose narrative in English literature."[19] Many critics have now found much to admire in the novel. "Anne would have been considered a genius in any other family, but her sisters overshadowed her."[20]

Emily and Anne realized too late that their publisher had done a poor job with their novels. There were many printing errors, and they had received no money. They were being cheated of their earnings. They didn't know what to do.

All three sisters were working on their next novels. In the evenings, after their father went to bed, they followed their long-standing habit of walking around and around the dining room table, for exercise and to discuss their current problems and future plans. They had stopped reading their works-in-progress to one another—probably because of Charlotte's strong disapproval of both Emily's and Anne's novels. She would later openly criticize them.

When they were together, however, their sometimes-prickly arguments did not affect their close bonds as sisters.

Anne finished her second novel, *The Tenant of Wildfell Hall*, about a woman who escaped from an abusive husband. Her work was inspired by a sad and troubling tale she had heard years earlier from one of her father's parishioners, a Mrs. Collins, who had come to Mr. Brontë for help and advice. Her life and her children's had been ruined by her curate husband's brutality to her and his addiction to alcohol. Mr. Brontë advised her to leave her husband, again showing himself to be an unusual and enlightened man. The Victorian norm would have been to advise a wife to stay.

Anne also had knowledge of the sometimes lax behavior of the wealthy families she had worked for as a governess. And, sadly, she was aware of her once-promising brother's heartbreaking weaknesses for alcohol and opium. Branwell continued to be a problem, worsening in fact, as his health deteriorated. He continued to drink, and was suffering from fainting fits. While drunk one night he set his bed clothes on fire. Anne tried, without success, to wake him. She then ran for Emily, who pulled Branwell off the bed. The burning bedding was pulled onto the floor and the flames extinguished. Mr. Brontë had always been afraid of fire in the house and had buckets at hand.

After that frightening event, Branwell was moved to his father's room to save him from himself, and the family from him. It's unlikely the concerned father slept much after that. Branwell subjected the entire family to days and nights of upset and fear with his erratic behavior. Though painful and distressing, it was not on a par with the cruel and abusive behavior of either Mr. Collins or the characters in Anne's book.

Anne had sold *Tenant* to the same publisher, Thomas Newby, who had done such a poor job with her first book. She soon regretted her choice. Why did Emily and Anne stay with Thomas Newby? Charlotte urged them to change to her honest and helpful publishing house, Smith, Elder. Could their decision not to do so be a statement of their stubborn desire to make their own choices and be free from Charlotte's dictates? Or was Mr. Newby a fast-talking scoundrel who somehow convinced them to stay with him? It was probably both.

The Tenant of Wildfell Hall was ahead of its time. It has been named one of the very first important feminist novels. The mildest-seeming and most pious of the Brontë sisters wrote a radical tale of the evils and abuses that can occur due to a lack of women's rights. The novel sold well—because it was considered so shocking—and soon went into a second printing. One critic gave a half-appreciative, half-condemning, review: "our object . . . is to warn our readers, and more especially our lady-readers, against being induced to peruse it, either by the powerful interest of the story, or the talent with which it is written. Did we think less highly of it in these particulars, we should have left the book to its fate."[21]

The book received its share of very harsh reviews. One claimed it was "unfit for . . . the very class of persons to whom it would be most useful . . . owing to the profane expressions, inconceivably coarse language, and revolting scenes and descriptions by which its pages are disfigured."[22] Modern readers will find the plot powerful and its message still pertinent. The scenes Victorian readers found shocking are mild seen in the light of today's world.

It is odd that so many critics failed to recognize that *Jane Eyre, Agnes Grey,* and *The Tenant of Wildfell Hall* were each written not only to entertain but also to expose wrongs, with strong moral purpose. Both Charlotte and Anne were upset at the repeated charges of coarseness and brutality in each of their books, and it hurt to be so misunderstood as to their intent. Emily, too, was upset at the harsh comments of the critics of *Wuthering Heights.*

Charlotte received a letter from her publisher indicating that "their American correspondent had written to them complaining that the first sheets of a new work by Currer Bell had been already received, and not by their house, but by a rival publisher, and asking the meaning of such false play; it enclosed an extract from a letter from Mr. Newby . . . affirming that to the best of his belief *Jane Eyre, Wuthering Heights,* and *Agnes Grey,* and *The Tenant of Wildfell Hall* (the new work) were all the production of one author." Charlotte wrote to Mary Taylor about the confusion. "The upshot of it was that on the very day I received Smith and Elder's letter, Anne and I packed up a small box, sent it down to Keighley, set out ourselves after tea, walked through a . . . storm to the station, got to Leeds, and whirled up by the night train to London with the view of proving our separate identity to Smith and Elder, and confronting Newby with his *lie.*"[23]

19

A Letter from London

We are three sisters . . .

Charlotte and Anne arrived the next morning at eight o'clock at Euston Station, London. Both young women were exhausted, but Anne, who had never been to London, must have been alert to all the new sights. A horse-drawn cab took them to dark and narrow Paternoster Row, in the shadow of St. Paul's Cathedral. The medieval lane received its name from the monks of St. Paul's, who had proceeded daily along the narrow lane and back, reciting their Paternoster prayers. The lane was closed to carriages, hidden from the noise and rush of traffic on the London streets.

Halfway down the Row, lined with book stores, stationers, and publishers, was the two-story Chapter Coffee House. Its most fashionable years were long gone. In the eighteenth century, the great literary figures of the day had frequented its rooms. Mr. Brontë had first lodged there when he was a young university student. It was, at that time, a busy hostel catering to famous writers, publishers, and journalists as well as students and literature-loving clerics up from the country. Charlotte, Emily, their father, and friends stayed there previously, on their way to Brussels. They must have realized that the two-hundred-year-old building was not the thriving hostelry it once had been, but didn't realize that even then it was not the best choice for the group of travelers.

More changes had taken place since Charlotte's last visit—it was now used only as a men's meeting house. (In six years it would be turned into a tavern.) Few ever slept there, and it was not quite a proper lodging for ladies. The only other female in the house was the maid. Charlotte and Anne were nevertheless welcomed and treated well, especially by an elderly waiter who tried to ensure their comfort.

The sisters were shown up a wide shallow staircase to their room on an upper floor. It had a low, beamed ceiling with wainscoting halfway up the walls and high, narrow windows looking out on the narrow Row. The house was so quiet only the occasional sound of footfalls on the flagged street below could be heard, but there would be the sound of bells from nearby St. Paul's to wake them in the morning. They washed their faces, tried to eat a bite of breakfast, and then rested while trying to calm themselves.

It was a momentous day. Both Charlotte and Anne were excited, as well as apprehensive, about visiting the publishers they had never met. They meant to take a horse cab to Charlotte's publisher, but were so nervous they set out walking, through the confusion of crowds, and traffic hindering their progress. It took them nearly an hour to walk the half-mile to their destination: 65 Cornhill. What happened when they arrived is best described in a letter Charlotte wrote to Mary Taylor.

"We found 65 to be a large bookseller's shop, in a street almost as bustling as the Strand. We went in, walked up to the counter. There were a great many young men and lads here and there; I said to the first I could accost: 'May I see Mr. Smith?' He hesitated, looked a little surprised. At last we were shown up to Mr. Smith. 'Is it Mr. Smith?' I said, looking up through my spectacles at a tall young man. 'It is.' I then put his own letter into his hand directed to Currer Bell. He looked at it and then at me again . . . I laughed at his perplexity—a recognition took place. I gave my real name: Miss Brontë. We were in a small room—ceiled with a great skylight—and there explanations were rapidly gone into. . . . Mr. Smith hurried out and returned quickly with one whom he introduced as Mr. Williams, a pale, mild, stooping man of fifty. . . . Then followed talk—talk—talk; Mr. Williams being silent, Mr. Smith loquacious."[1]

George Smith was a handsome twenty-five-year-old, with dark eyes and hair and a trim build. He was thrilled at the revelation that he had the famous author of *Jane Eyre* in his office. He immediately, excitedly, suggested ideas for entertaining the two country ladies. He invited them to be his guest in his home, which would not have been improper as he shared the house with his mother and sister. They declined. He was enthusiastic about the excitement and drama of introducing them to the great writers he knew.

Charlotte quietly told Mr. Smith and Mr. Williams of their intention to remain anonymous, as the Bell brothers. Only the publishers were being allowed to know their secret. Charlotte must have worried this would not be possible for long. There were already rumors in Haworth connecting Charlotte to *Jane Eyre*. Mr. Smith, probably reluctantly, agreed to keep their secret but must have hoped the reclusive authors would soon decide to announce their true identities. Theirs was the literary story of the year—the unmarried daughters of a country parson were authors of the most talked-about, even revolutionary, books of the year! Sales of *Jane Eyre*—of all three of the Bell brothers' novels—would surely multiply.

The sisters did not want to lose their privacy. They also knew that if their secret came out, their books would be considered even more shocking by some, having been written by women. They explained that the loss of their privacy would be very upsetting to them, and they knew when they got home their sister Emily would be furious with them for having given away her secret identity as well as their own, for Charlotte had announced there were no Bell *brothers*. She told George Smith and Mr. Williams that "we are three sisters."[2] But their new acquaintances were gentlemen, and businessmen, who wanted to keep Currer Bell as a client. They would not reveal their secret.

George Smith wished to take them to the opera that evening. They were reluctant to be seen at such a glittering event, knowing they would be noticeable in their plain dresses. They declined the invitation, as they "had no fine, elegant dresses with us, or in the world."[3] But when the young publisher arrived at their lodgings that night with his sisters in their elegant gowns, Charlotte and Anne gave in. In their unfashionable dresses they had sewn themselves, they were surrounded by a vision from their childhood dreams of beautiful, wealthy ladies and gentlemen in fine clothes. They were met at the opera house by Mr. Williams in formal dress as well.

Charlotte wrote Mary she was very aware of how she and Anne looked, and of "the contrast, which must have been apparent between me and Mr. Smith as I walked with him up the crimson-carpeted staircase of the Opera House and stood amongst a brilliant throng at the box door. . . . Still, I felt pleasantly excited in spite of headache and sickness and conscious clownishness, and I saw Anne was calm and gentle, which she always is."[4] The sisters must have felt they were in one of the Glasstown or Angrian stories of beauty, opulence, and music. It was what they and their siblings had wanted, from childhood— to be published, to be in London, amid the wealthy and the titled they had read about and written about.

They didn't return to the inn until one in the morning and had been awake all the night before. The next morning they were escorted to church by Mr. Williams, and later "Mr. Smith came in his carriage with his mother, to take us to his house to dine . . . the rooms, the drawing-room especially, looked splendid to us."[5]

The next three days were a whirlwind of activity and sightseeing. There were visits to the Royal Academy and the National Gallery, and they dined again with Charlotte's publisher.

The young women took time to shop, splurging on new gloves and parasols. They were laden down with books from Mr. Smith and gifts they had purchased for Emily, Tabby, and Martha Brown.

Anne and Charlotte apparently also visited the publisher, Thomas Newby, perhaps only as representatives of the Bell Brothers. They surely would not have given away their identities to him, as he had proved to be so untrustworthy. They would, however, have warned him again against making his false claim that there was only one author of all the Bell novels.

Their trip cost the equivalent of three-quarters of what a governess earned in a year, but it was a success. Their dreams were coming true.

On the long train ride home on that important and memorable day, did Charlotte and Anne think of the other long journey they had taken, from their first tiny books to the years of writing and dreaming of being authors? Did they talk of the bright future they hoped would be theirs, as Emily and Anne had repeatedly wished for in their diary papers? Their novels were published. Charlotte's *Jane Eyre* was a great success, and her future as a writer looked promising. While they were in London the reviews of Anne's *Tenant of Wildfell Hall* had been published. Many were quite good. The best review recommended her book as "the most interesting novel which we have read for a month."[6] Though many were harsh, even they commented on the author's "considerable abilities."[7] It seemed the sisters had each found an audience of readers. They had achieved literary notice. Any new books by the Bell brothers would be read. All three of their novels had already gone into second printings.

London had been exciting, but the exhausted sisters must have welcomed the idea of home, their comfortable routines, and the resumption of work on their new novels. Perhaps Charlotte wouldn't have to confess giving away Emily's identity. Perhaps there was still hope for Branwell to regain health and self-respect. Perhaps they even talked about what they would do when they got home. After they had rested, how welcome it would be to put on their boots and shawls and bonnets, and join Emily and their dogs for a long walk on Haworth Moor.

20

Take Courage

. . . gone like dreams . . .

Strong-willed, brave, and infuriating Charlotte would achieve almost all she had dreamed of in the happy, hopeful period of her childhood. She would, however, do so without her fellow dreamers—Branwell, Emily, and Anne. Only two months after Charlotte and Anne's successful trip to London, Branwell shockingly died suddenly. His symptoms of tuberculosis had been hidden by his addiction to alcohol and laudanum. At the last he asked his family to forgive him for his misspent life, and prayed with his father—dying in his arms.

Charlotte mourned Branwell, but she was bitter, too, for his wasted life—what she called an *obscure* life. "My poor father naturally thought more of his *only* son than of his daughters, and much and long as he had suffered on his account, he cried out for his loss. . . . 'My son! My son!' and refused to be comforted."[1]

Charlotte would soon write about Branwell more gently: "All his errors—to speak plainly, all his vices—seemed nothing to me in that moment; every wrong he had done, every pain he had caused, vanished; his sufferings only were remembered. . . . He is at rest."[2]

Years later an engineer friend from Branwell's days in Luddendenfoot wrote his impressions of his friend: "Branwell Brontë was no domestic demon—he was just a man moving in a mist, who lost his way."[3]

It rained the day of Branwell's funeral, and a drenched and chilled Emily caught cold. As the weeks passed, her health did not improve. She had all the symptoms of tuberculosis, but she stubbornly refused to seek medical aid until her last day. This caused her family great pain, though it had become clear nothing could be done. A frantic Charlotte had searched the wintry moors for a last sprig of heather for her sister, but Emily seemed not to recognize the bloom. She insisted on feeding the dogs the evening before she died; on the last day, she dressed herself, and combed her hair, though the comb fell from her hand into the fireplace. She made her way downstairs, even attempting to sew. But by afternoon, she was gone, only three months after the loss of Branwell.

"No need now to tremble for the hard frost and the keen wind. Emily does not feel them. She died in a time of promise. We saw her taken from life in its prime,"[4] Charlotte wrote to Ellen Nussey.

Devastated, Mr. Brontë was grateful that kind and capable Mr. Nicholls led the funeral service. Emily was buried next to her mother, brother, two sisters, and aunt in the family vault beneath the floor of her father's church. Her dog, Keeper, who had stayed at her side during her illness, walked beside Mr. Brontë at the head of the small procession from house to church. He followed Emily's coffin to the vault and lay in the family pew during the service. He then took his place outside the door of Emily's bedroom, howling pitifully for days. Charlotte's father told her "you must bear up! I shall sink if you fail me."[5]

Frighteningly, Anne's illness worsened, and her symptoms were the same as Emily had suffered. So to please her family she accepted the nauseating medicine and painful blistering treatment that had not helped her sister Maria years before. It did not help Anne, either, and the doctor told the family there was no hope of her recovering. Describing her fears, Anne wrote a poem that includes these lines:

> . . . .
> A dreadful darkness closes in
>   On my bewildered mind;
> O let me suffer and not sin,
>   Be tortured yet resigned . . .[6]

Still she clung to the thought of the healing properties of fresh air and sunshine in Scarborough, though she knew the finality of the doctor's diagnosis. She prayed to recover, and added more verses that were less desperate, expressing her yearning to live as well as her acceptance of death, if that was her fate.

> If Thou shouldst bring me back to life,
>   More humbled I should be;
> More wise, more strengthened for the strife,
>   More apt to lean on Thee.
>
> Should death be standing at the gate,
>   Thus should I keep my vow:
> But, Lord! whatever be my fate,
>   Oh, let me serve Thee now![7]

Anne believed she would either survive, or she would have a last wish—to see the sea again. Her doctor advised her that the sooner she traveled to the coast the better. A legacy of £200 she had received at the death of her godmother could be used for the trip.

Charlotte was against Anne traveling and delayed the journey as long as she could, until a determined Anne enlisted Ellen to convince Charlotte of her wishes and to accompany them on the trip. Charlotte finally agreed. Mr. Brontë, Tabby, Martha, and perhaps even Mr. Nicholls must have found saying goodbye very painful. As a last parting, Anne would have given Keeper and Flossy a last hug and kiss.

In Scarborough, Anne was able to ride in a donkey cart on the beach (where she begged the driver to take better care of the donkey pulling the cart). From their rented clifftop lodgings (where Anne had previously stayed with the Robinsons), she enjoyed the view of the sea, the castle, and the wide sandy beaches. But only three days after their arrival she died, calmly and peacefully, having told her sister, "Take courage, Charlotte; take courage."[8] Anne was buried in Scarborough on a hill overlooking the sea, in the shadow of the ancient castle ruins. She is the only member of the family not buried in her father's church.

When Charlotte arrived home, "The dogs seemed in strange ecstasy . . . the dumb creatures thought that as I was returned—those who had been so long absent were not far behind."[9]

In a letter to her friend, William Smith Williams, Charlotte wrote, "Waking, I think, sleeping, I dream of them."[10] Three months after Anne's death, Charlotte wrote about the loss of her siblings "had a prophet . . . foretold the autumn, the winter, the spring of sickness and suffering . . . I should have thought—this can never be endured. It is over. Branwell—Emily—Anne are gone like dreams."[11]

Writing saved Charlotte as it had done so often for her siblings and herself. She had begun her next novel, *Shirley*, before the loss of her family members. The characters were inspired by her family and friends, but with the loss of her siblings, the story changed. The title character was based on Emily, if she had had the benefit of good health, wealth, and security. The story was about the Luddite riots her father had talked about when she was a child, set in the area where she had gone to school.

James Taylor, the manager of Smith, Elder, offered to deliver the finished manuscript to the publishing office. Charlotte tried to prevent his visit by using her favorite excuse—her father—for just about anything she wanted to avoid. This added Mr. Taylor and others at the publishing house to the list of those who pitied Charlotte and thought her father selfish, difficult, and eccentric.

The determined Scotsman persevered and arrived at the parsonage to collect Charlotte's novel. Mr. Taylor and Charlotte had become pen-friends, but when she met him in person she didn't like him. She was probably shocked to discover that he had a strong resemblance to Branwell. Short in stature, he had red hair and a prominent nose. He would later also be her third suitor.

Amazingly, *Shirley* was published only five months after Anne's death. Though not as popular as *Jane Eyre*, the novel was a success and sold well. The Taylors, the Nusseys, and other inhabitants of Gomersal and Birstall all recognized themselves. This surprised Charlotte who always claimed she didn't use real people in her novels. She sent a copy to Mary. Her old friend wrote back, "What a little lump of perfection you've made me!"[12]—but she liked the novel.

Charlotte seemed to be trying to avoid the parsonage as much as she could by visiting friends. That first Christmas after Anne's death, Charlotte went to visit Ellen Nussey; Mr. Brontë spent the holiday alone.

By early 1850, it was widely suspected in Yorkshire that Charlotte Brontë was Currer Bell. Finally a newspaper piece in the *Bradford Observer* on February 28 announced, "It is understood that the only daughter of the Rev P Brontë, incumbent of Haworth is the authoress of *Jane Eyre* and *Shirley*." Charlotte had finally—after Anne's death—admitted to Ellen the secret of the writing Bell "brothers"—long after she had told Mary Taylor. Now the closely guarded secret was out. She wrote to Mr. Williams that "I no longer walk invisible."[13]

Charlotte was invited to visit her publisher, George Smith, and his family in London. Mary Taylor later wrote that Charlotte's idea of literary fame was being able to join "the society of clever people."[14] London was where she would find them. There she was treated to sightseeing, an art exhibition, Shakespearean plays, and a dinner party where she met several famous literary critics as well as her idol, William Thackeray, who had handled her awkward dedication to him with such ease. She and Mr. Smith were becoming good friends, forming a comfortable, teasing relationship. In Victorian England, there may have been eyebrows raised by their lack of formality.

Some of Charlotte's friends believed Carolyn Helstone in *Shirley* was based on Anne (or even Charlotte herself), though Ellen Nussey believed she, herself, was the inspiration for the important character. Charlotte had included unflattering portraits of her father's curates in the novel, including Arthur Bell Nicholls. In her letters to Mr. Williams, she commented on the curate's reactions to their portrayal in *Shirley*: " each characteristically finds solace for his own wounds in crowing over his brethren."[15]

Charlotte must have approved of Mr. Nicholls's response to his own characterization, which indicated a sense of humor and lack of ego. Charlotte wrote, "Mr. Nicholls has finished reading *Shirley*; he is delighted with it. John Brown's wife [Nicholls's landlady] seriously thought he had gone wrong in the head as she heard him giving vent to roars of laughter as he sat alone, clapping his hands and stamping on the floor. He would read all the scenes about the curates aloud to Papa. He triumphed in his own character." He had fared better than the rest of the curates, and was described as "decent, decorous, and conscientious." But Charlotte added, "Being human . . . he had his faults; these, however, were proper, steady-going, clerical faults: the circumstance of finding himself invited to tea with a dissenter would unhinge him for a week; the spectacle of a Quaker wearing his hat in the church . . . these things could make strange havoc in Mr. Macarthey's [Arthur Nicholls's] physical and mental economy; otherwise he was sane and rational, diligent and charitable."[16]

Before her next trip to London, Charlotte bought pretty new dresses, a striking lace cape, and an outwardly sober bonnet that was lined with bright pink silk. Trying to look more stylish, Charlotte had pinned a false hair piece—which apparently did not look realistic—to her own hair. It resulted in an amused reaction (especially from society ladies she met), which she had not noticed. With her identity now known, her company was sought by famed writers, critics, and other members of society, including William Thackeray. Mr. Smith or Mr. Williams escorted her to operas, museums, and the Royal Academy. She was taken to the Chapel Royal, where she saw the Duke of Wellington and was able to follow him to get a better look so she could share with her father the excitement and nostalgia of seeing the great man.

But Charlotte was haunted, too. She saw the faces of her lost loved ones in people she met. In London, she saw Emily in the face of literary critic J. H. Lewes. She wrote Ellen, "the aspect of Lewes' face almost moves me to tears; it is so wonderfully like Emily—her eyes, her features, the very nose . . . even, at moments, the expression." She saw Mary Taylor's charming little sister in the face of Julia Kavanagh, a young author she met—"it was Martha (Taylor) in every lineament."[17]

Writing about her years later, George Smith described Charlotte as having a "quaint old-fashioned look. . . . I believe that she would have given all her genius and her fame to have been beautiful. Perhaps few women ever existed more anxious to be pretty than she, or more angrily conscious of the circumstance that she was *not* pretty."[18]

Charlotte reluctantly allowed Mr. Smith to arrange to have her portrait done as a gift from him. Celebrated artist George Richmond had drawn and painted many of the most famous literary figures of the day. When the artist had her remove the false hair piece, the humiliation upset her so much that the artist would not allow her to see the portrait until it was finished. She burst into tears when she saw it, believing the portrait was more a likeness of Anne than herself. The artist had created a flattering representation

GEORGE SMITH

WILLIAM SMITH WILLIAMS

of Charlotte, choosing to downplay her crooked mouth and square jaw. But everyone agreed Richmond had accurately captured the beauty of her large, luminous eyes.

Mr. Smith sent the portrait and another thoughtful gift—a small, framed likeness of the Duke of Wellington—which father and daughter were pleased to receive. Mr. Brontë and Tabby believed the portrait of Charlotte made her look too old. Tabby, whose eyesight was very poor, thought the representation of the Duke was of "the Master" (Mr. Brontë), so her opinion was not helpful!

In July, Charlotte joined George Smith and his sister and brother for a brief holiday in Scotland. A trip down the Rhine River with Mr. Smith and his sister was being considered by the friends. In London, there were gossipy rumors of marriage. Ellen believed Charlotte was again in love—with cheerful, considerate, and handsome George Smith. A sign of their easy, even affectionate, relationship was Charlotte's use of her publisher's first name—only used by close friends of the opposite sex in the Victorian era. His mother was not pleased. Charlotte was eight years older than her son and—knowing about the family history of tuberculosis—she did not believe Charlotte was healthy.

Ellen asked Charlotte if she was marrying George Smith. Charlotte admitted she had thought of the possibility, writing, "Were there no vast barrier of fortune, etc., etc., there is perhaps enough of personal regard to make things possible which are now impossible."[19] Her feelings for him were stronger than she admitted to Ellen.

Sir James Kay-Shuttleworth, a wealthy doctor and celebrated education reformer who had retired due to ill health, was one of the people eager to meet Charlotte. He enjoyed entertaining and cultivating the acquaintance of literary figures, and was thrilled Charlotte Brontë lived just across the moors from his home in Lancashire. He was determined to take a reluctant Charlotte under his wing, introducing his trophy to famous and important people. His motives seem to have been a combination of kindness and self-interest.

Upon meeting Sir James, Charlotte wrote, "I wish he may be as sincere as he is polished. He shows his white teeth with too frequent a smile."[20] When she could no longer avoid the invitations, she visited their stately home, Gawthorpe Hall (so reminiscent of an Angrian mansion!). Charlotte admitted she had enjoyed her visit, as she later enjoyed a visit with them in the Lake District, where she met fellow guest and novelist Elizabeth Gaskell. But

Charlotte wished to avoid a stay in Kay-Shuttleworth's London home, where she would be paraded before his society friends. In London, she preferred to stay with the Smiths.

Mr. Smith wanted to publish new editions of *Wuthering Heights* and *Agnes Grey*. Charlotte insisted on including a biographical notice; she would present her sisters in the way she wished them to be seen and remembered. She would answer the critics who had labeled them as coarse and brutal because of the books they had written. Her representation of Emily and Anne was of two innocent, naïve young women who were uneducated, had rarely been away from home, and were so unsophisticated in their secluded lives that they hardly knew what they were writing. She included some of Emily and Anne's poetry, but she had edited them—often even changing their meanings. About Emily she wrote, "An interpreter ought always to have stood between her and the world."[21] Charlotte considered herself that interpreter. She did not admit she had rewritten or, in one case, probably composed an entirely new poem herself, claiming it was Emily's.

Charlotte wished to regain the approval of society for herself and her sisters. Even Miss Wooler disapproved of *Jane Eyre*. Charlotte was conflicted in many areas of her life—she wrote controversial books, but she wished to be seen as the proper Victorian lady she was. She loved her sisters, but her actions indicate condescension, disapproval, and even jealousy. She was sometimes secretive about Emily, perhaps overaccentuating Emily's differences—her *singularities*. Charlotte did not understand either sister. Lack of Emily's—and Anne's—personal papers is not the only reason we know little about them. Charlotte was an unreliable witness to their lives.

Even after her sisters' deaths, Charlotte was interfering with the lives they had lived and the work they had produced. They had always tried to ignore her attempts to direct and control them. But now there was no one to stop her.

Charlotte had complained all her life that she was misunderstood, but it was Charlotte, herself, who first created a fictitious version of her sisters—and of herself. Elizabeth Gaskell would later add Branwell and Mr. Brontë to the myth. Charlotte wished to protect her sisters' reputations (and her own). Perhaps the most unkind decision she made concerned Anne's *Tenant of Wildfell Hall*. She told George Smith—who wanted to reprint *Tenant*—not to do so. She didn't like the novel, even though it had many admirers and had been selling well, rivaling the sales of *Jane Eyre*. It would be many years before Anne's novel would be republished. It is still in print. Anne is now appreciated for her talent, her brave and progressive effort to promote justice and equal rights for women, and for being the first innovative writer whose female heroine was realistic, ordinary, and plain. There is an unanswered question concerning Emily's purported work-in-progress—her second book, mentioned in a letter from her publisher. Did Emily destroy her own manuscript, or did Charlotte—disliking it as she had disliked *Wuthering Heights* and Anne's *Tenant of Wildfell Hall*?

James Taylor was being sent to India for five years to start a branch of the Smith publishing house. Before leaving he visited the parsonage, where it was obvious to Charlotte (and her father) that he intended to propose. Mr. Brontë favored him as a suitor, but Charlotte found herself recoiling in his presence, and did not encourage him. Her father was annoyed by her reluctance—he favored a long engagement, and welcomed the idea that after his own death a successful gentleman would take care of Charlotte. Charlotte wrote Ellen, "if Mr. Taylor be the only husband fate offers to me, single I must always remain."[22]

Charlotte was a difficult guest. In London, she barely spoke to assembled guests at William Thackeray's house. They expected to hear the entertaining conversation of the famous Currer Bell, but she preferred to sit in a corner speaking to the family governess. At another time, an indignant Charlotte was overly outspoken and sharp-tongued in a heated discussion she instigated with Mr. Thackeray. He had made her angry at a lecture by introducing her to his mother, in a loud voice, as Jane Eyre instead of Miss Brontë. George Smith later wrote of Charlotte, "Strangers used to say that they were afraid of her. She was very quiet and self-absorbed, and gave the impression that she was always engaged in observing and analyzing the people she met."[23] Some found such analysis of themselves off-putting.

Charlotte was escorted to the Great Exhibition of 1851. It was held in the Crystal Palace, an amazing glass building resembling a giant greenhouse. Charlotte described the technological marvels as a spectacular bazaar. It was a creation worthy of the young Brontës' most elaborate Glasstown structures.

Charlotte was intrigued by a belief, fashionable at the time, that one's character and personality could be determined by the shape of one's head: the bumps—"organs"—and indentations in the skull. Charlotte had even included references in her novels to phrenology. It was a quick way to establish a character's qualities. In *Jane Eyre*, character Blanche Ingram comments, "Really your organs of wonder and credulity are easily excited."[24] Mary Taylor wrote, "Charlotte said she could get on with any one who had a bump at the top of their heads (meaning conscientiousness)."[25]

Charlotte and George Smith, pretending to be brother and sister, visited a London phrenologist. Dr. Browne's reading of Charlotte's character seemed remarkably accurate. "Her attachments are strong and enduring—indeed, this is a leading element of her character." She was described as intelligent, nervous, sensitive, and poetic, with a love of beauty. She was ambitious yet insecure, and a perfectionist. "This lady possesses a fine organ of language."[26] Charlotte considered Mr. Smith's reading to be accurate, too, and enjoyed teasing him about it. He believed, "The estimate of my own head was not so happy."[27]

After Mr. Taylor moved to Bombay, he and Charlotte exchanged letters briefly, but she still gave him no reason to believe she would marry him. When he stopped writing, Charlotte missed receiving his letters. She found him interesting—from a distance. But when she asked Mr. Williams—who was a good judge of character—for his thoughts on Mr. Taylor, she was told that the heat in India had not agreed with him. He was well known there for his irritable temper. He was apparently disliked by all. Charlotte had again escaped from a most likely unhappy marriage, and was relieved she had not encouraged his proposal.

Celebrity, the experience she had craved as a young girl dreaming of the lives of wealthy and beautiful people, did not make her happy. Without her siblings to share it with, nothing was as rewarding as she had imagined. Despite her comment as a dramatic twelve-year-old that she would never marry, she wrote Ellen: "the Future sometimes appals me . . . not that I am a *single* woman and likely to remain a *single* woman, but because I am a *lonely* woman and likely to be *lonely*."[28]

Emily's dog, Keeper, died in his sleep close to the anniversary of Emily's death, and was buried in the garden. Flossy was "dull and misses him,"[29] Charlotte wrote. It was another lost connection to Emily.

Charlotte finally began writing a new novel, *Villette*, using as inspiration her experiences at the Pensionnat Heger. As in *Shirley*, most of the characters were based on people she knew. The main character, Lucy Snowe (her name reflecting the frozen misery of the protagonist), was recognizable as Charlotte herself. A critic would later comment, "An atmosphere of pain hangs about the whole."[30] For someone so private, Charlotte had imbued the character of Lucy Snowe with her own unhappiness, loneliness, and frustration.

Monsieur and Madame Heger, and even George Smith and his mother, were characterized in the novel. "Madame Beck" was recognizable as Madame Heger, and it was a very unflattering portrait. Characters and actual places were given new names that Charlotte must have meant to be satirical and humorous but were also insulting. Brussels was called Villette, meaning a small, insignificant town pretending to be a city. The port of Ostend became Boue-Marine, or Sea Mud. Belgium became Labassecour, which can be translated as barnyard. Charlotte was anxious about George Smith's reaction to the novel's plot once he realized he had been included in the story as a man beloved by Lucy Snowe. Despite her fears, Mr. Smith was pleased to recognize himself as handsome, charming Dr. John Bretton, even to his Scottish background, dark hair, and the cleft in his chin. When Mr. Smith asked Charlotte what would happen to his character in the novel, Charlotte told him, "Lucy must not marry Dr. John."[31] Charlotte, herself, may have sabotaged any closer relationship with George Smith by that decision.

As she finished the novel, she panicked that he would not like the ending she had chosen. She did not hear from him for ten days after she sent him the finished manuscript. She was right to worry. He was disappointed—his character had almost disappeared from the novel, replaced by Lucy Snowe's beloved Monsieur Paul (based, of course, on Monsieur Heger). Charlotte tried to explain that "[t]he spirit of romance would have indicated another course . . . but this would have been unlike real life . . . at variance with probability."[32]

George Smith may have been attracted to Charlotte, even toying with the idea of marrying the famous and talked-about author. He was a very ambitious man and enjoyed his own place in society. He wrote, fifty years later, that he had never been in love with her. Had he felt rebuffed by Charlotte's decision concerning Lucy Snowe and Dr. John Bretton? He seems to have taken personally the choice Charlotte made for her novel's plot—much more than a publisher's usual involvement in the production of a writer's work. She admitted that her reading public would probably have preferred the other ending—which was George Smith's strong belief. But Charlotte stubbornly went her own way. Among the criticisms of the novel was that choice, as well as disapproval and disbelief that a woman could love two men at the same time. But the reviews were mostly favorable, and *Villette* was more widely appreciated than *Shirley*. Some critics said it was her best novel yet. It sold well, too. It was a success. Mr. Smith continued to enjoy Charlotte's company and was proud of his reputation of having discovered the famous Charlotte Brontë, but Charlotte's relationship with George Smith may have begun to change.

21

The Purest Gem

"We have been so happy!"

Since Arthur Nicholls's arrival in Haworth years before, villagers and friends had speculated about him and Charlotte being a suitable match. Charlotte hated gossip about herself and had been mostly hostile to him, or any references to him. After the loss of most of her family, however, she had become more pleasant to him, perhaps because he had been so kind and helpful and had mourned with the family the too-early deaths of her siblings. Mr. Nicholls was also a strong, reliable support to Mr. Brontë, and had taken on more and more of the parish work.

Charlotte Brontë, for all her described plainness, eccentricities, and excessive shyness, clearly had charms that appealed to more than one Victorian gentleman. Very possibly when she allowed herself to be known, when she was relaxed and comfortable in another's company, she possessed enough charm, personality, humor, and wit to make up for her lack of beauty. Arthur Nicholls had seen her in all her moods, good and bad, for almost eight years. He knew she was opinionated and moody and had a fiery temper—and he had fallen in love with her. In December 1852, he proposed to her. She had suspected from his recent manner that he would do so, from "his constant looks, and strange, feverish restraint."[1] Mr. Brontë seems to have noticed his odd behavior as well, and had become less friendly to him. The strength of

Arthur Nicholls's love shocked Charlotte. "Shaking from head to foot, looking deadly pale, speaking low, vehemently, yet with difficulty, he made me
for the first time feel what it costs a man to declare affection where he doubts
response,"[2] she wrote to Ellen.

Her father's fury was shocking, too. His anger was so great she feared he
would have a stroke, and quickly turned down the proposal without considering it. Her father was apparently not against Charlotte marrying eventually—he had promoted a long engagement to James Taylor. His reasons
were many—and complex. He did not think his low-paid curate, whom he
believed was from a humble Irish background, was worthy of his now-famous
daughter and believed that Mr. Nicholls might want to marry Charlotte for
her money. He believed she could now find a better prospect. A man of his
times, he was also offended his curate did not ask his permission to propose
to Charlotte. Perhaps his main worry was that young, and surely ambitious,
Arthur Nicholls would take his one remaining child away from Haworth to
seek his own curacy.

But Charlotte now saw Mr. Nicholls as a devoted, rejected suitor, and
couldn't stand to witness his misery or her father's continued hostile treatment of his curate. She escaped to London and the Smith family home. There
was, however, a feeling of mutual unease there as well—especially with Mrs.
Smith since Charlotte had used her hosts as characters in her novel. Still, she
felt less awkward with them than she had felt at home with her furious father
and the now-tragic Mr. Nicholls.

A thought had nagged her for months, that her friends at the publishing
house, and even George Smith's mother, had befriended her for business reasons rather than out of true regard. At the same time, she was concerned that
George Smith was working too hard. He often did, and looked particularly
ill, exhausted, and preoccupied during the visit. It's likely she saw little of
him—possibly an intentional choice on his part. It was a quiet visit, though
Charlotte made a few excursions around London.

William Thackeray wrote to a friend about his opinion of Charlotte, "The
poor little woman of genius! the fiery little eager brave tremulous homely-
faced creature! I can read a great deal of her life as I fancy in her book, and
see that rather than have fame . . . she wants some Tomkins or another to
love her and be in love with. But you see she is a little bit of a creature without a penny worth of good looks, thirty years old I should think, buried in

the country, and eating up her own heart there, and no Tomkins will come. You girls with pretty faces and red boots . . . will get dozens of young fellows fluttering about you—whereas here is one a genius, a noble heart longing to mate itself and destined to wither away into old maidenhood with no chance to fulfil the burning desire."[3] Charlotte, by that time, had received four proposals of marriage.

Once so joyful at the sight of the parsonage when she returned from journeys near and far, Charlotte now dreaded going home. Her father was still furious with Mr. Nicholls, who decided he must leave his position and had dramatically applied for a missionary post in Australia. He would be leaving Haworth in May. Charlotte found his depression painful to be around. He soon withdrew his rash application for the post in Australia. Mr. Brontë and the entire Brown family didn't hide their dislike of him. (Tabby's opinion at this time isn't known.) This antagonism made Charlotte pity him more. She confided in Ellen, "I may be losing the purest gem, and to me far the most precious, life can give—genuine attachment."[4] She again visited friends, trying to escape the dreary atmosphere at home. But she could not stay away long.

After returning to the parsonage from one of her trips, Charlotte found that her father had had the piano moved upstairs from his study. An annoyed Charlotte said the piano was a good place to display books. It was a thoughtless reaction. She had apparently not considered the possibility that her elderly father might sit and stare at the silent piano, remembering the sound of the music once played by his lost children, and their laughter.

Arthur Nicholls broke down during a final Sunday communion service. He "lost command over himself—stood . . . white, shaking, voiceless."[5] Sympathetic women parishioners sobbed throughout the service. Unfortunately Mr. Brontë was told about Mr. Nicholls's behavior, and he did *not* sympathize. The townspeople gossiped and speculated about why Mr. Nicholls was leaving Haworth, but they raised a subscription to show respect for him. The local gentry and other clergymen in town presented him with a gold watch in appreciation of his years of service.

He found another post forty miles away at Kirk Smeaton, and before leaving, he stopped by the parsonage to say goodbye. Charlotte didn't wish to see him, but he lingered so long at the gate to the lane, "sobbing as women never sob," that Charlotte went to speak to him. She could not offer him any hope or encouragement. "I trust he must know . . . that I am not cruelly blind and indifferent to his constancy and grief. . . . However he is gone—gone, and there's an end of it."[6]

Charlotte became ill with nerves. Mr. Brontë, also stressed and perhaps feeling guilty, experienced what Charlotte had feared—a stroke that left him blind. Some vision slowly returned but the loss was serious, and he may have regretted both his fury and the absence of his responsible, formerly valued curate. His replacement was a poor substitute, and his daughter and an efficient curate were needed more than ever to help him with his parish responsibilities.

Tabby had become deaf, but she still expected to be told everything that concerned the household. To avoid being overheard having loud conversations about private matters, Charlotte took Tabby for walks on the moors so she could tell her the latest news. Tabby's eyesight was also failing. She still tried to do her chores, but Charlotte began to secretly redo Tabby's work, repeeling potatoes and perhaps rewashing dishes.

Charlotte confided in her new friend, Elizabeth Gaskell, who visited her in the autumn. She told her about her suitor, and her father's opposition to him. Mrs. Gaskell formed a negative opinion of Charlotte's father, which would result in harm to Mr. Brontë's image and reputation, even to this day. She was concerned about Charlotte's misery and loneliness. "No one comes to the house; nothing disturbs the deep repose; hardly a voice is heard; you catch the ticking of the clock in the kitchen, or the buzzing of a fly in the parlour, all over the house."[7]

Martha told Mrs. Gaskell about Charlotte's lonely pacing every night. "Tabby says . . . Miss Brontë and Miss Emily & Miss Anne used to put away their sewing after prayers, and walk all three one after the other round the table in the parlour till near eleven o'clock. Miss Emily walked as long as she could, and when she died Miss Anne and Miss Brontë took it up—and now my heart aches to hear Miss Brontë walking, walking on alone." Did Mrs. Gaskell, listening at the top of the stairs, believe she heard Charlotte in the parlor late at night? Envisioning the scene, she wrote, "I am sure I should fancy I heard the steps of the dead."[8] She went home determined to make Charlotte's suitor more worthy in Mr. Brontë's eyes. She was an efficient and determined woman who knew many powerful people, and she managed to arrange for Mr. Nicholls to be offered a pension, which puzzled him, and impressive curacies, which he declined.

Charlotte had planned to escape again to London, but at the end of November, she received a brief, awkward letter from George Smith that seemed to hint that something was about to happen. Charlotte wrote his mother for an explanation, and Mrs. Smith responded quickly with the reason for the odd note. Her son was about to be engaged to a young woman he had met at a ball in the spring. She was beautiful and wealthy, and he fell in love with her at first sight.

Charlotte was hurt and perhaps embarrassed at what she might have shown of her attachment to him, and bitter that he may have hinted he might care for her. Charlotte may also have believed Mrs. Smith had interfered with her relationship with him. Charlotte canceled her intended trip to London. She sent back the latest shipment of books kindly lent by Smith, Elder, with a curt note to Mr. Williams not to send more. To George Smith, she wrote a cold and abrupt reply when she received his wedding announcement. Her pain and disappointment were obvious, and it even seemed doubtful her relationship with Mr. Smith and his publishing house would continue.

Charlotte began to think differently about Arthur Nicholls after he was gone and the unpleasantness at the parsonage was ended. She found the thought of him more interesting and appealing. Once considered boring, he was now a romantic, almost tragic figure. Did she realize he resembled a character she could have conjured up for one of her novels? After he had written her a series of unanswered letters she finally relented, and the two began a secret correspondence—a romantic experience worthy of a work of fiction.

Ellen had suffered another disappointment concerning her latest possible suitor. She and Charlotte had exchanged many letters through the years discussing men Ellen thought were going to propose, but no one ever had. She didn't want Charlotte to marry while it appeared she never would. She wrote to determinedly single Mary Taylor, believing she would have an ally, but Mary was not an ally. She believed if Charlotte wanted to marry Mr. Nicholls she should do so. Ellen's disapproval of Charlotte's interest in Arthur Nicholls and her strong opposition to him angered Charlotte. They argued and parted. Incredibly, it appeared their long friendship was over.

Charlotte felt deserted and alone. Mary Taylor was far away. She was estranged from her father and the friends she relied on the most—George Smith and Ellen Nussey. The exchange of letters with Arthur Nicholls continued. Elderly Tabby, set in her ways, insisted on collecting and handing out the mail each day, but Charlotte didn't worry about being found out. Tabby would keep Charlotte's secret. Mr. Nicholls arranged two clandestine meetings with Charlotte on country lanes near Haworth. Here was someone who, like herself, had deep emotions and was faithful and devoted. Perhaps Charlotte also thought about how satisfying it would be to send George Smith an announcement of her own wedding? All the months of loneliness and confusion were almost over, and Charlotte knew what she wanted to happen next and proceeded to bring it about.

She told her father she had been exchanging letters with Arthur Nicholls and had even met with him. She insisted she wished to get to know him better. Stubbornly, her father believed Charlotte should marry someone more important than a poor curate. Charlotte answered him: "I must marry a curate if I marry at all; not merely a curate but *your* curate. Not merely *your* curate but he must live in the house with you, for I cannot leave you."[9]

Charlotte's father didn't speak to her for a week, and she was ill again from stress. Tabby stood up for the last of the children she had helped raise, asking Mr. Brontë if he wished to kill his daughter. The emotional havoc was not good for anyone in the household. Mr. Brontë relented—sanctioning their letters, their meetings, and inevitably their marriage.

Charlotte had decided to marry Arthur Nicholls. If there was not love on her part, there would be enough of affection. Just as she had told her father of her intentions, she probably informed her fiancé that they would be staying in Haworth to take care of her father. He would take up his old position as her father's curate as soon as the present assistant could find another curacy. Charlotte reported to Miss Wooler that her father was now content, interested in the wedding preparations, and all was returning to normal.

Charlotte's fictional creations in her stories since childhood (probably as well as her greatest love—Constantin Heger) were strong, even domineering men. But Charlotte, in real life, was an independent-minded, managing woman. At the end of *Jane Eyre*, Mr. Rochester is a blind, weakened version of himself. She has the man she wants, but she is now in charge—at least for a while. That's Charlotte Brontë's real character, which she showed in her planning of her life with Arthur Nicholls.

After months of estrangement, Miss Wooler interceded between Charlotte and Ellen. They put aside their anger and became friends again, though Charlotte soon informed Ellen she would be marrying Arthur Nicholls.

Charlotte did not send a wedding announcement to George Smith, but her news was clear in a curt note she sent regarding a business matter. The absence of polite good wishes to him was an obvious indication of her continued ill will. His response and congratulations, however, was lengthy, kind, and friendly as he always was. She sent a reluctant reply, which included good wishes to the members of the Smith family she knew, but about his new wife she pointedly wrote, "I hardly know in what form of greeting to include your wife's name, as I have never seen her. Say to her whatever may seem to you most appropriate and most expressive of goodwill."[10] Without embarrassment, Charlotte made no effort to conceal her jealousy and disappointment.

June 29 was chosen for Charlotte and Arthur's wedding day. The night before, Mr. Brontë said he did not feel well enough to attend the wedding. Charlotte believed him, but whether it was illness or his own complex reasons for not attending is not known. Mr. Brontë was an old man, probably still frightened of losing Charlotte. And some believe the absence of the rest of his children at such an important family event would have been too painful to witness. After a flurry of confusion, it was decided motherly Miss Wooler could act as his proxy and give the bride away. Ellen was bridesmaid, and Sutcliffe Sowden, the groom's best friend (who had also been an old friend of Branwell), officiated at the ceremony.

Charlotte wore an embroidered white muslin dress; a white bonnet decorated with flowers, leaves, and lace; and a short veil. She wrapped a lace mantle around her shoulders in the cool morning air. She was described by the few invited guests—close friends, Tabby, Martha and her father, John Brown—as looking like a snow drop. It was common practice to be married in the morning, so there was a festive wedding breakfast. The church, house, and breakfast table were decorated with as many flowers as Martha Brown could obtain from the neighbors' gardens. The young maid, who had probably already returned to her former positive opinion of Mr. Nicholls, would have enjoyed the excitement and romance of the day. Tabby may have shed tears, seeing her "bairn" finally married.

The couple left the same day for their honeymoon, spending several days in Wales and then crossing by packet steamer to Ireland. In Dublin, where Mr. Nicholls had attended university, he shared his favorite places with his new wife. Arthur introduced Charlotte to his brother and cousins, including his cousin Mary Anna, whom Charlotte described as "a pretty lady-like girl

CHARLOTTE & ARTHUR

with gentle English manners."[11] They escorted the newlyweds to Banagher, eighty miles away, where Charlotte met Mrs. Bell, Arthur's aunt (who, with her late husband, had raised Arthur). She was dignified, well bred, and had briefly attended a girls' school in London, which impressed determinedly English Charlotte. Arthur's uncle had been the well-respected director of a boys' school at large and impressive Cuba House—now the residence of his widow and daughter.

Charlotte, with a tendency to look down on the Irish despite her father's heritage and her own half-Irish lineage, may have believed she was marrying beneath her. She and her father had considered him to be a poor Irishman with few advantages. Charlotte admitted, "My dear husband . . . appears in a new light in his own country. . . . More than once I have had deep pleasure in hearing his praises on all sides. Some of the old servants and followers of the family tell me I am a most fortunate person, for that I have got one of the best gentlemen in the country."[12]

She could see for herself the Bell family was refined and comfortably well off, with gracious manners and a fine home. Her husband was loved and respected. She had underestimated Arthur Nicholls. Mr. Brontë would have found the news gratifying.

Charlotte had no intention of visiting her own, less impressive, Irish relatives. She did not wish to see how they lived or to introduce them to her new husband. Charlotte and Arthur continued their wedding trip, visiting the wild west coast with its dramatic views of the ocean. They then traveled on through the spectacular beauty of southwest Ireland. She had worried that Arthur was not intellectual, but he'd had a fine education. She also found she shared a sense of humor with Arthur, and appreciated that he was not a braggart and (importantly) didn't hurry her when she wished to linger over the beauties of nature. He was perceptive and sensitive to her feelings, and he loved her for herself, not her fame. She was gratified to realize that she and her new husband were a compatible couple. He had turned out to be the strong and romantic man she had always dreamed of, who was just dominant enough. It was clear, from letters she wrote to friends, that she was very happy.

Considering Charlotte was timid when it came to animals even as docile as cows, it's surprising she consented to a trip through a dangerous section of the Gap of Dunloe on horseback. Charlotte's horse panicked, and she fell to the ground—just escaping being trampled—to the consternation of her husband. She was not hurt, and the frightening incident didn't mar the trip, but at the end of the month a happy Charlotte was ready to return to the parsonage to begin her life as a cleric's wife.

Mr. Nicholls immediately plunged back into the work of the parish, and Charlotte was busy helping him with his work. Apparently the position of curate's *wife* made the work less tiresome than when she was a curate's daughter, for her letters mentioning her duties were cheerful and uncomplaining. She was content, and when she wasn't filled with anxieties, her health was excellent. She was in better health than she had been in years.

Her father was pleased to have a smoothly running parish again. He had come to terms with having a son-in-law in the parsonage. Charlotte had redone the storage room behind the parlor, turning it into an office for her husband with new paint and wallpaper, and green and white curtains she made herself. Her father's work space and schedule were not disrupted. He may have admitted to himself quite soon that he liked his curate again.

So happy in their own marriage, Charlotte and Arthur had tried to play matchmaker for Ellen with Sutcliffe Sowden. But their cleric friend showed no interest in long-suffering Ellen, who had been so unlucky in attracting a husband.

There were speculations among her friends that Mr. Nicholls would keep Charlotte from writing after their marriage. He wrote later of an icy, windy evening, sitting before the fire, when Charlotte told him it was just such a night when she would have been writing. She ran upstairs and brought down the beginnings of a new novel she had worked on briefly, months before. She read it to him, explaining how she usually wrote several beginnings before she was satisfied. A storyteller since childhood, it's likely she would have eventually decided it was time to bring out her writing box to seriously work on her new novel. Arthur Nicholls expressed no objections to her continuing to write.

Arthur later wrote to a friend that he never interfered with anything Charlotte chose to do. During their marriage, they were together every day and never had a disagreement between them of any kind.

It had been a year since Keeper's death when the entire household was saddened by the death of Anne's beloved dog. Charlotte wrote Ellen, "our poor little Flossy is dead. . . . He drooped for a single day, and died quietly in the night without pain. The loss . . . was very saddening, yet perhaps no dog ever had a happier life or an easier death."[13]

Ellen and Charlotte were exchanging letters again when Ellen was given a new reason to dislike Arthur Nicholls. Charlotte wrote her that her husband thought women's letters were incautious, and should never be kept. He had said, "they are dangerous as lucifer matches."[14] Charlotte didn't seem to mind or to consider her husband was interfering with her writing to her friends. In fact, she thought the idea of her letters being dangerous was amusing—but Ellen was furious. Because of Charlotte's fame, Mr. Nicholls was seriously concerned that her letters might be read by someone other than Ellen who might find insult or scandal in her words. He said Charlotte's letters must be burned or there should be no more, and he wanted Ellen's promise or he would censor their correspondence. His dictatorial attitude would have been common in a Victorian husband.

Charlotte didn't mind the dictate. She had probably not saved any of Ellen's letters, but Ellen had preserved all of Charlotte's since they were girls, and they were even more precious now that Charlotte was famous. She intended to keep them. Ellen sent a note agreeing to the pledge if he would not interfere with their correspondence. She never intended to burn them, however, and future fans and literary scholars have been grateful for her decision, however dishonest it was. She justified her inaction by the fact that she believed Mr. Nicholls would not stop censoring Charlotte's letters. Charlotte, however, told Ellen, "we may now write any dangerous stuff we please to each other."[15]

At the six-month anniversary of her marriage, Charlotte reported to Ellen how happy she was with her husband: "he is 'my dear boy,'—certainly dearer now than he was six months ago."[16]

Charlotte caught a lingering cold, followed by nausea and faintness that did not go away. She was pregnant and unable to eat or drink. Tabby was deathly ill from typhus, and it was painful for Charlotte to be unable to see the dearly loved old friend one last time—as it must have been for the elderly woman. Tabby was buried by the wall close to the parsonage, her grave visible from Charlotte's window.

Martha urged Charlotte to think ahead to the happy time when her baby was born, but Charlotte could still keep neither food nor drink down, and her continuing sickness was frightening. She managed to write a short note to Ellen. "I find in my husband the tenderest nurse, the kindest support, the best earthly comfort that ever woman had. His patience never fails, and it is tried by sad days and broken nights. . . . Our poor old Tabby is *dead and buried!*"[17]

By the time Charlotte could eat small amounts it was, tragically, too late. Doctors of the period had nothing to offer as treatment. She was too dehydrated and too worn down to recover. At the last, hearing her husband desperately praying for her recovery, she whispered, "I am not going to die—am I? *He* will not separate us! We have been *so* happy!"[18]

St. Michael's bells tolled for Charlotte the day of her funeral, calling the mourners—father, husband, and friends. It tolled for "the villagers who had known her from a child, and whose hearts shivered within them as they thought of the two . . . desolate and alone in the old grey house."[19]

Epilogue

Forever Known

. . . men and women of deep feelings . . .

In the months after Charlotte's death, the devastated Arthur Nicholls and Patrick Brontë became closer than they had ever been. They could share their grief and were companionable company for one another, living together in the old parsonage.

An article in *Sharpe's London Magazine* included ridiculous claims about Charlotte's life. At first, Mr. Brontë and Arthur laughed about the article, but both Ellen and Elizabeth Gaskell suggested there should be an accurate biography of Charlotte. Charlotte's father quickly decided he wanted Mrs. Gaskell to take on the project, which was originally thought would be a magazine article. Though Mr. Nicholls objected, he didn't like to go against the wishes of Charlotte's father. Mrs. Gaskell was delighted. She had already begun planning to write Charlotte's story. Ironically, and unknown to Charlotte's father and widower, she had been the scandal-monger responsible for the inaccurate details in *Sharpe's*.

Mrs. Gaskell barely consulted Mr. Brontë and Mr. Nicholls as she researched Charlotte's life. In an effort to excuse the image of Charlotte as the author of books described as coarse, brutal, and even anti-Christian, she decided to blame Charlotte's father and the manner in which she and her siblings were raised (their happy childhood!) for what was considered at the time to be the shocking lack of morality in his daughters' novels. She also held accountable the town where they were raised.

Ellen didn't like Mr. Brontë or Mr. Nicholls, nor did a few local gossips Mrs. Gaskell spoke to in Haworth. They became her main sources. She made no effort to verify the stories she was told. She listened to Ellen's biased and resentful opinions, and used Charlotte's private letters (which Mr. Nicholls believed had been burned) for much of the biography. Ellen contributed to the myth being created about the entire Brontë family. She edited anything that didn't show Charlotte in the way she wished her to be remembered. She may also have destroyed what Charlotte had written about Emily and Anne (presuming there was more than what has survived). Mrs. Gaskell had obtained Charlotte's letters to her father from Mr. Brontë, but Arthur Nicholls expected to express his wishes about Mrs. Gaskell's use of them. He wrote to Ellen with the expectation that any letters she had kept would be used "not for publication, but merely to give the writer [Mrs. Gaskell] an insight into her [Charlotte's] mode of thought."[1] Mrs. Gaskell wrote to Mary Taylor in New Zealand, asking for reminiscences. Mary complied but was careful not to share any confidences. For the rest of her life, she refused to be interviewed about the Brontës.

Mrs. Gaskell traveled to Brussels and spoke to Monsieur Heger, asking about his opinion of Charlotte and Emily, and taking away essays the sisters had written. She wanted to speak to Madame Heger, who refused the request, having read a pirated French version of *Villette*. She was still angry—probably about almost every detail of the novel.

Not included in the biography was Charlotte's obsessive love for Monsieur Heger. Charlotte's flirtatious feelings for William Weightman were also left out. She did, however, unkindly include Charlotte's lack of enthusiasm in accepting Arthur Nicholls's emotional initial proposal.

Sir James Kay-Shuttleworth joined forces with Mrs. Gaskell, and by treachery, dishonesty, and lies, descended on the parsonage. Sir James ignored Mr. Nicholls's protests and took what he wanted for the biography. Charlotte's last unfinished story, the young Brontes' tiny handmade books, and the manuscript of *The Professor*, all pried from Mr. Brontë's—and especially Mr. Nicholls's—reluctant hands, for Mrs. Gaskell's research and curiosity. Though Mr. Nicholls had previously refused permission, the overbearing Sir James announced that a photographer would be sent to the parsonage to take a photograph of Charlotte's portrait, to be used in the biography. Sir James and Mrs. Gaskell believed *The Professor* should now be published, wishing to edit it themselves. Arthur Nicholls, who reluctantly agreed to its publication, insisted that only he would edit it. Charlotte's first, flawed, novel—which had been rejected previously many times—would be published by Smith, Elder but receive little notice.

Even George Smith, who could be ruthless when business was involved, had helped Mrs. Gaskell in her efforts to obtain what she wanted for the biography. When she realized Ellen did not own the copyright to Charlotte's letters to her, Mrs. Gaskell schemed with George Smith to get Mr. Nicholls's signature transferring the copyright of everything used in the biography to her. Arthur Nicholls would not sign. George Smith then accused him of refusing to honor an arrangement previously made with Mrs. Gaskell. "I never authorized her to publish a single line of my wife's MS & correspondence . . . such a thing was never mentioned." Arthur Nicholls was angry and frustrated, but he signed the document. The project had "from beginning to end . . . been a source of pain . . . nothing but an unwillingness to thwart Mr. Brontë's wishes could have induced me to acquiesce."[2]

Charlotte's trusting, still-grieving father and husband were not up to the task of dealing with the determined and grasping trio.

Mrs. Gaskell didn't show the biography to Charlotte's father and widower before it went to press, though they had requested she write it and believed they could read it before publication. She did show it to Ellen. *The Life of Charlotte Brontë* was a huge success. Mrs. Gaskell was given £800 for the English copyright of the biography—more than Charlotte had ever received for any of her novels. (Emily and Anne never received any money from their novels.) Mrs. Gaskell sent £100 to Mr. Nicholls for a new pump for Haworth village.

The popularity of the biography did help the sale of Charlotte's novels, as well as Emily's and Anne's, and in Haworth a tourist industry was being created. The curious came to visit the town and were puzzled it bore no resemblance to Mrs. Gaskell's dramatic and very unflattering version of a Haworth a hundred years in the past. Though the townspeople had been angered by the inaccurate description of the town in the biography, they benefited from the many tourists who stayed at inns and visited taverns and shops.

The Life of Charlotte Brontë, with its misrepresentations, omissions, unkind characterizations, and outrageous claims, is an absorbing recounting of Charlotte's life, written by a contemporary. It is considered a landmark biography. Its ongoing success ensured the fascination with the Brontës would last—constantly renewing interest in them, their novels, and even the town where they lived.

The reputations of Charlotte, and even her sisters, were restored. Mrs. Gaskell had presented Charlotte as sacrificing, unselfish, suffering, and saintly. Mr. Brontë's and Branwell's reputations were destroyed in the eyes of readers. Emily and Anne are portrayed as naïve and uneducated. The continuing myth of Charlotte's life was the image of her as a martyr. The reading public forgave the perceived coarseness and brutality in the sisters' novels. But the biography was invasive and—written so soon after Charlotte's death—was painful to Arthur Nicholls, who was so private himself and so protective of Charlotte.

The parsonage became a magnet for admirers of the Brontës and their work. Mr. Nicholls attempted to fend off most of the visitors who wished to meet him or Charlotte's father, but Mr. Brontë liked to talk with Charlotte's admirers. When they asked for souvenirs, he gave them snippets of Charlotte's handwriting from letters she had written him. Americans were among her greatest admirers and seem to have been preferred visitors at the parsonage. Several made it past Arthur Nicholls. When one expressed how different the town and Mr. Brontë, himself, were from Charlotte's biography, both he and Mr. Nicholls smiled and said, "Well, I think Mrs. Gaskell tried to make us all appear as bad as she could."[3]

One visitor to the parsonage would have astonished the young Brontës, driving in their disreputable gig to Bolton Abbey many years before. If they had known that one day the Duke of Devonshire would invite their father (and Charlotte's husband!) to visit him at his grand house at Bolton Abbey, would they have been astonished? Or would they have accepted it as an example of their childhood belief that their dreams could come true? Certainly it would have seemed that anything could be possible.

The most maligned individual in the biography was Mr. Brontë, who was called a "monster" by one reviewer. He was accused of cruelty to his wife and children and of having a violent temper. His friends were incensed and wrote articles in the press about Mrs. Gaskell's malicious and inaccurate portrait of him. But Mr. Brontë, exhibiting his lack of ego, complained very little.

There were loud complaints about the book from others. The recently remarried Lady Scott (Branwell's Lydia Robinson) threatened a lawsuit, as did William Carus Wilson (of Cowan Bridge School). Mr. Brontë didn't want to complain too loudly about his own misrepresentation. He didn't want the veracity of the biographer doubted. He wanted his daughters—Charlotte, especially, with her greater fame—to be loved and respected. But he did ask Mrs. Gaskell to remove reference to the Garrs sisters being wasteful, as they were hurt and fearful their reputations would be harmed. He also wanted the worst of her claims about him to be removed—burning hearthrugs, sawing the arms off furniture, cutting up his wife's dress, denying his children meat, and burning their boots. He told his friends, "I never was subject to those explosions of passion ascribed to me, and never perpetuated those excentric [sic] and ridiculous movements."[4] It took until the third edition before the statements purported to be libelous and the ridiculous lies about Mr. Brontë were removed from the biography.

Arthur Nicholls kept his promise to stay in Haworth, looking after his father-in-law. Mr. Brontë preached at least one sermon on Sundays and performed what other duties he could manage, but, by 1855, Mr. Nicholls had assumed all of the work of the parish. Mr. Brontë was able to spend his last years in the parsonage that had been his home since 1820.

Mr. Brontë's health continued to decline. Confined to bed, with Martha Brown to care for him, he still retained a clear head. He was happy when an old cleric friend managed to travel through a snowstorm to visit him on his eighty-fourth birthday in 1861. Two and a half months later, he died, with Arthur Nicholls and Martha Brown by his bedside. He had lived to see many improvements in Haworth, which he had worked for forty years to bring about. He had even finally managed to convince the Board of Health in London to investigate the unhealthy conditions in Haworth that had been responsible for so many deaths. Changes had come and plans made to supply the town with fresh water. His will had been made six years before his death, leaving all but some small bequests (to relatives and to Martha Brown) to his "beloved and esteemed son-in-law . . . for his own absolute benefit."[5]

The shops in Haworth closed voluntarily the day of his funeral. Hundreds attended, spilling out of the church into the churchyard. No close family members had outlived him to mourn his death. Arthur Nicholls, Martha Brown and her sister and mother, Nancy Garrs, and Sutcliffe Sowden were the chief mourners who followed the coffin into the church. Arthur Nicholls was overcome with grief.

Patrick Brontë, whose death had been feared most of his children's lives, had outlived them all. The brief life spans of the siblings were not unusual for their time and place, but they were made more poignant by the fact that most of their friends and acquaintances lived long lives. Arthur Nicholls and George Smith lived into the next century. Ellen Nussey, Mary Taylor, Miss Wooler, the Garrs sisters, Martha Brown, and the Hegers all lived into old age.

Arthur Bell Nicholls, shockingly, was deprived of the Haworth curacy due to church politics. He returned to Ireland, to farm. He was eventually married, happily, to his cousin Mary Anna, "the pretty lady-like girl" Charlotte had met and liked on their honeymoon trip.

Neither Mary Taylor nor Ellen Nussey ever married. Mary returned from New Zealand, having prospered from her hard work there. She lived the rest of her life in comfort. Ellen, who never sought employment, lived a long life of genteel poverty, relying on her brothers' support.

Martha Brown also never married. For the rest of her life, she traveled back and forth to Ireland as the guest of the Nichollses, apparently still considered a member of the Brontë family.

Images of Charlotte and her family's lives were preserved as written by Elizabeth Gaskell in her *Life of Charlotte Brontë* and repeated in a profusion of future biographies. As new information has come to light, efforts are being made to discover more of the truth of their lives. Emily and Anne, with their papers destroyed and their preference for confiding primarily in each other, will probably always be mysteries.

The unusual upbringing their father gave his four remarkable children provided them with freedom to learn and create. Branwell's influence on his sisters should never be discounted in the development of their talents. Creative play—writing—occupied much of their lives as children. Writing became their lives as adults.

The common belief that the Brontës' lives were grim, unrelieved tragedy, and despair is false. Many of their childhood dreams were fulfilled. Their short lives, as do most lives, included tragedy, but also included much satisfaction and happiness.

The remote, evocative world of parsonage, hill town, and moors provided a beloved haven of safety for them all. The Brontë story is one of family love, their actions often governed by their love of, and need for, one another. The old parsonage on the edge of Haworth Moor drew the siblings like a magnet when they were too long away. The moors stretching beyond their gate pulled at them, too, representing freedom. Despite their reputations for eccentricity, remoteness, and preference for solitude, they were kind and warmhearted. In the town where they spent their lives they were fondly remembered. Sexton William Brown (John's brother) said Mr. Brontë "was the most truly kind & considerate man, for the feeling and rights of others that ever was known." The sisters were always described as gentle and kind. Branwell, while they acknowledged his faults and errors, was their favorite. "To him they attribute . . . every accomplishment . . . to them he was the perfection of a fine gentleman . . . he knew everything and could do anything."[6]

In discussing the characters in the novels of Currer Bell, critic G. H. Lewes could have been describing the Brontë family when he wrote, "They are men and women of deep feelings, clear intellects, vehement tempers. . . . Their address is brusque . . . individual, direct. . . . The power that is in them makes its vehement way right to your heart."[7]

The solitary, creative childhood Charlotte, Emily, and Anne led gave their work originality, and originality made their novels memorable. Even after almost two hundred years, their novels are considered among the most beloved in the English language.

Mr. Brontë was proud of the achievements of all his children. At the end of his life, he wrote, "I do not deny that I am somewhat excentrick [sic]. Had I been numbered amongst the calm, sedate, *concentric* men of the world, I should not have been as I now am, and I should, in all probability, never have had such children as mine have been."[8]

Notes

PROLOGUE

1. Elizabeth Gaskell, *The Life of Charlotte Brontë* (London: Smith, Elder, 1870), 219.

CHAPTER 1

1. Clement K. Shorter, *Charlotte Brontë and Her Circle* (London: Hodder & Stoughton, 1896), 34–35.

2. Elizabeth Gaskell, *The Life of Charlotte Brontë* (London: Smith, Elder, 1870), 423.

3. Marion Harland, *Charlotte Brontë at Home* (New York: Putnam, 1899), 23.

4. Richmal Mangnall, *Historical and Miscellaneous Questions, for the Use of Young People* (London, Longman, 1812), 78–79, https://www.google.com/books/edition /Historical_and_miscellaneous_questions_N/FwlhAAAAcAAJ?hl=en&gbpv=1&bsq =Druids.

CHAPTER 2

1. J. A. V. Chapple and Arthur Pollard, eds., *The Letters of Mrs Gaskell* (Manchester, UK: Mandolin, 1997), 124.

2. William Scruton, *Thornton and the Brontës* (Bradford, UK: John Dale, 1898), 62.

3. Marion Harland, *Charlotte Brontë at Home* (New York: Putnam, 1899), 32.

4. Harland, *Charlotte Brontë at Home*, 32.

5. Elizabeth Gaskell, *The Life of Charlotte Brontë* (London: Smith, Elder, 1870), 41.

6. Christine Alexander and Margaret Smith, eds., *The Oxford Companion to the Brontës* (Oxford, UK: Oxford University Press, 2006), 457.

7. John Lock and W. T. Dixon, *A Man of Sorrow: The Life, Letters and Times of the Rev. Patrick Brontë 1777–1861* (London: Nelson, 1965), 237.

8. Chapple and Pollard, *Letters of Mrs Gaskell*, 243.

9. Mrs. Ellis H. Chadwick, *In the Footsteps of the Brontës* (New York: Brentano's, 1914), 68.

10. Gaskell, *The Life of Charlotte Brontë*, 90.

11. Clement K. Shorter, *The Brontës: Life and Letters* (New York: Scribner, 1908), 1:45.

CHAPTER 3

1. John Lock and W. T. Dixon, *A Man of Sorrow: The Life, Letters and Times of the Rev. Patrick Brontë 1777–1861* (London: Nelson, 1965), 6.

2. James Senior, *Patrick Brontë* (Boston: Stratford, 1921), 33.

3. J. Horsfall Turner, ed., *Brontëana: The Reverend Patrick Brontë, His Collected Works and Life* (Bingley, UK: Harrison, 1898), 178.

4. Charlotte Brontë, *Jane Eyre, an Autobiography* (New York: Putnam, 1897), 57.

5. Mrs. Ellis H. Chadwick, *In the Footsteps of the Brontës* (New York: Brentano's, 1914), 75.

6. Elizabeth Gaskell, *The Life of Charlotte Brontë* (London: Smith, Elder, 1870), 49.

7. Brontë, *Jane Eyre*, 44.

8. Gaskell, *The Life of Charlotte Brontë*, 49.

9. Clement K. Shorter, *The Brontës: Life and Letters* (New York: Scribner, 1908), 1:60.

10. Christine Alexander and Margaret Smith, eds., *The Oxford Companion to the Brontës* (Oxford, UK: Oxford University Press, 2006), 457.

11. Gaskell, *The Life of Charlotte Brontë*, 55.

12. Emily Brontë, *Wuthering Heights* (New York: Doubleday, Page, 1907), 43.

13. Gaskell, *The Life of Charlotte Brontë*, 57.

CHAPTER 4

1. Elizabeth Gaskell, *The Life of Charlotte Brontë* (London: Smith, Elder, 1870), 62–63.

2. Juliet Barker, *The Brontës: Wild Genius on the Moors* (New York: Pegasus, 2013), 177.

3. Gaskell, *The Life of Charlotte Brontë*, 62.

4. Gaskell, *The Life of Charlotte Brontë*, 60.

5. Gaskell, *The Life of Charlotte Brontë*, 61.

6. Juliet Barker, ed., *Charlotte Brontë: Juvenilia, 1829–1835* (London: Penguin, 1996), 21.

CHAPTER 5

1. Elizabeth Gaskell, *The Life of Charlotte Brontë* (London: Smith, Elder, 1870), 61–62.

2. Clement K. Shorter, *The Brontës: Life and Letters* (New York: Scribner, 1908), 1:132.

3. Juliet Barker, *The Brontës: Wild Genius on the Moors* (New York: Pegasus, 2013), 181.

4. Juliet Barker, ed., *Charlotte Brontë: Juvenilia, 1829–1835* (London: Penguin, 1996), 7.

5. Barker, *Juvenilia*, 108.

6. Deborah Lutz, *The Brontë Cabinet: Three Lives in Nine Objects* (New York: Norton, 2015), 6.

7. Barker, *Juvenilia*, 104.

8. Barker, *Wild Genius*, 191.

9. Barker, *Juvenilia*, 96.

10. Barker, *Juvenilia*, 96.

11. Barker, *Juvenilia*, 98.

12. Barker, *Juvenilia*, 97.

13. Barker, *Juvenilia*, 98.

14. Barker, *Juvenilia*, 98.

15. Barker, *Juvenilia*, 98.

16. Barker, *Juvenilia*, 99.

CHAPTER 6

1. Elizabeth Gaskell, *The Life of Charlotte Brontë* (London: Smith, Elder, 1870), 78.

2. Gaskell, *The Life of Charlotte Brontë*, 76.

3. Clement K. Shorter, *The Brontës: Life and Letters* (New York: Scribner, 1908), 1:81.

4. Gaskell, *The Life of Charlotte Brontë*, 68.

5. Ellen Nussey, "Reminiscences of Charlotte Brontë," *Scribner's Monthly* 2 (1871): 19, https://www.google.com/books/edition/Scribner_s_Monthly_an_Illustrated _Magazi/TsVZAAAAYAAJ?hl=en&gbpv=1&bsq=reminiscences.

6. Nussey, "Reminiscences," 20.

7. Nussey, "Reminiscences," 21.

8. Gaskell, *The Life of Charlotte Brontë*, 76.

9. Shorter, *Life and Letters*, 1:156.

10. Juliet Barker, *The Brontës: Wild Genius on the Moors* (New York: Pegasus, 2013), 209.

11. Mrs. Ellis H. Chadwick, *In the Footsteps of the Brontës* (New York: Brentano's, 1914), 85.

12. Clement K. Shorter, *Charlotte Brontë and Her Circle* (London: Hodder & Stoughton, 1896), 191.

13. C. Holmes Cautley, "Old Haworth Folk Who Knew the Brontës," *Cornhill Magazine*, n.s., 29 (1910): 78, https://www.google.com/books/edition/The_Cornhill_Magazine/i2ZOAAAAIAAJ?hl=en&gbpv=1&bsq=Haworth%20Folk.

14. Nussey, "Reminiscences," 30.

15. Shorter, *Charlotte Brontë and Her Circle*, 76.

16. Nussey, "Reminiscences," 24.

CHAPTER 7

1. Juliet Barker, *The Brontës: A Life in Letters* (Woodstock, NY: Overlook, 1998), 87.

2. Barker, *Life in Letters*, 87.

3. Marion Harland, *Charlotte Brontë at Home* (New York: Putnam, 1899), 67.

4. Francis Gribble, *The Love Affairs of Lord Byron* (London: Eveleigh Nash, 1910), 132.

5. Ellen Nussey, "Reminiscences of Charlotte Brontë," *Scribner's Monthly* 2 (1871): 26, https://www.google.com/books/edition/Scribner_s_Monthly_an_Illustrated_Magazi/TsVZAAAAYAAJ?hl=en&gbpv=1&bsq=reminiscences.

6. Nussey, "Reminiscences," 29.

7. Nussey, "Reminiscences," 30.

8. Elizabeth Gaskell, *The Life of Charlotte Brontë* (London: Smith, Elder, 1870), 57.

9. Nussey, "Reminiscences," 26.

10. Nussey, "Reminiscences," 26–27.

11. Nussey, "Reminiscences," 27.

12. Clement K. Shorter, *Charlotte Brontë and Her Circle* (London: Hodder & Stoughton, 1896), 179.

13. Nussey, "Reminiscences," 27.

14. Nussey, "Reminiscences," 27.

15. Nussey, "Reminiscences," 27.

16. C. Holmes Cautley, "Old Haworth Folk Who Knew the Brontës," *Cornhill Magazine*, n.s., 29 (1910): 81, https://www.google.com/books/edition/The_Cornhill_Magazine/i2ZOAAAAIAAJ?hl=en&gbpv=1&bsq=Haworth%20Folk.

17. Charlotte Brontë, *Jane Eyre, an Autobiography* (New York: Putnam, 1897), 311.

18. Mrs. Ellis H. Chadwick, *In the Footsteps of the Brontës* (New York: Brentano's, 1914), 111.

19. Arthur C. Benson, ed., *Brontë Poems: Selections from the Poetry of Charlotte, Emily, Anne and Branwell Brontë* (London: Smith, Elder, 1915), 232.

20. Emily Brontë, *Wuthering Heights* (New York: Doubleday, Page, 1907), 257.

21. Nussey, "Reminiscences," 27.

22. Juliet Barker, *The Brontës: Wild Genius on the Moors* (New York: Pegasus, 2013), 229.

23. Barker, *Wild Genius*, 230.

24. Barker, *Wild Genius*, 230.

25. Gaskell, *The Life of Charlotte Brontë*, 91.

CHAPTER 8

1. Juliet Barker, *The Brontës: A Life in Letters* (Woodstock, NY: Overlook, 1998), 29.

2. Barker, *Life in Letters*, 29–30.

3. Barker, *Life in Letters*, 30.

4. Elizabeth Gaskell, *The Life of Charlotte Brontë* (London: Smith, Elder, 1870), 424.

5. Sarah Fermi, "'The Pillar Portrait' Reconsidered," *Brontë Studies* 35, no. 3 (2010): 285, https://doi.org/10.1179/147489310X12798868308120.

6. Gaskell, *The Life of Charlotte Brontë*, 346.

CHAPTER 9

1. Clement K. Shorter, *The Brontës: Life and Letters* (New York: Scribner, 1908), 2:419.

2. Christine Alexander, ed., *The Brontës: Tales of Glass Town, Angria, and Gondal* (Oxford, UK: Oxford University Press, 2010), 158.

3. Alexander, *Tales*, 173–74.

4. Elizabeth Gaskell, *The Life of Charlotte Brontë* (London: Smith, Elder, 1870), 101.

5. Winifred Gerin, *Charlotte Brontë: The Evolution of Genius* (Oxford, UK: Clarendon, 1967), 103.

6. Alexander, *Tales*, 163.

7. Alexander, *Tales*, 158.

8. Gerin, *Evolution of Genius*, 106.

9. Gerin, *Evolution of Genius*, 103–4.

10. Gerin, *Evolution of Genius*, 104.

11. Gerin, *Evolution of Genius*, 103.

12. Clement K. Shorter, ed., *The Complete Poems of Emily Brontë* (London: Hodder & Stoughton, 1910), 93.

13. Rev. Charles Cuthbert Southey, ed., *The Life and Correspondence of Robert Southey* (London: Longman, Brown, Green, and Longmans, 1850), 6:328–29.

14. Gerin, *Evolution of Genius*, 103.

15. J. Horsfall Turner, ed., *Brontëana: The Reverend Patrick Brontë, His Collected Works and Life* (Bingley, UK: Harrison, 1898), 102.

16. Arthur C. Benson, ed., *Brontë Poems: Selections from the Poetry of Charlotte, Emily, Anne and Branwell Brontë* (London: Smith, Elder, 1915), 233.

17. Juliet Barker, *The Brontës: A Life in Letters* (Woodstock, NY: Overlook, 1998), 53.

18. Barker, *Life in Letters*, 53–54.

19. Margaret Smith, ed., *Charlotte Brontë: Selected Letters* (Oxford, UK: Oxford University Press, 2007), 6.

20. Gaskell, *The Life of Charlotte Brontë*, 105.

CHAPTER 10

1. Arthur C. Benson, ed., *Brontë Poems: Selections from the Poetry of Charlotte, Emily, Anne and Branwell Brontë* (London: Smith, Elder, 1915), 236.

2. Clement K. Shorter, *The Brontës: Life and Letters* (New York: Scribner, 1908), 1:151.

3. Shorter, *Life and Letters*, 1:151–52.

4. Juliet Barker, *The Brontës: Wild Genius on the Moors* (New York: Pegasus, 2013), 357.

5. Emily Brontë, *Wuthering Heights* (New York: Doubleday, Page, 1907), 2.

6. Benson, *Brontë Poems*, 269.

CHAPTER 11

1. Juliet Barker, *The Brontës: Wild Genius on the Moors* (New York: Pegasus, 2013), 350.

2. Winifred Gerin, *Charlotte Brontë: The Evolution of Genius* (Oxford, UK: Clarendon, 1967), 138.

3. Clement K. Shorter, *The Brontës: Life and Letters* (New York: Scribner, 1908), 1:150.

4. Clement K. Shorter, *Charlotte Brontë and Her Circle* (London: Hodder & Stoughton, 1896), 296.

5. Marion Harland, *Charlotte Brontë at Home* (New York: Putnam, 1899), 120.

6. Harland, *Charlotte Brontë at Home*, 122.

7. Harland, *Charlotte Brontë at Home*, 121.

8. Shorter, *Life and Letters*, 1:150.

9. Anne Brontë, *Agnes Grey* (Edinburgh: John Grant, 1905), 27–28.

10. Shorter, *Life and Letters*, 1:155.

11. Shorter, *Life and Letters*, 1:155.

12. Shorter, *Life and Letters*, 1:158.

13. Shorter, *Life and Letters*, 1:158.

14. Elizabeth Gaskell, *The Life of Charlotte Brontë* (London: Smith, Elder, 1870), 133.

15. Gaskell, *The Life of Charlotte Brontë*, 133.

16. Shorter, *Charlotte Brontë and Her Circle*, 303.

17. Arthur C. Benson, ed., *Brontë Poems: Selections from the Poetry of Charlotte, Emily, Anne and Branwell Brontë* (London: Smith, Elder, 1915), 114.

18. Benson, *Brontë Poems*, 264–65.

19. William Scruton, *Thornton and the Brontës* (Bradford, UK: John Dale, 1898), 129.

20. Gaskell, *The Life of Charlotte Brontë*, 135.

21. Scruton, *Thornton and the Brontës*, 131–32.

CHAPTER 12

1. Clement K. Shorter, *The Brontës: Life and Letters* (New York: Scribner, 1908), 1:444.

2. Shorter, *Life and Letters*, 1:179.

3. Shorter, *Life and Letters*, 1:179.

4. Shorter, *Life and Letters*, 1:175.

5. Mrs. Ellis H. Chadwick, *In the Footsteps of the Brontës* (New York: Brentano's, 1914), 167.

6. Shorter, *Life and Letters*, 1:176.

7. Clement K. Shorter, *Charlotte Brontë and Her Circle* (London: Hodder & Stoughton, 1896), 234.

8. Shorter, *Life and Letters*, 1:228.

9. Shorter, *Life and Letters*, 1:189.

10. Shorter, *Charlotte Brontë and Her Circle*, 283.

11. Arthur C. Benson, ed., *Brontë Poems: Selections from the Poetry of Charlotte, Emily, Anne and Branwell Brontë* (London: Smith, Elder, 1915), 342.

12. Currer Bell, Ellis Bell, and Acton Bell, *Poems* (London: Smith, Elder, 1846), 125.

13. Francis A. Leyland, *The Brontë Family: With Special Reference to Patrick Branwell Brontë* (London: Hurst and Blackett, 1886), 1:266–67.

14. Wikipedia, s.v. "Summit Tunnel," accessed December 9, 2022, https://en:wiki pedia.org/wiki/Summit_Tunnel.

CHAPTER 13

1. Clement K. Shorter, *Charlotte Brontë and Her Circle* (London: Hodder & Stoughton, 1896), 301.

2. Shorter, *Charlotte Brontë and Her Circle*, 238.

3. Clement K. Shorter, *The Brontës: Life and Letters* (New York: Scribner, 1908), 1:204.

4. Shorter, *Life and Letters*, 1:206.

5. Shorter, *Life and Letters*, 1:211.

6. Shorter, *Charlotte Brontë and Her Circle*, 239.

7. Shorter, *Charlotte Brontë and Her Circle*, 238.

8. Marion Harland, *Charlotte Brontë at Home* (New York: Putnam, 1899), 225–26.

9. Shorter, *Charlotte Brontë and Her Circle*, 238.

10. Harland, *Charlotte Brontë at Home*, 133.

11. Shorter, *Charlotte Brontë and Her Circle*, 147.

12. Arthur C. Benson, ed., *Brontë Poems: Selections from the Poetry of Charlotte, Emily, Anne and Branwell Brontë* (London: Smith, Elder, 1915), 177–78.

13. Emily Brontë, *Wuthering Heights* (New York: Doubleday, Page, 1907), 82.

14. Currer Bell, Ellis Bell, and Acton Bell, *Poems* (London: Smith, Elder, 1846), 163.

15. Shorter, *Charlotte Brontë and Her Circle*, 147.

16. Shorter, *Charlotte Brontë and Her Circle*, 147.

17. Shorter, *Charlotte Brontë and Her Circle*, 148.

18. Shorter, *Charlotte Brontë and Her Circle*, 148–49.

19. Shorter, *Charlotte Brontë and Her Circle*, 148.

20. Shorter, *Life and Letters*, 1:208.

21. Francis A. Leyland, *The Brontë Family: With Special Reference to Patrick Branwell Brontë* (London: Hurst and Blackett, 1886), 1:268–69.

22. Victor A. Neufeldt, ed., *The Works of Patrick Branwell Brontë*, vol. 3, *1837–1848* (New York: Garland, 1999), 335.

23. Neufeldt, *Works of Patrick Brontë*, 3:339.

24. Shorter, *Life and Letters*, 1:315.

CHAPTER 14

1. Marion Harland, *Charlotte Brontë at Home* (New York: Putnam, 1899), 131.

2. Elizabeth Gaskell, *The Life of Charlotte Brontë* (London: Smith, Elder, 1870), 157.

3. Clement K. Shorter, *The Brontës: Life and Letters* (New York: Scribner, 1908), 1:238.

4. Shorter, *Life and Letters*, 1:237.

5. Gaskell, *The Life of Charlotte Brontë*, 167.

6. Gaskell, *The Life of Charlotte Brontë*, 167.

7. Winifred Gerin, *Charlotte Brontë: The Evolution of Genius* (Oxford, UK: Clarendon, 1967), 207.

8. Juliet Barker, *The Brontës: A Life in Letters* (Woodstock, NY: Overlook, 1998), 106.

9. Mrs. Ellis H. Chadwick, *In the Footsteps of the Brontës* (New York: Brentano's, 1914), 226.

10. Chadwick, *Footsteps of the Brontës*, 225.

11. Francis H. Grundy, *Pictures of the Past: Memories of Men I Have Met and Places I Have Seen* (London: Griffith and Farran, 1879), 83–84.

12. Anne Brontë, "To --------," Public Domain Poetry, accessed February 3, 2023, https://www.public-domain-poetry.com/anne-bronte/to-9538.

13. Juliet Barker, *The Brontës: Wild Genius on the Moors* (New York: Pegasus, 2013), 475.

CHAPTER 15

1. Clement K. Shorter, *The Brontës: Life and Letters* (New York: Scribner, 1908), 1:262.

2. Shorter, *Life and Letters*, 1:237.

3. Shorter, *Life and Letters*, 1:267.

4. Shorter, *Life and Letters*, 1:268.

5. Shorter, *Life and Letters*, 1:267.

6. Elizabeth Gaskell, *The Life of Charlotte Brontë* (London: Smith, Elder, 1870), 200.

7. Currer Bell, Ellis Bell, and Acton Bell, *Poems* (London: Smith, Elder, 1846), 323.

8. William Scruton, *Thornton and the Brontës* (Bradford, UK: John Dale, 1898), 130.

9. Shorter, *Life and Letters*, 1:273.

10. Juliet Barker, *The Brontës: Wild Genius on the Moors* (New York: Pegasus, 2013), 501.

11. Shorter, *Life and Letters*, 1:275.

12. Gaskell, *The Life of Charlotte Brontë*, 210.

13. Shorter, *Life and Letters*, 1:284.

14. Currer Bell, *Villette* (New York: Harper & Brothers, 1855), 299–300.

15. Barker, *Wild Genius*, 493.

16. Edith M. Weir, "New Brontë Material Comes to Light," *Brontë Society Transactions* 11, no. 4 (1949): 256–57, https://doi.org/10.1179/030977649796550157.

17. Clement K. Shorter, *The Brontës and Their Circle* (London: Dent, 1914), 96.

18. Bell, Bell, and Bell, *Poems*, 126.

CHAPTER 16

1. Victor A. Neufeldt, ed., *The Works of Patrick Branwell Brontë*, vol. 3, *1837–1848* (New York: Garland, 1999), 401.

2. Emily Brontë, *Wuthering Heights* (New York: Doubleday, Page, 1907), 130.

3. Currer Bell, Ellis Bell, and Acton Bell, *Poems* (London: Smith, Elder, 1846), 104–5.

4. Juliet Barker, ed., *The Brontës: Selected Poems* (London: Dent, 1991), 82–83.

5. Juliet Barker, *The Brontës: A Life in Letters* (Woodstock, NY: Overlook, 1998), 114.

6. Clement K. Shorter, *The Brontës: Life and Letters* (New York: Scribner, 1908), 1:277.

7. Shorter, *Life and Letters*, 1:306.

8. Shorter, *Life and Letters*, 1:303.

9. Clement K. Shorter, *Charlotte Brontë and Her Circle* (London: Hodder & Stoughton, 1896), 153–54.

10. Shorter, *Life and Letters*, 1:305.

11. Shorter, *Life and Letters*, 1:305–6.

12. Shorter, *Life and Letters*, 1:303.

13. Francis H. Grundy, *Pictures of the Past: Memories of Men I Have Met and Places I Have Seen* (London: Griffith and Farran, 1879), 87.

14. Grundy, *Pictures of the Past*, 87–88.

15. Shorter, *Life and Letters*, 1:321.

16. Shorter, *Life and Letters*, 1:276–77.

17. Barker, *Life in Letters*, 139.

18. Francis A. Leyland, *The Brontë Family: With Special Reference to Patrick Branwell Brontë* (London: Hurst and Blackett, 1886), 2:133.

CHAPTER 17

1. Clement K. Shorter, *The Brontës: Life and Letters* (New York: Scribner, 1908), 1:317.

2. Shorter, *Life and Letters*, 1:333.

3. Currer Bell, Ellis Bell, and Acton Bell, *Poems* (London: Smith, Elder, 1846), 31–32.

4. Bell, Bell, and Bell, *Poems*, 10–11.

5. Bell, Bell, and Bell, *Poems*, 112–13.

6. Shorter, *Life and Letters*, 1:452.

7. "Poetry of the Million," *Athenaeum*, July 4, 1846, 682.

8. Miriam Allott, ed., *The Brontës: The Critical Heritage* (London: Routledge & Kegan Paul, 1974), 59–60.

9. Francis A. Leyland, *The Brontë Family: With Special Reference to Patrick Branwell Brontë* (London: Hurst and Blackett, 1886), 2:173.

10. Shorter, *Life and Letters*, 1:332.

11. Juliet Barker, *The Brontës: Wild Genius on the Moors* (New York: Pegasus, 2013), 585.

CHAPTER 18

1. Clement K. Shorter, *The Brontës: Life and Letters* (New York: Scribner, 1908), 1:335–36.

2. Shorter, *Life and Letters*, 1:336.

3. J. A. V. Chapple and Arthur Pollard, eds., *The Letters of Mrs Gaskell* (Manchester, UK: Mandolin, 1997), 245.

4. Juliet Barker, *The Brontës: Wild Genius on the Moors* (New York: Pegasus, 2013), 614.

5. Miriam Allott, ed., *The Brontës: The Critical Heritage* (London: Routledge & Kegan Paul, 1974), 227.

6. Allott, *Critical Heritage*, 70.

7. Allott, *Critical Heritage*, 79.

8. "Recent Novels: French and English," *Fraser's Magazine* 36, no. 216 (December 1847): 690–91.

9. Charlotte Brontë, *Jane Eyre, an Autobiography* (New York: Putnam, 1897), 242.

10. Brontë, *Jane Eyre*, 102.

11. Augustine Birrell, *Life of Charlotte Brontë* (London: Walter Scott, 1887), 110.

12. Allott, *Critical Heritage*, 228.

13. Allott, *Critical Heritage*, 241.

14. Emily Brontë, *Wuthering Heights* (New York: Doubleday, Page, 1907), 81.

15. Allott, *Critical Heritage*, 236.

16. Allott, *Critical Heritage*, 227.

17. Barbara Lloyd Evans and Gareth Lloyd Evans, *Everyman's Companion to the Brontës* (Lonon: Dent, 1982), 381.

18. George Moore, *Conversations in Ebury Street* (New York: Boni and Liveright, 1924), 253.

19. Moore, *Conversations*, 257.

20. Mrs. Ellis H. Chadwick, *In the Footsteps of the Brontës* (New York: Brentano's, 1914), 380.

21. Allott, *Critical Heritage*, 263.

22. Allott, *Critical Heritage*, 265.

23. Shorter, *Life and Letters*, 1:435–36.

CHAPTER 19

1. Clement K. Shorter, *The Brontës: Life and Letters* (New York: Scribner, 1908), 1:436–37.

2. Shorter, *Life and Letters*, 1:442.

3. Shorter, *Life and Letters*, 1:437.

4. Shorter, *Life and Letters*, 1:437.

5. Shorter, *Life and Letters*, 1:438.

6. "Reviews: *The Tenant of Wildfell Hall*," *Athenaeum*, no. 1080, July 8, 1848, 670–71.

7. Miriam Allott, ed., *The Brontës: The Critical Heritage* (London: Routledge & Kegan Paul, 1974), 250.

CHAPTER 20

1. Marion Harland, *Charlotte Brontë at Home* (New York: Putnam, 1899), 200.

2. Clement K. Shorter, *Charlotte Brontë and Her Circle* (London: Hodder & Stoughton, 1896), 140.

3. Francis H. Grundy, *Pictures of the Past: Memories of Men I Have Met and Places I Have Seen* (London: Griffith and Farran, 1879), 92.

4. Harland, *Charlotte Brontë at Home*, 209.

5. Harland, *Charlotte Brontë at Home*, 210.

6. Arthur C. Benson, ed., *Brontë Poems: Selections from the Poetry of Charlotte, Emily, Anne and Branwell Brontë* (London: Smith, Elder, 1915), 366.

7. Benson, *Brontë Poems*, 367–68.

8. Elizabeth Gaskell, *The Life of Charlotte Brontë* (London: Smith, Elder, 1870), 297.

9. Margaret Smith, ed., *Charlotte Brontë: Selected Letters* (Oxford, UK: Oxford University Press, 2007), 6:139.

10. Harland, *Charlotte Brontë at Home*, 215.

11. Smith, *Selected Letters*, 6:138.

12. Shorter, *Charlotte Brontë and Her Circle*, 251.

13. Shorter, *Charlotte Brontë and Her Circle*, 356.

14. Gaskell, *The Life of Charlotte Brontë*, 181.

15. Gaskell, *The Life of Charlotte Brontë*, 327.

16. Shorter, *Charlotte Brontë and Her Circle*, 468.

17. Gaskell, *The Life of Charlotte Brontë*, 332–33.

18. George M. Smith, "Charlotte Brontë," *Cornhill Magazine*, n.s., 9 (1900): 784–85, https://www.google.com/books/edition/The_Cornhill_Magazine/ouULAQAAIAAJ?hl=en&gbpv=1&bsq=Charlotte%20Bronte.

19. Clement K. Shorter, *The Brontës: Life and Letters* (New York: Scribner, 1908), 2:194.

20. Shorter, *Life and Letters*, 2:118.

21. Charlotte Brontë, "Biographical Notice of Ellis and Acton Bell," in *"Wuthering Heights," by Emily Brontë; and "Agnes Grey," by Anne Brontë* (London: Smith, Elder, 1870), xiii.

22. Harland, *Charlotte Brontë at Home*, 231.

23. Smith, "Charlotte Brontë," 788.

24. Charlotte Brontë, *Jane Eyre, an Autobiography* (New York: Putnam, 1897), 183.

25. Gaskell, *The Life of Charlotte Brontë*, 88.

26. Smith, "Charlotte Brontë," 786–87.

27. Smith, "Charlotte Brontë," 787.

28. Shorter, *Life and Letters*, 2:274.

29. Gaskell, *The Life of Charlotte Brontë*, 382.

30. Miriam Allott, ed., *The Brontës: The Critical Heritage* (London: Routledge & Kegan Paul, 1974), 172.

31. Gaskell, *The Life of Charlotte Brontë*, 399.

32. Gaskell, *The Life of Charlotte Brontë*, 403.

CHAPTER 21

1. Clement K. Shorter, *Charlotte Brontë and Her Circle* (London: Hodder & Stoughton, 1896), 472.

2. Shorter, *Charlotte Brontë and Her Circle*, 473.

3. Miriam Allott, ed., *The Brontës: The Critical Heritage* (London: Routledge & Kegan Paul, 1974), 197–98.

4. Shorter, *Charlotte Brontë and Her Circle*, 479.

5. Shorter, *Charlotte Brontë and Her Circle*, 479.

6. Shorter, *Charlotte Brontë and Her Circle*, 481.

7. Elizabeth Gaskell, *The Life of Charlotte Brontë* (London: Smith, Elder, 1870), 422–23.

8. J. A. V. Chapple and Arthur Pollard, eds., *The Letters of Mrs Gaskell* (Manchester, UK: Mandolin, 1997), 247.

9. Chapple and Pollard, *Letters of Mrs Gaskell*, 289.

10. George M. Smith, "Charlotte Brontë," *Cornhill Magazine*, n.s., 9 (1900): 795, https://www.google.com/books/edition/The_Cornhill_Magazine/ouULAQAAIAAJ ?hl=en&gbpv=1&bsq=Charlotte%20Bronte.

11. Juliet Barker, *The Brontës: A Life in Letters* (Woodstock, NY: Overlook, 1998), 390.

12. Marion Harland, *Charlotte Brontë at Home* (New York: Putnam, 1899), 266.

13. Clement K. Shorter, *The Brontës: Life and Letters* (New York: Scribner, 1908), 2:383.

14. Shorter, *Life and Letters*, 2:378.

15. Shorter, *Life and Letters*, 2:379.

16. Harland, *Charlotte Brontë at Home*, 269.

17. Harland, *Charlotte Brontë at Home*, 272.

18. Harland, *Charlotte Brontë at Home*, 275.

19. Gaskell, *The Life of Charlotte Brontë*, 439.

EPILOGUE

1. Clement K. Shorter, *Charlotte Brontë and Her Circle* (London: Hodder & Stoughton, 1896), 12.

2. Juliet Barker, *The Brontës: Wild Genius on the Moors* (New York: Pegasus, 2013), 937.

3. T. Wemyss Reid, *Charlotte Brontë, a Monograph* (New York: Scribner, Armstrong, 1877), 195.

4. Dudley Green, ed., *The Letters of the Reverend Patrick Brontë* (Stroud, Gloucestershire, UK: Nonsuch, 2005), 254.

5. Shorter, *Charlotte Brontë and Her Circle*, 55.

6. "An American Visitor at Haworth, 1861," *Brontë Society Transactions* 15, no. 2 (2013): 129–30, https://doi.org/10.1179/030977667796498750.

7. Miriam Allott, ed., *The Brontës: The Critical Heritage* (London: Routledge & Kegan Paul, 1974), 185.

8. Green, *Letters of the Reverend Patrick Brontë*, 258.

Selected Bibliography

Alexander, Christine, ed. *The Brontës: Tales of Glass Town, Angria, and Gondal.* Oxford, UK: Oxford University Press, 2010.

Alexander, Christine, and Margaret Smith, eds. *The Oxford Companion to the Brontës.* Oxford, UK: Oxford University Press, 2006.

Allott, Miriam, ed. *The Brontës: The Critical Heritage.* London: Routledge & Kegan Paul, 1974.

"An American Visitor at Haworth, 1861." *Brontë Society Transactions* 15, no. 2 (1967): 126–38. https://doi.org/10.1179/030977667796498750.

Barker, Juliet. *The Brontës: A Life in Letters.* Woodstock, NY: Overlook, 1998.

———. *The Brontës: Selected Poems.* London: Dent, 1991.

———. *The Brontës: Wild Genius on the Moors.* New York: Pegasus, 2013.

———, ed. *Charlotte Brontë: Juvenilia, 1829–1835.* London: Penguin, 1996.

Beer, Frances, ed. *The Juvenilia of Jane Austen and Charlotte Brontë.* London: Penguin, 1986.

Bell, Currer. *Villette.* New York: Harper & Brothers, 1855.

Bell, Currer, Ellis Bell, and Acton Bell. *Poems.* London: Smith, Elder, 1846.

Benson, Arthur C., ed. *Brontë Poems: Selections from the Poetry of Charlotte, Emily, Anne and Branwell Brontë*. London: Smith, Elder, 1915.

Birrell, Augustine. *Life of Charlotte Brontë*. London: Walter Scott, 1887.

Brontë, Anne. *Agnes Grey*. Edinburgh: John Grant, 1905.

———. *The Tenant of Wildfell Hall*. London: Smith, Elder, 1873.

———. "To --------." Public Domain Poetry, accessed February 3, 2023. https://www.public-domain-poetry.com/anne-bronte/to-9538.

Brontë, Charlotte. "Biographical Notice of Ellis and Acton Bell." In *"Wuthering Heights," by Emily Brontë; and "Agnes Grey," by Anne Brontë*, xiii. London: Smith, Elder, 1870.

———. *Jane Eyre, an Autobiography*. New York: Putnam, 1897.

———. *Shirley*. New York: Harper, 1899.

Brontë, Emily. *Wuthering Heights*. New York: Doubleday, Page, 1907.

Cautley, C. Holmes. "Old Haworth Folk Who Knew the Brontës." *Cornhill Magazine*, n.s., 29 (1910): 76–84. https://www.google.com/books/edition/The_Cornhill_Magazine/i2ZOAAAAIAAJ?hl=en&gbpv=1&bsq=Haworth%20Folk.

Chadwick, Mrs. Ellis H. *In the Footsteps of the Brontës*. New York: Brentano's, 1914.

Chapple, J. A. V., and Arthur Pollard, eds. *The Letters of Mrs Gaskell*. Manchester, UK: Mandolin, 1997.

Fermi, Sarah. "'The Pillar Portrait' Reconsidered." *Brontë Studies* 35, no. 3 (2010): 278–86. https://doi.org/10.1179/147489310X12798868308120.

Gaskell, Elizabeth. *The Life of Charlotte Brontë*. London: Smith, Elder, 1870.

Gerin, Winifred. *Charlotte Brontë: The Evolution of Genius*. Oxford, UK: Clarendon, 1967.

Glen, Heather, ed. *Charlotte Brontë: Tales of Angria*. London: Penguin, 2006.

Green, Dudley, ed. *The Letters of the Reverend Patrick Brontë*. Stroud, Gloucestershire, UK: Nonsuch, 2005.

Gribble, Francis. *The Love Affairs of Lord Byron*. London: Eveleigh Nash, 1910.

Grundy, Francis H. *Pictures of the Past: Memories of Men I Have Met and Places I Have Seen*. London: Griffith and Farran, 1879.

Harland, Marion. *Charlotte Brontë at Home*. New York: Putnam, 1899.

Leyland, Francis A. *The Brontë Family: With Special Reference to Patrick Branwell Brontë*. 2 vols. London: Hurst and Blackett, 1886.

Lloyd Evans, Barbara, and Gareth Lloyd Evans. *Everyman's Companion to the Brontës*. London: Dent, 1982.

Lock, John, and W. T. Dixon. *A Man of Sorrow: The Life, Letters and Times of the Rev. Patrick Brontë, 1777–1861*. London: Nelson, 1965.

Lutz, Deborah. *The Brontë Cabinet: Three Lives in Nine Objects*. New York: Norton, 2015.

Mangnall, Richmal. *Historical and Miscellaneous Questions, for the Use of Young People*. London: Longman, 1812.

Moore, George. *Conversations in Ebury Street*. New York: Boni and Liveright, 1924.

Neufeldt, Victor A., ed. *The Works of Patrick Branwell Brontë*. Vol. 3, *1837–1848*. New York: Garland, 1999.

Nussey, Ellen. "Reminiscences of Charlotte Brontë." *Scribner's Monthly* 2 (1871): 18–31.

"Recent Novels: French and English." *Fraser's Magazine* 36, no. 216 (December 1847): 690–91.

Reid, T. Wemyss. *Charlotte Brontë, a Monograph*. New York: Scribner, Armstrong, 1877.

Scruton, William. *Thornton and the Brontës*. Bradford, UK: John Dale, 1898.

Senior, James. *Patrick Brontë*. Boston: Stratford, 1921.

Shorter, Clement K. *The Brontës and Their Circle*. London: Dent, 1914.

———. *The Brontës: Life and Letters*. Vol. 1. New York: Scribner, 1908.

———. *The Brontës: Life and Letters*. Vol. 2. New York: Scribner, 1908.

———. *Charlotte Brontë and Her Circle*. London: Hodder & Stoughton, 1896.

———, ed. *The Complete Poems of Emily Brontë*. London: Hodder & Stoughton, 1910.

Smith, George M. "Charlotte Brontë." *Cornhill Magazine*, n.s., 9 (1900): 778–95.

Smith, Margaret, ed. *Charlotte Bronte: Selected Letters*. Oxford, UK: Oxford University Press, 2007.

Southey, Rev. Charles Cuthbert, ed. *The Life and Correspondence of Robert Southey*. Vol. 6. London: Longman, Brown, Green, and Longmans, 1850.

Taylor, Mary. *Miss Miles, or A Tale of Yorkshire Life 60 Years Ago*. New York: Oxford University Press, 1990.

Turner, J. Horsfall, ed. *Brontëana: The Reverend Patrick Brontë, His Collected Works and Life*. Bingley, UK: Harrison, 1898.

Weir, Edith M. "New Brontë Material Comes to Light." *Brontë Society Transactions* 11, no. 4 (1949): 249–61. https://doi.org/10.1179/030977649796550157.

Wright, Sharon. *The Mother of the Brontës: When Maria Met Patrick*. London: Pen & Sword, 2019.

Index

eccentricities, 22; education of,
21–22; education of children by,
9–10, 14, 21–22, 43, 56; eyesight,
179–82, 211; favoritism toward son,
133–34, 137–38, 195; fondness for
William Weightman, 116, 137, 140,
147; grief over loss of family, 13,
31–32, 195–97; illnesses, 51–52, 211,
224; kindness to servants, 8, 26–27,
112, 224; love of family, 25, 36; love
of music, 78–79; love of nature, 7,
9, 22; love of pets, 32, 40, 181; name
change, 21; opposition to Arthur Bell
Nicholls as Charlotte's suitor, 208–
10, 213; pride in Charlotte's success,
185–86; relationship with Arthur
Bell Nicholls, 180, 183–84, 208,
220, 224–25; science and ecology
interests of, 26; writer and
storyteller, 22, 35, 45, 69, 92, 180,
183–84
Brontë, Patrick Branwell. See Brontë,
Branwell
Broughton-in-Furness, 113–15
Brown, John, 88–89, 113–14, 163, 165,
168, 199
Brown, Martha, 84, 112, 148, 154, 193;
bequest of Patrick Brontë to, 224;
chief mourner at Patrick's funeral,
225; description of, 111; devotion to
Brontë family, 27, 225; employed by
Brontës, 111; friendship with Arthur
Bell Nicholls after Brontë family
deaths, 225; lifespan, 225; Patrick
Brontë nursed by, 224
Brussels, Belgium, 140, 142–48, 151–56,
169, 206, 221. See also Pensionnat
Heger (Brussels school)

Burder, Mary, 16
Byron, George Gordon, Lord, 49, 65–66,
72, 75, 80

Calvinism, 29, 93–94, 162
Chapter Coffee House, 190–91, 193
Clergy Daughters School. See Cowan
Bridge (Clergy Daughters School)
Coleridge, Hartley, 115–16, 128
Cornwall, 11–12, 15–16, 18, 26, 64, 174
Cowan Bridge (Clergy Daughters
School), 20–21, 27, 55, 113;
Charlotte's education at, 24–25,
30–31; description of, 23–24; Emily's
education at, 27, 29–31; founder's
threat of lawsuit over biography, 224;
harsh conditions at, 23–25, 29–31;
illness and death at, 30–31; Jane Eyre
inspired by, 182

Dewsbury Moor. See Heald's House
(school)
Dixon family, 146, 153
Duke of Wellington, 37, 59, 82, 142, 200,
202; in juvenilia, 15, 36, 41, 48–49
Dury, Isabelle, 16

Franks, Elizabeth Firth, 15, 59, 86, 122

Garrs, Nancy, 8–9, 13–15, 31–32; arrival
in Haworth, 1–6; caregiver, friend,
and playmate to Brontë siblings, 27;
chief mourner at Patrick's funeral,
225; death in workhouse of, 180;
devoted to Brontë family, 26–27;
hired as nursemaid for Charlotte, 8;
kept in touch with Brontë family, 27;
lifespan, 225

About the Author

Diane Browning is an award-winning author/illustrator whose star-reviewed picture book, *Signed, Abiah Rose*, was named a Booklist Top Ten Title for Youth in both the art and history categories. She studied with acclaimed writer/illustrator Uri Shulevitz in New York, and at Art Center College of Design (now in Pasadena). Browning has lived in Dallas, Hollywood, London, and San Francisco. Now living in Southern California, she is a member of the Brontë Society and a longtime member of the Society of Children's Book Writers and Illustrators.